The
Victorian
Country Child

When I was a child, I spake as a child, I understood as a child, I thought as a child: but when I became a man, I put away childish things.

I Corinthians 13:11

The Victorian Country Child

PAMELA HORN

ALAN SUTTON

First published in the United Kingdom in this edition in 1990 by Alan Sutton Publishing
Limited · Phoenix Mill · Far Thrupp · Stroud · Gloucestershire

First published in the United States of America in this edition in 1991 by Alan Sutton
Publishing Inc · Wolfeboro Falls · NH 03896–0848

First published 1974 by The Roundwood Press
First published by Alan Sutton Publishing in Sovereign 1985

British Library Cataloguing in Publication Data
Horn, Pamela, *1936–*
The Victorian Country Child. – New ed.
1. England. Rural regions. Children. Social aspects, history
I. Title
305.230942

ISBN 0–86299–776–3

Library of Congress Cataloguing in Publication Data applied for

Jacket picture: The Ride *by William Bromley (fl. 1835–88)*

Typeset in Bembo 10/13.
Typesetting and origination by
Alan Sutton Publishing Limited.
Printed in Great Britain by Dotesios Printers Limited

Contents

Acknowledgements

I should like to thank all those who have helped me with this book, either by providing material or in other ways. In particular, my thanks are due to the staff at the Bodleian Library, Oxford and to staff at many County Record Offices – including Bedfordshire, Berkshire, Buckinghamshire, Hampshire, Northampton-shire, Oxfordshire and Warwickshire. I should also like to express my gratitude to the Museum of English Rural Life at the University of Reading; the British Library Newspaper Library, Colindale; Birmingham Reference Library; Oxford City Library; Winchester City Library; Cowper and Newton Museum, Olney; Abbot's Hall Museum of Rural Life of East Anglia, Stowmarket.

Many individuals have likewise given help and to them my thanks are equally due. They include: the late Mrs Gertrude M.L. Anderson of Abingdon, and her son, the late Mr J.R.L. Anderson; Mrs L. Bookham of Headington, Oxford; Mrs M. Dring, Headington, Oxford; Mrs H. Eriksen, Cropredy, Oxfordshire; Mrs R. Evans, Culham, Oxfordshire; Mr J. Hawkins, Pitstone, Bucking-hamshire; Miss E.N.H. Ibbotson, Ilmington, Warwickshire; Miss A. Hall and Miss M.A. Hall of Stratford-upon-Avon, Warwickshire; Miss C. Pearce, Chippenham, Wiltshire; my former colleague, Mr P. Smith of Oxford Poly-technic; Mrs T. Tidmarsh, Swindon, Wiltshire. I am also grateful to the Director of Education for Oxfordshire and Mr M. Goodliffe of Oxford Polytechnic for help in the provision of illustrations.

My brother- and sister-in-law, Mr and Mrs I. Horn, of Ivinghoe, Bucking-hamshire, have generously given assistance on rural life in that county and particularly on nineteenth-century cottage lacemaking. Their aid has been much appreciated.

To my parents my thanks are also due. My mother, indeed, knew at first hand something of the life of a country child early in the present century.

Finally, as always, I owe an especial debt to my husband. He has not only helped me with research but has listened patiently to my monologues on the subject of the Victorian country child! His guidance and assistance have been invaluable and without them this book would not have been written.

EDUCATIONAL MILESTONES
(1850–1900)

1862 Introduction of the Revised Code for Elementary Education – the 'payment by results' system.

1867 Agricultural Gangs Act – prohibited the employment of children under the age of eight in public agricultural gangs and required all gangmasters to be duly licensed by the local magistrates. Public gangs of mixed sex were prohibited.

1867 Factory and Workshops Regulation Act – laid down that no child below the age of eight was to be employed in a handicraft. Between the ages of eight and thirteen, he or she could be employed only in accordance with the half-time system already used in factories. The definition of a workshop was widened.

1870 Education Act – designed to provide elementary education for all children. It authorized the establishment of rate-aided board schools, where necessary; these could impose compulsory school attendance for children in their area. But as late as 1895 only 1.9 million of the nation's children attended board schools, as opposed to 2.4 million who were attending voluntary schools of one kind or another.

1873 Agricultural Children Act – largely ineffective. It sought to prohibit the employment of children below the age of eight in agriculture, and to secure minimum school attendance for those aged eight to twelve. Minimum age for work in a public gang raised to ten.

1876 Education Act – required the setting up of school attendance committees in areas where there were no school boards; the committees were empowered (but not compelled) to demand compulsory attendance of children in the age range of five to thirteen inclusive.

1880 Education Act – imposed the compulsory attendance of all children between the ages of five and ten and thereafter until fourteen, unless exemption could be gained on grounds of educational attainment or of average level of attendance.

1891 Elementary Education Act – made possible free elementary education; a government grant of 10s a year was to be payable for each pupil in a public elementary school and fees could either be reduced by that amount or abolished entirely.

1893 Minimum school leaving age raised to eleven.

1899 Minimum school leaving age raised to twelve – although in agricultural areas eleven was apparently still accepted.

SHILLINGS AND PENCE
CONVERSION TABLE

1d	½p	1s 7d	8p
2d		1s 8d	8½p
or	1p	1s 9d	
3d		or	9p
4d	1½p	1s 10d	
5d	2p	1s 11d	9½p
6d	2½p	2s	10p
7d	3p	2s 6d	12½p
8d	3½p	2s 9d	
9d		or	14p
or	4p	2s 10d	
10d		3s	15p
11d	4½p	5s	25p
1s	5p	7s 6d	37½p
1s 1d	5½p	10s	50p
1s 2d		12s 6d	62½p
or	6p	13s 6d	67½p
1s 3d		15s 0d	75p
1s 4d	6½p	18s 0d	90p
1s 5d	7p	20s 0d	100p
1s 6d	7½p	i.e. £1	
		£1 5s 0d	£1.25

NOTE ON THE SYSTEM OF REFERENCES

The reference numbers in the text refer the reader to the corresponding entry in the Bibliography section at the end of the book. Notes on additional material used have been added at the end of each chapter, where necessary. Information on the organization of individual schools has been obtained from the *school log books* preserved at the relevant County Record Offices, unless an indication to the contrary is given.

NB: When Flora Thompson's *Lark Rise to Candleford* (1963 edn.) is quoted, the north Oxfordshire hamlet where she lived and its adjoining village are given their correct names of Juniper Hill and Cottisford respectively, rather than the fictional Lark Rise and Fordlow used in the book.

Introduction

Throughout Queen Victoria's reign agricultural labourers formed by far the largest single group of male workers in rural England. Indeed, when the Queen ascended the throne in 1837 they comprised the biggest category of workers of *any* type in the whole country. Although they reached their peak in absolute terms in the middle of the nineteenth century, as late as the 1891 Census of Population they still numbered about three quarters of a million; in 1851, at around one and a quarter million they had formed over one-fifth of the nation's entire adult work force.

Given this background, therefore, it is inevitable that any study of the 'average' country child must be weighted heavily in favour of the sons and daughters of farm workers. Nevertheless, the children of rural craftsmen and the smaller farmers cannot be forgotten, even though in certain respects at least their lives and those of the labourers' children ran along very similar channels.

This book seeks to trace the day-to-day experiences of youngsters who were often deprived of the material possessions which are nowadays regarded as essential for a contented life. Yet, despite this, most of them enjoyed a happy childhood, secure in the love of their own family. However, it must be remembered that at least some family circles did *not* display mutual regard and pleasure in one another's company. For children employed in the cottage industries of the early and mid-Victorian period especially, the day-to-day routine was little more than drudgery. For them, occasional highdays and holidays provided the only break from a harsh and monotonous daily toil.

Finally, the documents at the end of the book illustrate some of the varied aspects of the life of the country child – in most cases, as seen through the eyes of their contemporaries.

CHAPTER ONE

Early Life and Home Background

For the majority of Victorian country children – the offspring of farm workers and village craftsmen – life began in a small cramped cottage without any of the ceremonial which greeted the birth of a baby in the wealthier ranks of society. It was quite unusual even for a doctor to be present at the confinement, unless complications were feared, for few families could afford the fees involved in obtaining this sort of medical attention. (As a report in the *Norfolk News* of 10 April, 1875, shows, doctors might charge as much as £1 1s for 'services as accoucheur'. This was equal to almost two weeks' wages for the average labourer.) Occasionally the free services of the local poor law doctor might be secured, but this, too, was not common and normally the village midwife would preside. She was usually a respectable elderly woman – the wife or widow of a local labourer – whose only recommendation for holding her office was that she had herself borne several children. Her formal training was nil, but nevertheless experience and commonsense were in most cases sufficient to bring the patient through, and 'accidents were rare'.

For a small payment of perhaps 2s 6d, therefore, the midwife 'officiated at the birth and came every morning for ten days to bathe the baby and make the mother comfortable'.[144] Where an elder daughter was mature enough, she might be kept away from school to look after her mother as well, but this obviously depended very much on individual circumstances. Most women would struggle to their feet again as quickly as possible, in order to resume their duties of running the house and perhaps looking after other children.

For the first day or two the new mother would subsist on gruel or 'a basin o' bread sop, with a mite o' butter and salt and pepper'.[112] On rare occasions the ingredients for these would be provided by the local poor law guardians, but usually such help was reserved for the poorest families only. Most would be expected to cater for themselves – or to rely upon charity. At Steeple Claydon in Buckinghamshire, for example, there was a 'lying in society' which regularly provided clothing and extra groceries for the baby and its mother, while in the north Oxfordshire hamlet of Juniper Hill, the rector's daughter took a hand.

Although the mothers lived on the customary 'water gruel, dry toast, and weak tea' for the first three days, they were then given 'one large sago pudding, followed up by a jug of veal broth. After these were consumed they returned to their ordinary food, with a half-pint of stout a day for those who could afford it. No milk was taken, and yet their own milk supply was abundant. Once, when a bottle-fed baby was brought on a visit to the hamlet, its bottle was held up as a curiosity.'[144]

As soon as the immediate problems surrounding the baby's arrival had been solved, therefore, life quickly returned to normal. A home-made wickerwork basket or, in the worst-off families, an ordinary wooden box, would serve as a cradle, and bed clothes could easily be made up from the family's existing possessions. However, the provision of clothes for a new baby was more difficult. When children were older, they could wear clothes handed down to them, but it often seemed a wasteful outlay for a badly-off family to buy clothing suitable for the first weeks of a baby's life only. It was here that the many village lying-in charities played their part. Countless country children began their existence in borrowed garments.

At Juniper Hill, two boxes of baby clothing were made available by the rector's daughter. Each contained 'half a dozen of everything – tiny shirts, swathes, long flannel barrows, nighties, and napkins, made . . . by the clergyman's daughter. In addition to the loaned clothes, it would contain, as a gift, packets of tea and sugar and a tin of patent groats for making gruel.' At the end of a month the box was supposed to be returned 'with the clothes freshly laundered', but if a family's need was great enough it could be retained longer; 'many mothers were allowed to keep their box until, at six or seven weeks old, the baby was big enough to be put into short clothes; so saving them the cost of preparing a layette other than the one set of clothes got ready for the infant's arrival. Even that might be borrowed.'[144]

But for those who lived in parishes which lacked these advantages, or who were too independent to make use of them, then a few simple clothes would be gathered together within the family – and, if necessary, father's old shirt tails would come in very well for napkins. In all but the very poorest families, there would also be a special Sunday outfit for every member of the family, 'from the baby dressed in white muslin with pink ribbon on the shoulder to mother in her silk dress and father in his clean trousers and hard hat, with his hair and whiskers brushed and oiled'.[112]

At this stage in its life the baby was, of course, too young to notice the sort of environment into which it had been born. Understanding of that would come only with the years. Yet, sadly, the cottage accommodation in much of rural England was extremely unsatisfactory. This was especially the case in the 'open

Children at Home Farm, Kewstoke, on the Smyth Pigott estate, August 1885. For such youngsters the farmyard could be not only a place of work but of play – providing the farmer did not object. (Reproduced by courtesy of Woodspring Museum, Weston-super-Mare)

villages', where land ownership was widely dispersed among local tradesmen, builders, absentee landlords and others. Most cottage rents averaged between 1s and 2s per week, although in the more populous areas they could reach a slightly higher level, while for the worst cottages they might sink to a mere 6d per week. Such a low rate of return as this naturally discouraged the speculative builder from producing much-needed new dwellings, and yet, given the farm labourers' low basic wages, significantly higher rents were impossible. Cottage improvement thus rested all too often upon the philanthropic interest – or lack of it – of the larger landowners. Perhaps fortunately for the labourers, the first forty years of Victoria's reign saw a revival of interest in cottage building on these humanitarian grounds, with numerous books and articles appearing on the subject – like William Gray's *Rural Architecture* (1852); John Vincent's *Country Cottages* (1860), and many others. It was in this atmosphere that the Duke of Bedford could boast of the cottages he had been building on his estates, and could observe that 'while other landlords were building and improving cattle sheds they

3

should also build and improve dwellings for their labourers'.[154] In the 1860s Colonel Loyd-Lindsay (later Lord Wantage) likewise built model cottages for workers on his Berkshire estate at Ardington and Lockinge (see Document A), and in Somerset during the same decade, Lord Taunton was building good cottages made of 'red stone found on the spot, (costing) £220 a pair, besides pig-sty and privy, which are away at the back of the garden'. In shape, they were 'perfectly square . . . the block of two measuring 48 feet by 24 . . . The . . . cottages (were) let at £3 (per annum) a-piece.'[2]

Many of these model dwellings had three bedrooms, as well as a kitchen and scullery or pantry. There might also be a parlour and outhouses, including a wash-house and a bakehouse, although often the latter would be a communal one shared with neighbours.[87]

However, dwellings of this type were very much in the minority during the whole of Victoria's reign, and with the onset of low prices and growing imports of grain from the 1870s and of refrigerated meat and dairy produce from the 1880s, landlords found themselves in some financial difficulty and became increasingly unwilling to embark upon heavy expenditure to improve cottages. Far more characteristic of the village scene than these attractive cottages, therefore, were the ones described by the chairman of a parish council in a letter to *The Times* in 1898: ' . . . they are in a wretched state of neglect and overcrowding, whole families being still reared in the single bedroom . . . '[154] And even when the cottages were kept in a reasonable state of repair, they could be uncomfortable. As John Purser, who was born during the late 1890s, in the Warwickshire parish of Ilmington, recalled: 'The one or two bedrooms of the thatched cottages were in the roof, and were open to the rough rafters, which were branches cut straight from the tree. We easily bumped our heads. The only light and ventilation was from one small window, two foot by two foot six. In such cramped conditions, if one member of the family got influenza, others were sure to catch it.'[119] In earlier years even stronger indictments of English cottage accommodation had been given.

At the time of the 1867–69 *Royal Commission on the Employment of Children, Young Persons and Women in Agriculture*, for example, it was noted by one assistant commissioner – the Revd James Fraser – that out of 300 villages he had visited in Norfolk, Essex, Sussex, Gloucester and parts of Suffolk, in only *two* had the cottage provision been 'both admirable in quality and sufficient in quantity'. His condemnation was severe: 'The majority of the cottages that exist in rural parishes are deficient in almost every requisite that should constitute a home for a Christian family in a civilized community.' They are 'deficient in drainage and sanitary arrangements; they are imperfectly supplied with water; such conveniences as they have are often so situated as to become nuisances; they are full enough of draughts to generate any amount of rheumatism; and in many instances are lamentably dilapidated and out of repair . . .' He concluded: 'It is impossible to exaggerate the ill effects of such a state of things in every aspect – physical, social, economical, moral, intellectual . . .'

In Cumberland and Westmorland at around the same time, the need for cottage improvement was likewise regarded as the 'question of the day' by the local clergy. They felt, in particular, that attempts to raise educational standards were of little avail when the houses in which the children lived were 'over-crowded, dirty, and often without the requisite of decency and comfort'.[2] Indeed, of sixty-eight parishes and townships in Cumberland visited by the assistant commissioner, only thirty-seven had satisfactory accommodation, while in Westmorland, of twenty-four townships or parishes quoted, only nine were adequately provided with cottages.

Nor, as we have seen, had the situation improved very much by the end of the century. In fact, when in 1892 Mr Cecil Chapman carried out a survey in connection with the *Royal Commission on Labour* on cottage accommodation in certain districts of Oxfordshire, Buckinghamshire, Cornwall, Herefordshire, Berkshire, etc., his conclusions were a salutary reminder of the sort of conditions under which many country children were still spending their early days as the Queen's reign drew to an end. 'Cleanliness and tidiness are remarkable in most of the cottages, but it is often impossible to scrub the bedroom floor because the cracks in it let the water through into the sitting room . . . The number of privies are being generally increased, though in each place instances occur where one privy is shared by three or four cottages; and in [the] Truro [district] it is a common thing to find a whole row of cottages without any privy accommodation at all . . . One of the greatest difficulties of an agricultural labourer's life is the absence of good water . . . In the fens particularly it is true that "there is water everywhere but not a drop to drink." Cottages with thatched roofs depend upon the rainfall, and when that is insufficient the occupiers must buy water from their neighbours or drink what they can get from the dykes, brooks or ponds . . . A cesspool and a well are often close to each other . . . Occasional instances occur in every district of people having to fetch water from a distance of a quarter to half a mile, and it is a matter of frequent occurrence for a village to have but one village pump. Lazy people will, under such circumstances, prefer to drink out of a pond . . . '[13]

At Ilmington John Purser remembered that a 'few lucky ones had a well or a pump'. But when the season was dry the old pump was often difficult to work, and had to be coaxed into operation by pouring a jugful of water down its spout and then working away at the arm until water began to gush forth. 'One must keep at it till all had had enough, or he'd go on strike again quickly. We were fortunate, we had a well, though sometimes it was necessary to let down the bucket on the end of my older brother's shepherd's crook. In most other cases, water had to be carried a long distance, and this fell to the hard-pressed housewife during the day . . . with a yoke and two buckets. Such yokes were well made and fitted comfortably on the shoulders; even then, it was a heavy job for mothers. At one house where we lived for a time, it was my job to carry sufficient water on Saturday to supply us till Monday, and store it in a large glazed vessel holding several gallons.

'Washing was done on a bench outside in a large zinc vessel. All heating of water was done in a big iron pot. Even when empty, it was as heavy as a woman could lift.'[119]

Mrs Kate Edwards, whose childhood was spent in the Lotting Fen area of Huntingdonshire during the 1880s and 1890s, had similar memories of the water problem, 'Most houses 'ould have a rainwater tub, but that 'ould be green and shiny and full o' striddlebags, little wriggling creatures as 'ould turn into gnats afore long. That warn't very good tack to drink, but it were better than the muck from the dykes. Many's the time I'm seen a man or woman in the bottom o' the dyke, waiting for the water to seep into a tablespoon to be put into a kettle for the one cup o' tea o' the day. As late as 1921 we had a summer without water; it were so bad that year that we could only have one bowl o' water a day in the house for everybody to wash in. The first up in the morning was the lucky one, 'cos he had it clean, but everybody else all day had to have the same water used over and over again . . .'[112]

Yet if the general structure and amenities of the cottages were often poor, the interior and furnishings were equally so. A few plain wooden chairs, a table and perhaps a rough wooden dresser on which were displayed the owner's few pots and pans – these were the sum total of major items of furniture in the living room of most cottages. Sometimes a plant or two would brighten the windowsill and on the floor of the more energetic women's houses would perhaps be a home-made rag rug, hiding some at least of the bare flags or boards. In the days before cheap polish, many of the more houseproud cottage women would use a little thick home-made beer to give a golden brown colour to the wood of their furniture.[81]

However, where the family was a large one of young children and the cottage small and over-crowded, a mother might lack sufficient energy and time to provide these small extras. Often there would not even be enough seats for all of the children to sit down together for their meals, and so they would either have to stand or else sit on the doorstep or in a corner of the room, with their plates in their hands or on their laps. Some mothers even adopted a 'relay' system for feeding their children.[90]

EARLY LIFE AND HOME BACKGROUND

At a time when villagers had to fetch their water from wells, this youngster, complete with yoke, was carrying out an essential household task at Worle, Avon. (Reproduced by courtesy of Woodspring Museum, Weston-super-Mare)

Yet not all homes were as poverty-stricken as this. On the walls of many of them, especially in the slightly more prosperous late Victorian period, there would often be a few prints (usually with a religious theme) and perhaps a selection of the Staffordshire pottery chimney ornaments beloved by most cottagers. But few houses were as well fitted out as the home of a Cotswold labourer described just after the end of the Victorian period: 'The furniture of the room consist[ed] of a large deal table, an ancient sofa covered with faded red cloth, a chest of drawers, and half a dozen chairs, including the arm-chair by the fireside in which no one else must presume to sit when the carter [was] at home . . . There [were] no less than fifty ornaments on the mantelpiece . . . As with ornaments, so with pictures and photographs; there [were] nearly a hundred hanging upon the walls of the living-room. Of these the most conspicuous [were] a reproduction of "The Stolen Duchess" in colours, and two old Scriptural prints – "The Finding of Moses" and "Moses in the Land of Midian". The mirror, before which the carter [had] his weekly shave, [was] marked with the name of a certain embrocation, warranted "Good for Cattle", and the covering over the back of the good-wife's chair [was] a piece of hand-wrought embroidery depicting Joseph's flight with the infant Christ into Egypt. Hanging up [were] a hempen halter and a great horn lantern for use in the stables; upon the floor [were] a long brass-handled whip and a flag dinner basket.'[70]

In some of the more fortunate cottages there would be an oven built into the chimney corner, 'with the oven door so arranged that the escaping smoke would go up the house chimney'. The door was often nothing more than 'a heavy block of wood, with a handle for each hand, made to fit closely, although it might have to be packed with cloths to keep the heat in. The oven was shaped like a big, upturned dish, about four to six feet across inside.' When it was empty the children would perhaps play hide-and-seek in it, for the door was just big enough for a child to creep through.[119]

Yet, as we have seen, large numbers of cottages were without these amenities, and in most of them day-to-day existence in the one living-room was both cramped and uncomfortable. Where children were very young there was little room for them to move about, let alone play. But it was on wash days that such

Parents and children sharing the misery of eviction from their Dorset cottage in 1874. The men were being 'punished' for joining Joseph Arch's farm workers' trade union. (Blandford Museum Collection)

8

restricted conditions became well-nigh intolerable. As in John Purser's Ilmington, so elsewhere, it was normal for water to be boiled for the washing in small pots over the fire; once hot, it had to be taken out to the washing-tub, which stood in the yard on a bench or log of wood 'or anything else which [would] sufficiently heighten [it]'.[45] The business of washing was itself tiring, especially when the water was hard. In the Lotting Fen area of Huntingdonshire the dyke water was so hard, indeed, that 'a quarter of a stone o' soda and a bucket-ful of wood ashes' had to be added to it overnight before it could be used. This mixture certainly softened the water but it also coloured it a light brown shade, and 'it 'ould take a nice lot o' blue bag to get your clothes white in it . . .'[112]

But if the daytime accommodation in many country cottages left much to be desired, the conditions of poverty and overcrowding were often still more obvious in the bedrooms, which were out of the public gaze. After climbing the narrow staircase – frequently little more than a ladder – which gave access to the upper rooms, the bedroom or bedrooms would open off immediately. Many cottages lacked the refinement of even a small landing – instead one bedroom merely opened off the other, with the first room leading directly on to the stairs. A vivid picture of conditions at their worst was provided by F.G. Heath, a mid-Victorian visitor to a Somerset cottage: 'A wretched, ragged-looking bed was before me. It filled up the greater part of the room. An old, brown, worn, patched tester stretched over this bed, in which the father, mother, and the two youngest children slept . . . On the floor at the foot of the bedstead there was a nondescript heap of rags, amongst which the three eldest children slept. Seven human beings in this tiny, ill-lit room . . . There was only one small window. Several of the panes were out . . .'[49]

Similar conditions of overcrowding were reported elsewhere. Thus in 1867–68 of sixty-three parishes investigated in Staffordshire, 'no less than 25 per cent of the cottages had only one bedroom, and 9 per cent contained a family with three children or more living in that one bedroom . . .'[2] Again, at Hilborough in Norfolk a population of 252 was accommodated in fifty-three cottages – twenty-two of which comprised one bedroom and one living room only. Not surprisingly it was noted that 'the bedrooms [were] overcrowded with no proper separation of sexes'. One even had eleven people sleeping in what the relieving officer called 'a very small room!' And at Narborough, a few miles away, with a population of 261, twenty-one of the fifty-eight cottages in the parish had one bedroom only.[2] All over the country other villages could be found which mirrored these conditions and which gave rise to charges of 'gross immorality' or even incest from more fortunately placed neighbours. An official inquiry pointed out of the West Country in 1843: 'The sleeping of boys and girls, young

9

men and young women, in the same room, in beds almost touching one another, must have the effect of breaking down the great barriers between the sexes, – the sense of modesty and decency on the part of women, and respect for the other sex on the part of the men. The consequences of the want of proper accommodation for sleeping in the cottages are seen in the early licentiousness of the rural districts – licentiousness which has not always respected the family relationship.' (See also Document D (ii).) Similar statements were made throughout the first half of Victoria's reign – and even to the end of the century in a few areas.

Nevertheless in a large number of cases efforts *were* made to preserve modesty and privacy as between parents and children, or between children of different sex. Despite the general shortage of space, many labouring families would, for example, 'curtain off' their one room as best they could. It was also fairly common for the largest families to split up for sleeping purposes, so that one or two members would regularly sleep with neighbours, or perhaps with grand-parents, whose own children had left home.[90]

On the other hand, in this unfavourable environment some allowed themselves to degenerate still further. Even in the 1880s and 1890s in the Lotting Fen area of Huntingdonshire: '[The children's] beds were made of straw, so that when they wetted it, it 'ould all run through. Then when they got too bad, they could be burnt and have a fresh one. There warn't anything on'y straw beds in most folks's houses. Anybody as had chaff beds had a real luxury, and best of all were a bed of oat-flights, 'cos they'd be free from thistles. These straw beds were a real breeding place for fleas, and the poor little kids 'ould be bumped up all over with flea-bites. You could tell a child as come from a flea-pit; 'cos its neck 'ould all be spotted all over like a plum pudding . . .'[112]

However, where a family kept chickens there was the opportunity to save the feathers to fill pillows and even mattresses – at least for the adults. The feathers were first of all baked in the oven to kill any insects which might be in them, and then they were ready for use.

Bed clothes were another problem when financial resources were small and competing needs for money great; some families preferred to make do with sacking or rags – like the Somerset example already quoted. But in a number of villages, charity or blanket clubs might step in to fill the gap – very often organized by the clergy or gentry. Thus at Steeple Claydon in Buckinghamshire there was a blanket loan society financed by charity whose apparent custom it was to buy twenty pairs of blankets each year (at a cost of 11s 6d per pair) and to lend them out for the winter to needy families. At the end of each winter the blankets were cleaned and then sold off at 1s each to the villagers. Obviously where this practice was followed over a number of years, it would help to solve some of the bedding problems in a particular parish. Likewise in late Victorian

Blaxhall in Suffolk a little girl could remember that every family received an annual gift of a sheet and a yard of calico for each child – the latter intended to be made into underclothing. These gifts were normally handed over from tables erected near to the church porch.[85]

But apart from the comfort – or otherwise – of his or her home, another matter of great interest to the growing child was, of course, that of food. Once a baby had outgrown reliance upon its mother's milk for sustenance, there was often little suitable alternative food available. Fresh milk was surprisingly scarce in rural areas – and especially at the end of the nineteenth century the situation became acute, as large quantities were dispatched by rail to the big urban centres, while skim milk was used to fatten the pigs. Naturally both the more perceptive parents and medical men complained of this state of affairs, even if they were able to do little to remedy the situation. As a 'Warwickshire Labourer' wrote in 1872: '. . . but when milk cannot be bought for miles round, surelie it is better to gie skim milk to human beings than to pigs. I doont think th' Chamber o' Agriculture thout o' that, because poor children ha' to go wi'out what th'a owt to ha morst on.'[26] And in August 1864, a Sussex doctor wrote to *The Times* from Brighton: 'Only a few days ago a woman brought her child a distance of five miles for medical advice. Proper food was what was most needed, and I recommended the mother to get a good supply of fresh milk daily for the child. She replied that it was almost impossible for her to get milk of any kind. This short supply of milk is constant throughout the Weald of Sussex, though Brighton is well supplied with butter from its dairy farms.'

Evidence from elsewhere tended to bear out these claims, especially in regard to the southern counties. For example, a survey of labourers' diets produced by the Medical Officer of the Privy Council in 1863 revealed that of twenty families investigated in Dorset, only twelve had any milk at all – and their *weekly* average was under five pints, or less than one pint per family per day. In Oxfordshire, likewise, of eleven families investigated only seven had milk; in Essex, only two of six reported upon; and in Gloucestershire, of nine families interviewed only one had milk – and that was a mere two pints per week for a family of eight.[14] Although each of the thirty-four families investigated in Devonshire had milk (skimmed milk in the main), the amount involved was by no means adequate at under $2\frac{1}{2}$ pints per person per week; only Northumberland could perhaps be considered satisfactory. Here all of the seven families reported upon had milk, and the per capita average consumption was over 3 pints per week.

Furthermore, as already indicated, this problem had certainly not disappeared by the end of the century. In the 1880s the daughter of at least one family from the Lotting Fen area of Huntingdonshire was to recall that they only had 'a penn'orth o' skim milk once a week, on Sunday, to make a baked pudding with. All the rest o' the week we drunk our tea without milk, though sugar were cheap and we could have it as sweet as we liked . . .'[112] Often, the skimmed milk was not of very good standard anyway – it was so thin, indeed, that some said it 'looked blue with cold'.

However, if the lack of milk was harmful to the older children, it was particularly so for the youngest. By the end of the nineteenth century, admittedly, the unsatisfactory substitute of tinned milk was sold in most village shops, and many mothers relied upon it; but its nutritional value was small. Other mothers, in desperation, crammed their children 'with bread sop, arrow-root, and other farinaceous substances', or, according to a Wiltshire critic, even with herrings! She declared that they 'ought not to give (the youngsters) anything fermented until they [were] two years old . . .'[17] Unfortunately, family poverty and the milk shortage prevented most labourers' wives from complying with this advice.

To a certain extent, of course, the availability of milk depended upon an individual farm worker's relationship with his employer, and some families fared better in this respect than others. Yet few were as fortunate as the labourers of North Derbyshire in the late 1860s – some of whom, living in the Bakewell area of the county, were allowed to rent 'enough grass land to keep one or two cows, by the Duke of Devonshire'. Elsewhere farm servants received a quart of new milk per day (worth 2d) as a perquisite; and in other cases again, labourers were able to rent 'with their cottage six or eight acres of grass land with a shippon attached, and [were] thus enabled to keep two cows during both summer and winter' or they might 'borrow a cow from a farmer for £3–£4 during the summer months'. The ample milk supplies to which these schemes gave rise were regarded by observers as 'the secret of the comfort of the labourers' homes in North Derbyshire'.[2] Furthermore, the tending of the animals did not interfere with the man's employment, since this work would normally be left to the wife and children.

In the south of Derbyshire a few labourers also kept their own cow, feeding it in the winter on grains purchased from the Burton breweries, and relying in the summer on grazing the animal at the roadside. But by the later 1860s this practice of roadside grazing was being discouraged by the authorities, and so the number of cows kept in the area was dwindling.

Yet, for most families such opportunities did not exist and a little weak milkless tea and bread formed the great staple of life, especially for the mother and her children. The monotony of many diets was, indeed, underlined by an assistant commissioner who visited the county of Somerset in connection with the *Royal Commission on the Employment of Children, Young Persons and Women in Agriculture*, 1867–69. What he wrote was also applicable to most other rural areas at that time: 'There is little variety and little that is inviting in the food of the Somersetshire labourer. A little girl in the vale of Taunton Deane, being asked what she had for breakfast, said "bread and butter." What for supper? "bread and butter and cheese." It is a fair sample of what the agricultural labourer lives on, except that where no cheese or butter is produced he has nothing but the bread dipped in cider; the wife drinks tea, and there is sometimes a bit of bacon for the husband after his work, unless they are so poor that they have to sell every atom of the pig to pay the rent. There is besides a concoction, called tea kettle broth, given to the children; hot water flavoured with a few herbs or tag ends of bacon, sometimes little but the pure hot water.' For those too poor to buy even tea there was also 'frog water', as it was known in parts of Wiltshire. This consisted of a 'frog' – or a thick crust cut from the bottom of a loaf and blackened in the oven or before the fire. It was then placed in the teapot and boiling water poured upon it. After it had been allowed to stand for a few minutes, the liquor 'was fit for use'.[152]

In view of this, it is hardly surprising that a later critic could write of the mid-century plight of the labouring family: 'I do not think that there is much evidence from the low-wage districts that the food available was insufficient for men in normal health, but there is certainly medical evidence to show that if there was a disposition to disease, then the quality was found to be defective. Further, as the husband had necessarily to have the largest share of the food, and also the most strengthening diet, such as pork and bacon, the women and children frequently suffered from insufficient nourishment . . . the principal diet of the agricultural labourers was wheaten bread or other food made from flour. Barley bread was, however, frequently eaten in the western counties; and, in the north, barley bread, oat cake and porridge. In some counties nearly half a man's weekly wages appears to have been spent on bread for his family. Other articles of diet were bacon, pork (the latter frequently salted), cheese, dripping, lard, milk, potatoes, onions and other vegetables. The high price of tea prohibited much being drunk. Fresh meat (beef or mutton) was seldom eaten, except in some of the northern and north midland counties (chiefly on Sundays) . . .

'In the low-wage counties the monotony of the bread diet was relieved by eating it soaked in broth or spread with dripping or lard. Toast water was often taken in lieu of tea. Skim milk or butter-milk was also drunk. Bacon or pork was, as a rule, eaten on Sundays only; and, at times when this could not be obtained for the Sunday dinner, potatoes were eaten with melted butter or grease.

'In some of the western counties potatoes, swedes and cheese made from skim milk formed a considerable portion of the diet.'[87]

By the end of the Victorian period, the slight rise in money wages of perhaps one-fifth, as compared with the 1860s and the fall in food prices which had taken

East Anglian girl peeling potatoes. (From P.H. Emerson, *Pictures from Life in Field and Fen*, 1887)

place since the 1870s, as cheaper grain, meat and dairy produce were imported, had helped to raise living standards to some extent. Nevertheless, even in the 1890s many labourers were still reported to be living six days a week on vegetables, bacon and bread – with roast meat only on Sundays (usually roast pork rather than the more expensive joints of beef or mutton).[13] Tinned foods perhaps added variety to the diet, for most village stores were now stocking canned meats, fish and fruit. (See Documents B and C.)

But apart from poverty, lack of fuel and poor cooking facilities often discouraged any culinary experimenting in the labourer's home. In most cases the one hot meal of the day would be cooked in a single iron pot suspended over the kitchen fire. This would consist, by the 1880s, of a small square of bacon, 'cabbage or other green vegetables in one net, potatoes in another, and the roly-poly swathed in a cloth. It sounds a haphazard method . . . but it answered its purpose, for, by carefully timing the putting in of each item and keeping the simmering of the pot well regulated, each item was kept intact and an appetising meal was produced . . .'[144]

A number of cottages had ovens of their own, or else a large oven might be shared with several neighbours. Provided fuel was easily and cheaply available, this was naturally a great boon and women would bake their own bread, cakes and pies. Unfortunately not all of the ovens worked very well. In the Purser family home at Ilmington there was a small oven at the side of the fireplace which Mrs Purser used from time to time to bake her bread, but the door was ill-fitting and it was difficult to discover when the oven was hot enough. As John Purser recalled, the fire to heat this particular sort of oven had to be kindled, with small branches, straight on the floor of the oven itself. Then, when it was thought hot enough, the 'ashes had to be scraped out clean, and the bread placed in quickly with a long-handled pole. There would be ten or more loaves; a bacon and potato pie, some scraps of pig-meat; and a dough cake with currants. If the oven was hot enough, and the bread taken out at just the right time, all was well, and very thankful we were . . . If the oven was not hot enough, the bread would be heavy, or "sad"; but we had to make the best of it. My mother was relieved when the local baker, seeing his trade diminishing . . . offered to bake for us at a ha'penny a loaf. For yeast, we depended on the one-armed donkey-carrier, Tom. I was sent once a week for "two penn'orth o' barm", which he used to bring in quantities from the Stratford brewery, and sell to the housewives for their bread-making.'[119]

Vegetables from garden or allotment were a vital part of any cottage family's diet. Equally important for a large number was the keeping of livestock – a pig or some chickens, for example. But this practice was by no means universally permitted. Even in the early 1890s it was noted that 'in villages the sanitary authorities are obliged to prevent men from keeping pigs in places where they may prove to be a nuisance, and on farms it is often thought necessary to prevent a man from keeping a pig if he has charge of a corn bin . . .' Furthermore, as a number of local labourers frankly admitted in the Wantage area of Berkshire, they could not 'afford to buy a pig, and [had] no place to keep it in when they [did]'. On the other hand, in the Crediton district of Devonshire nearly every cottage was supplied with a pig sty, erected by the landlord, and in this area pig-keeping was an accepted part of labouring life.[13]

Where a pig *was* kept, it soon became a focus of attention for all members of the family – even the youngest. It was fed upon scraps – the water 'in which food had been cooked', the potato parings, and other vegetable trimmings – as well as upon small potatoes. In addition, 'the children, on their way home from school, would fill their arms with sow thistle, dandelion, and choice long grass, or roam along the hedgerows on wet evenings collecting snails in a pail for the pig's supper'. Just before it was killed it would probably have additional feeds of barley meal to fatten it still further. 'Sometimes, when the weekly income would not run to a sufficient quantity of fattening food, an arrangement would be made with the baker or miller that he should give credit now, and when the pig was killed receive a portion of the meat in payment.'[144] Those who had large allotments were in the best position – like the Pursers at Ilmington. They fed their pig on 'barley meal, bran, bean meal and potatoes, all from the allotment'.

Nevertheless, whatever the problems which had attended the final rearing, the actual occasion of the pig killing was one of great excitement. A successful pig killing meant that the family's supply of meat was assured for some weeks to come, and although the younger children might be frightened by the frantic squeals of the pig and the general 'noisy, bloody business', most accepted it as inevitable. For 'country people of that day had little sympathy for the sufferings of animals, and men, women and children would gather round to see the sight. After the carcass had been singed, the pig-sticker would pull off the detachable, gristly, outer coverings of the toes, known locally as "the shoes", and fling them among the children, who scrambled for, then sucked and gnawed them, straight from the filth of the sty and blacked by fire as they were.'[144]

The next day, the mother of the family would start work upon the carcass. 'Hams and sides of bacon were salted, to be taken out of the brine later and hung on the wall near the fireplace to dry. Lard was dried out, hogs' puddings were made, and the chitterlings were cleaned and turned three days in succession under running water, according to ancient ritual.'[144] There was even food to spare – and many families would send 'small plates of fry and other oddments' to their friends as a gift at this time of celebration. Later on the gesture would probably be reciprocated when other families killed their pig; in this way neighbours could help one another.

Chickens were less common in the labouring household – partly because where labourers lived at farm cottages the farmer objected as he thought they were 'always feeding themselves at [his] expense'. In addition, there was the suspicion that labourers would steal grain for their chickens, if given the chance. One device, especially when threshing, was to slip as much as possible into the boots before a man went home, and for this reason, some farmers insisted that 'their threshers should empty their boots before leaving the threshing floor'.[84] A second cause of the relative unpopularity of chickens was their tendency 'to get into the neighbours' gardens and cause a disturbance'. Indeed, one observer noted in 1892 that there was 'not a more constant source of quarrelling' than straying chickens; he also thought that the 'absence of commons and village greens [had] probably caused men to give up keeping chickens, ducks or geese . . .'[13]

A few families kept bees, although in general these were 'not thought much of', while tame rabbits acted as pets for children and later as meat for the pot.[26]

In her quest for as high a degree of self-sufficiency for her family as possible, the careful housewife would also seize the opportunity to make her own beer, wines and preserves. As one Warwickshire labourer later wrote: 'My mother used to . . . brew some good beer, besides making elderberry wine and black-berry jam. We used to gather cowslip-pips for her on the second Monday in May, for cowslips are best and sweetest then. Before this, we gathered coltsfoot flowers . . .'[26] These could be used to make wines or medicines, and as the extract indicates, children were often kept at home by their parents in order to help in these household chores. Thus an entry in Blaxhall School log book in Suffolk for 11 August, 1871, reads: 'Great many absentees; required at home for brewing'.[81] At Helidon in Northamptonshire likewise: 'Picking cowslips, setting potatoes, and helping mother' were noted as 'frequent excuses' for absence early in May, 1872.

It was against this simple, often hard-pressed family background that the average country child grew up. There was little time for pampering – especially as families were frequently large and a new baby would be coming along almost every year. From early on, a spirit of independence and hardiness was encouraged in labouring children, and toddlers were often sent outside to play in the coldest weather. At Juniper Hill, Oxfordshire, in the 1880s, they were 'bundled into a piece of old shawl crossed on the chest and tied in a hard knot at the back . . .' and were then pushed outside to amuse themselves as best they could. Even in the winter time, when their limbs turned purple with cold, they would still 'stamp around', playing at 'horses and engines' or other games. They might, and often did, have running noses and chilblains on hands, feet and ear-tips, but most of them survived the spartan regime to grow into sturdy children.

"SPARE THE ROD AND SPOIL THE CHILD!"

Compassionate Curate. "WHAT'S THE MATTER WITH LITTLE BILLY, MRS. DODDER!"
Suffolk Mother (who has been correcting her Son). "MATTER WUTH 'M! THERE'S ALLUS SUFF'N THE MATTER WUTH 'M! YOU CAN'T DEW WRONG A-HIDIN' OF 'M! IF HE BEAN'T IN MISCHEIF, HE'S JUST A-GOIN' IN, THELSE JUST A-COMIN' OUT!!"

No question of spare the rod and spoil the child. (*Punch*, 1876)

During the summer months, when mothers helped in the harvest field or later went out gleaning, the small children would be brought along, too, often in the care of brothers and sisters only a little older than themselves. Then, while the women worked, the children would play or would wander around searching for crab apples and blackberries. 'If there was an apple or pear tree in the fences unguarded it would of course prove a superior attraction.'[33]

At other times – provided the farmer was willing – toddlers would perhaps play in the nearby farmyard, or in the sheds, at hide and seek among the carts and waggons, 'or scamper about among the trusses of hay and straw on the ground, or peep through the fence and watch their fathers milking the cows or foddering the young cattle . . .'[151] A small boy might stand at the stable door 'watching the harnessing of the great carthorses, which are from the very first the object of his intense admiration. When the horses are gone he visits the out-house, where the steam-engine is driving the chaff-cutter, or peers in at the huge doors of the barn, where with a wide wooden shovel the grain is being moved. Or he may be met with round the hayricks, dragging a log of wood by a piece of tar cord, the log representing a plough.'

One such small Wiltshire lad (perhaps three or four years of age) was described by Richard Jefferies in 1880, in the following terms: 'His hat [was] an old one of his father's, a mile too big, coming down over his ears to his shoulders, well greased from ancient use . . . He [wore] what [had been] a white jacket, but [was] now the colour of the prevailing soil of the place; a belt; and a pair of stumping boots, the very picture of his father's, heeled and tipped with iron. His naked legs [were] red with cold, but thick and strong; his cheeks [were] plump and firm, his round blue eyes bright, his hair almost white, like bleached straw . . . He [would] potter about the farmyard the whole morning, perhaps turning up at home for a lunch of a slice of bread well larded. His little sister, not so old as himself, [was] there already, beginning her education in the cares of maternity, looking after the helpless baby that crawls over the wooden threshold of the door with bare head despite the bitter cold . . .'[50]

Most of these children had, of course, very few toys, and the ones they did possess had probably been purchased with hard-earned pennies from local fairs and markets, or had been received as presents at Christmas celebrations organized by the clergy or gentry. The toys were, in any case, normally of a cheap and fairly crude variety. For example, the dolls sold at St Giles's fair, Oxford, in the late nineteenth century were little more than a wooden ball stuck on to another piece of wood, with legs made of very thin sticks, 'but the kids used to like 'em cos they used to put a cape round 'em, or some kind of apparatus . . . like a frock . . . or a shawl . . . an' their little eyes was a bit of black . . . , some 'ad black 'air an' that was a doll you see . . .'[61] More sophisticated toys were few and far between for labouring children; golliwogs, for instance, made their first 'noticed appearance' at St Giles's fair in 1881, when 'a row of them appeared as prizes in a coconut shy'. As for other toys, the older children would perhaps play with marbles, skipping ropes and hoops, which were widely available, while a little ingenuity could rig up a see-saw from a wooden bench and a plank of wood. Where a father was clever with his hands, he might make a doll or kite or small cart for his children.

Not all pre-school children, however, were as free to wander about outside as earlier paragraphs indicate. Where a mother went out to work herself, perhaps on one of the local farms, a young child's liberty might be very much more closely circumscribed. Sometimes older brothers and sisters would be kept away from school to look after the babies, and in the winter months, this often meant that they would all have to be shut in the house together for long hours. On occasion, the youth of the boy or girl in charge could lead to tragedy, where the youngsters were too immature to accept their responsibilities. This is exemplified by a case reported in the *Norfolk News* of 27 March, 1875, when a five-year-old girl from Fletwell in Norfolk died 'after severe suffering from being burnt . . .' Her mother had gone to work in the fields, leaving three children at home under the care of the eldest – a boy of ten years. He had gone out of the house for a few minutes to get some fuel, when the little girl 'by some means got her clothes on fire, and ran out of the house all in flames . . .' In other communities similar tragedies occurred from time to time; for example, a labourer and his wife interviewed near Marlborough in Wiltshire in 1868 in connection with the *Royal Commission on the Employment of Children, etc. in Agriculture* declared that they had lost one of their children through a house fire. While they were at work, the children had been 'locked up in their cottage' and one of them had got too close to the fire and had been burnt to death. Again, Mr Bullock, a Warwick doctor, reported at around the same time that he had attended eight such cases in the fairly recent past – four of them proving fatal. Another observer, pointing to the dangers where babies were left for hours in the care of 'youthful inefficient nurses', claimed that accidents caused 'by fire and water and dangerous falls, sufficiently indicate the . . . evils connected with the mother's absence'.[56] Yet, given the number of women still employed on the farms in the 1870s, at least on a seasonal, part-time basis, the surprising thing is that the tragedies proved comparatively rare. For the number of children at risk must have been a high one.

But if life had its darker side for a minority of country children, for most, the early years were happy ones. Unlike their fellows in the towns, there was plenty of room for them to play, and even if, as we have seen, toys were scarce, they could often make their own amusements – as at Juniper Hill, where, for example, they outlined 'houses with scraps of broken crockery', furnishing them with pieces of moss and stones. Or, in winter, they would make snow men and slide on the frozen puddles.[144] However, when they reached the age of four or five (and sometimes even earlier), this quiet day-to-day routine was left behind, for most of them must attend school. For those who did not (at least prior to the education legislation of the 1870s), then the serious business of earning a living would soon present itself, with small boys and girls perhaps obtaining work as bird scarers on a local farm, or at some other simple but monotonous rural task.

NOTES ON ADDITIONAL SOURCES USED
For information on Steeple Claydon village charities, see Clergy Visitation Returns, Bucks. Archdeaconry, 1872 – MS.Oxf. Dioc. Pp. c.337 at Oxfordshire Record Office.

CHAPTER TWO

Going to school

'Ah, there's too much of that sending to school in these days! It only does harm. Every gatepost and barn's door you come to is sure to have some bad word or other chalked upon it by the young rascals: a woman can hardly pass for shame sometimes. If they'd never been taught how to write they wouldn't have been able to scribble such villainy. Their fathers couldn't do it, and the country was all the better for it.' – Captain Vye in Thomas Hardy's *The Return of the Native* (1971 edn.), p. 115. The book was first published in 1878.

T he age at which a country child first attended school largely depended, at least in the earlier Victorian period, upon the circumstances and attitude of its parents – as well as upon the availability or otherwise of a school building in the neighbourhood. However, where the mother was employed outside the home or where she had other younger children, attendance might begin as early as two years of age, as at Wadenhoe School in Northamptonshire, in the 1860s. During the months of October – December 1866, no less than three children were accepted there whose age was noted as '3 years next birthday'. And even in 1897 children of three were still being admitted to the school. On the other hand, at Helidon in the same county, it was decided in July, 1874, that the minimum 'entry age' must be raised from three to four years. Yet while some schools followed this example, others continued along the old lines. At Steppingley in Bedfordshire efforts were still being made in the mid–1870s to enforce a minimum age of three, and as late as May, 1896, the mistress at Wasperton in Warwickshire was lamenting 'the very small number of attendances made by the children admitted at three years of age'.

The teachers, for their part, accepted these 'babies' because they realized that in many of the larger families if they did not, then 'the older ones [would be] kept away to take care of them . . .'[2] Or else they acted out of pity for a mother in obvious difficulty. Thus at Blaxhall in Suffolk, Katie Ling, who remembered first attending school at the age of three (in 1873), found herself admitted because her mother and a younger child were both ill. 'To relieve the mother the schoolmistress offered to take Katie on the school "roll".' The little girl spent her first day sitting 'on a small stool in front of the fire'.[81] Yet, from the educational point of view, the presence of a considerable number of possibly lively, very young children was extremely unsatisfactory – for it is unlikely that they were all as amenable to good order and discipline as the small Katie Ling appears to have been. It was on this account, therefore, that one Government Inspector declared as early as 1858 that children *under* three 'should certainly not be admitted to an infant school, unless it [was] provided with a baby room or crèche . . .'[28] An investigation of school log books soon reveals that his advice was widely ignored.

On the other hand, by no means all children *did* attend school in the days before compulsory elementary education was introduced by the Education Acts of 1876 and 1880. In the late 1860s a landowner from Alveston in Warwickshire, for example, spoke of the need to send children to school who were 'found habitually in the roads collecting manure, or otherwise loitering and playing', while in areas where there were cottage industries like lacemaking, straw plaiting and glove-making – in which children were involved – the education of the young workers was sadly neglected.[2] And as late as the 1890s there are examples of reluctant scholars making their first attendance at the age of ten years – despite the careful provisions of the Education Acts for instruction to commence at five.

Nevertheless, most children would spend at least part of their early years at school, either because their parents were simply anxious 'to be free from the care of them', or, more encouragingly, because they wanted the youngsters to learn to read. At Tysoe in Warwickshire, it was noted that 'there were only one or two families whose children did not go to [school] at all, twenty years before compulsion came . . .'[63] This was often the case elsewhere – and most particularly in the very north of the country, in Northumberland. Even in the late 1860s an official observer could write of education in that county: 'The standard of instruction was of course unequal, but there was an absence of that gross ignorance which is said to prevail in other less favoured counties . . . Northumberland may justly be proud of her system of farming, which produces a superior class of occupiers of land, and an intelligent and contented peasantry.'[2] It is, therefore, against a background of fairly general parental acceptance of the need for some measure of education that the day-to-day lives of the children should be examined.

For most nineteenth-century country families the motto was 'early to bed, early to rise'. In the case of the fathers of labouring families 'early to rise' normally meant getting up in time to start work at 6 a.m. in summer – although for the horsemen, who had to arrive before the rest of the labourers, in order to

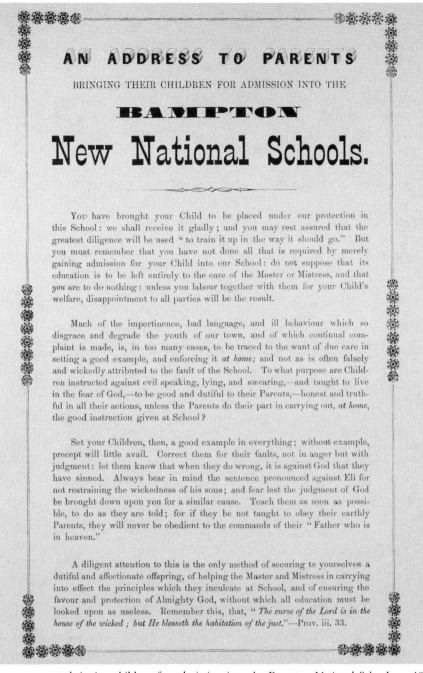

AN ADDRESS TO PARENTS

BRINGING THEIR CHILDREN FOR ADMISSION INTO THE

BAMPTON

New National Schools.

You have brought your Child to be placed under our protection in this School: we shall receive it gladly; and you may rest assured that the greatest diligence will be used "to train it up in the way it should go." But you must remember that you have not done all that is required by merely gaining admission for your Child into our School: do not suppose that its education is to be left entirely to the care of the Master or Mistress, and that *you* are to do nothing: unless you labour together with them for your Child's welfare, disappointment to all parties will be the result.

Much of the impertinence, bad language, and ill behaviour which so disgrace and degrade the youth of our town, and of which continual complaint is made, is, in too many cases, to be traced to the want of due care in setting a good example, and enforcing it *at home;* and not as is often falsely and wickedly attributed to the fault of the School. To what purpose are Children instructed against evil speaking, lying, and swearing,—and taught to live in the fear of God,—to be good and dutiful to their Parents,—honest and truthful in all their actions, unless the Parents do their part in carrying out, *at home,* the good instruction given at School?

Set your Children, then, a good example in everything; without example, precept will little avail. Correct them for their faults, not in anger but with judgment: let them know that when they do wrong, it is against God that they have sinned. Always bear in mind the sentence pronounced against Eli for not restraining the wickedness of his sons; and fear lest the judgment of God be brought down upon you for a similar cause. Teach them as soon as possible, to do as they are told; for if they be not taught to obey their earthly Parents, they will never be obedient to the commands of their "Father who is in heaven."

A diligent attention to this is the only method of securing to yourselves a dutiful and affectionate offspring, of helping the Master and Mistress in carrying into effect the principles which they inculcate at School, and of ensuring the favour and protection of Almighty God, without which all education must be looked upon as useless. Remember this, that, "*The curse of the Lord is in the house of the wicked; but He blesseth the habitation of the just.*"—Prov. iii. 33.

Address to parents bringing children for admission into the Bampton National Schools, c. 1871.
(The Bodleian Library, Oxford, John Johnson Collection: Education 12)

feed the horses, 4 a.m. would be the time most usual for rising. Given the small and overcrowded condition of many cottages, therefore, the movements of the men and boys getting ready for work must have awakened the remainder of the family.

Once the children were up they would finish dressing themselves before having a wash, many of them having slept in at least some of their underclothing. This would perhaps consist for the girls, of quilted stays with buttons down the front, a calico chemise and knickers. Often, as at Blaxhall in Suffolk, the calico used would be a gift from a village charity, or a Christmas present from the local gentry. But in parishes where such annual gifts were lacking, underclothes were sometimes allowed to become very ragged, as all the efforts of the mother were devoted to keeping up a good external appearance.[117] (Indeed, in the Newent area of Gloucestershire, to take a rather extreme example, it was said that in a number of labouring families 'the flannel undervest [was] perhaps only taken off when it [was] worn out'.[2])

Water for washing had to be brought to the house the night before and in warmer weather the bowl of water used was regularly kept outside on a specially constructed wooden stool or table. Indeed, as Kate Edwards of Lotting Fen in Huntingdonshire recalled: 'Nobody ever washed theirselves [sic] in the house more 'n once a week, when they had a "bath" and changed their clothes. Other times they washed in a bowl what stood on a plank stool . . . outside the door . . . There'd be a half a coconut shell containing a bit of yellow, strong soap, as hard as flint, and a square of an old shirt tail or a worn out blanket for a face flannel.'[112] But not all children made even these limited concessions to hygiene, and as school log books reveal, a small minority would regularly either be sent home to wash by the teacher or else would have to wash on the school premises. Thus at Souldern in Oxfordshire, offenders were compelled to wash at school in this way, while periodic lectures were given to the assembled pupils on the evils of 'coming dirty to school'. At Bloxham parish school in the same county, rules issued in January, 1855, made a similar point: 'All children must come clean, and with their hair combed, and must bring pocket-handkerchiefs.'

For the girls there was the problem of keeping their fashionably long hair in a clean and tidy condition. At Lotting Fen, it was the custom only to wash the hair 'about twice a year when there was plenty o' soft water. Then we should be sent to get two-penn'orth of "air-ile", and mother would allus doctor it with a drop or two o' "saint" (scent – usually lavender water). We used to wear our hair in one long plait down over our backs, and keep the snarls out of it with a little besom brush.'[112] Unfortunately, under these circumstances it was extremely easy for long hair to become infested with vermin – one of the major hygiene problems in most Victorian schools. If mothers were careless, or overburdened with large families, then children would be sent to school with 'dirty heads', and the nuisance would rapidly spread to others. Teachers on occasion intervened to send offenders home for treatment, until they were fit 'to mix with the other children' but this often led to considerable unpleasantness between the parents concerned and a teacher. Of course, certain of the more cautious mothers always made their daughters wear their hair cut short like a boy – so that they could 'keep a clean head'.[81] (Indeed, a surviving school photograph from Cropredy in north Oxfordshire, dated about 1888, shows a majority of girls with short hair, but photographs from other villages at about the same time indicate that such a wholehearted attitude as this was unusual.)

After the children had washed and finished dressing there was breakfast to eat – usually weak tea and bread smeared with lard, dripping or butter, although for those with milk to hand, there might be a mixture of warmed milk and wheaten flour known in parts of Wiltshire as 'bang belly'. (In north Warwickshire it had the rather more elegant title of 'Lumpy Tom'.) Then, for the children with a mile or two to walk, it was time to leave home – often as early as 7 a.m. – in order to arrive at school in plenty of time for the attendance bell at 9 a.m. For unpunctuality was, like uncleanliness, an especial sin in the eyes of school teachers, and persistent unpunctuality was soon punished by 'keeping in', or a few taps on the hand, or (less logically) by sending the child straight home again. For the would-be truant, this latter solution was no doubt a heaven-sent opportunity.

On the journey to school, provided the weather was fine, the children would play together as they trotted along. Sometimes the bigger boys would bully the smaller children, but normally there were sufficient older brothers, sisters or cousins to prevent any serious damage. This journey would also give the children an opportunity, at the appropriate seasons, of supplementing their meagre breakfast by picking berries and nuts from the hedgerows or munching turnips gathered surreptitiously from a field. In the spring the large buds and young leaves of the hawthorn (called 'bread and cheese') would be consumed, while primrose and cowslip petals and stalks would be sucked or, in the summer, the fruit of brambles, crabs, etc. gathered. At almost all times of the year there was *something* which could be eaten, and in the winter a few children might even carry 'two hot potatoes which had been in the oven, or in the ashes, all night, to warm their hands on the way to school, and to serve as a light lunch on arrival'.[144]

If the weather were wet, however, attendance at school was usually seriously affected, for the clothing and especially the boots of the children of most agricultural labourers were often too shabby to keep out the rain. In any case, if the children did attend, there were normally no facilities for drying out wet clothes, so that they would have to sit in their wet things all day. A common entry in school log books on a rainy day, therefore, was: 'Wet day; few children attended' – such as was made at Souldern school in Oxfordshire on 28 May 1869.

Although smock frocks were now dying out for the children of labourers, some still wore them – at least until the last quarter of the nineteenth century. But at Waterstock, Oxfordshire, in the 1890s, the boys refused to wear smocks provided by a local charity. Many youngsters were dressed in clothes cut down from older members of the family – and for the boys this often meant that they would be made of serviceable cord, which soon became the characteristic dress of the Victorian farm worker. Although most of the handed-down clothes were ill-fitting, as an examination of photographs of Victorian school children will soon reveal, at least they were preferable to the 'skirts and pinafores' worn by some unlucky lads, who were so attired 'because custom and household economy demanded that [they] should wear their older sister's clothes as they grew into them'. A photograph of children from the Warwickshire village of Hill Wootton shows boys dressed in this fashion as late as August 1890.[153] 'The age when you graduated into trousers depended on whether, and when, the family possessed a pair that would fit you.' At the north Oxfordshire hamlet of Juniper Hill, in the 1880s small boys were normally dressed in petticoats 'until they were six or seven'. In school, likewise, the younger boys as well as the girls might wear calico pinafores.

Nevertheless, despite all this 'make do and mend', mothers still had to use their ingenuity to obtain enough money to clothe their children. Alfred Dodman (1879–1971) recollected that in his early youth at West Rudham, Norfolk, his mother used to mend old umbrellas at 6d a time, in order to get money to buy clothing; she would mend other things, too, such as 'old lamps with plaster of Paris . . .' so as to earn the odd extra vital pennies. Fieldwork, charing or washing for the better-off members of village society were other methods adopted, while in some villages mothers would contribute to a clothing club. Here the contributions of a family were usually supplemented by gifts from the local gentry and clergy, and every year – sometimes twice a year – distributions would be made from the fund. Very often, as at Odell in Bedfordshire, the school room would be used for this latter purpose.

Boots were, however, an even bigger problem than clothes, both because they were often stiff and uncomfortable to wear and because they were expensive to buy. While poorer children might wander around home or village barefoot, particularly during the summer, they must invariably have suitable footwear to attend school. In the Lotting Fen area of Huntingdonshire, Kate Edwards recalled that the children's boots always seemed to be wet, especially in the winter months. At night they would be hastily dried in front of the fire, but this treatment, coupled with the fact that the footwear was made of strong, hard

Annie Eliza Johnson, c. 1885. Annie was baptized at Fifield, Oxfordshire, in 1881 and was the daughter of a coachman. Note that despite her elaborate costume she is wearing the traditional heavy boots common to labouring children in the Victorian countryside. (Mrs M. Dring)

leather, made them extremely unpleasant to wear. In an attempt to remedy this, the boots would be rubbed with 'shoe oil' each week to soften them, and they would also be cleaned with shoe blacking, applied to the boots with a rabbit's paw, and 'brushed off with the one and only shoe brush the family possessed'.[112] Nevertheless, despite this treatment the boots remained stiff and children's heels would be rubbed raw with blisters and chilblains. At the worst times of year, the 'little children 'ould start to cry with their feet afore they'd gone a quarter of a mile. . .Most. . .'ould be crying about something afore we got to school . . .'[112]

In these circumstances, therefore, it is scarcely surprising that school attendance was interrupted from time to time by a child's lack of suitable footwear. At the Oxfordshire village of Launton, in June, 1866, for example, a Mrs Sansome, the wife of a local labourer, informed the schoolmaster that she had been unable to send her seven-year-old daughter, Sarah, to school or to church on Sunday, 'because her shoes were so very bad'. She appealed to the master to let the little girl 'come to school this week (and) she would try to get her some new ones for next'. In Lincolnshire, too, lack of boots was seen by at least one observer as an insuperable barrier to compulsory education, since children would not be allowed to attend school barefoot. In the late 1860s the Roman Catholic parish priest of Louth pinpointed the problem when he declared: 'As to compulsory education, I can only say that it is a question of clothes, and especially of shoes; and I don't see how to get over that difficulty . . .'[128]

Again, when there was snow or frost about, poorly shod children might suffer so badly with chilblains or 'bad feet' that they could not attend school. At Asthall School in Oxfordshire as late as 1 March 1895, it was noted that several of the older children had been kept at home with chilblains – 'can't get their boots on'. 'Broken chilblains' were given as a cause of absence in this and many other country schools during the winter months.

Yet at least by the end of the century some of the problems were being overcome. Cheaper machine-made boots were now becoming available at a cost of perhaps 8s a pair, as opposed to those made to order by the village shoemaker, which had been sold for about 14s a pair.[13] And even if the machine-made footwear did not last as long as the other, the existence of this cheaper alternative probably meant that fewer children had to go to school in broken boots handed down from one member of the family to another, or in those worn long past the end of their effective life.

Nevertheless, as we have seen, cast-off *clothing* still formed a major source of the children's wardrobe, and in Wiltshire it was declared in the early 1890s that without it 'the families of labourers earning 10s to 12s a week . . . would be nearly naked'.[13]

By the end of the century, most parents were making an effort to dress their children tidily for school. The little girls would perhaps wear a 'dress of drab cloth stuff, print pinafore, dark stockings, and stout heavy square nailed boots, blacked weekly. When it [was] fine they [came] unencumbered; if it [looked] stormy they half [carried] and half [dragged] a little jacket of coarse material on one side of them . . .' The boys usually wore their hair fairly 'long and bristly – sticking up for fine weather, as they jokingly said – and home cut. Their clothes [were] mostly threadbare, made out of father's left-offs, more than likely, often with trousers reaching half-way down the legs, ridiculous to the critical eye of the townsfolk. They [wore] a woollen scarf around the neck in winter . . . Their boots [were] heavy, thick, and cumbersome, and well nailed; such as [came] from the farms in the fields [wore] leather gaiters in the winter and [kept] them on during the day.'[150]

Those children who came from a long distance would bring a small basket or a handkerchief with them in which they wrapped their midday meal of bread and butter, lard, jam or treacle. Some of the more fortunate might also have a little cheese or perhaps a piece of cake or a pasty.

Once they had arrived at school they would hang up hats and coats on the pegs provided and would then take their place in the large room which, together perhaps with a separate infants' classroom, usually comprised the total accommodation available. These schoolrooms were rather forbidding places with long rows of desks neatly arranged and with, very often, a gallery, or raised platform at one end of the room for the younger pupils. The gallery was so planned that a teacher could see clearly what each child was up to, while freedom of movement was reduced to a minimum. Heating arrangements were likewise most unsatisfactory. In the majority of schools an open fire would be the only form of heat available in the winter and would prove totally inadequate for its purpose, except for those who sat near it. At Austrey School, north Warwickshire, for example, the master noted disapprovingly in his log book on 21 March 1898: 'Temperature, two yards from the fire, 44°.' Again, at Weston-on-Avon, (then in Gloucestershire) the entry for 20 January 1879, read: 'Excessively cold. Hardly able to carry the school on properly, the children shivering frequently with cold.' On occasion, indeed, schools ran out of fuel for a time. At Launton in Oxfordshire in January, 1866, the master reported that they could 'only use one end of the school room . . . because the snow had beaten through one of the windows and made the other end very wet'; on the next day (12 January) he added that he had 'dismissed the school at 3.45 this afternoon because the fires were out and we had no more fuel at school'. Similarly, at Cublington school, Buckinghamshire, in April, 1877, the mistress noted that it was 'bitterly cold in school, no fires since last Wednesday. Have applied for firing but none came.' One Derbyshire head teacher was even forced to report that the 'ink was frozen'

East Adderbury Girls' School on 11 June, 1906. Note the picture showing water and boats on the rear wall. It was probably used as an illustration for 'object' lessons. (Oxfordshire Education Committee)

because of the cold weather![113] Although cases as extreme as this were fairly rare, there is little doubt that during the winter months a majority of schools were very cold and uncomfortable.

On the other hand, during summer and winter alike, the atmosphere could become extremely close and unhealthy through lack of ventilation. Mr E.H. Brodie, HMI noted in 1860 that he had 'constantly found ventilators, both in roof and floor, or at the sides closed; and on inspecting schools in the afternoon, too often the pestiferous atmosphere had manifested that the windows have not been opened in the interval between school hours to freely air and purify the room. From such closeness and foulness the health of teachers and pupils suffers daily . . .'[7] Two years earlier than this, his colleague, the Revd M. Mitchell, had observed that in Norfolk, Suffolk and Essex schools, 'picturesque lattice windows' seriously hampered ventilation and proper lighting; he gloomily recorded that there had been 'eleven cases' in his area where the teacher or a pupil teacher 'had broken down in health or collapsed' after teaching in a poorly ventilated room fitted with lattice windows. One wonders what the effect on the pupils had been. But it was no doubt this sort of situation which lay behind a July, 1870, log book entry at Steppingley School, Bedfordshire: 'Very hot; sent babies under the shed.'

Furthermore, by no means all schools – at least before the 1870s – were purpose-built. In north Oxfordshire, during the mid-century there are examples of schools being held not only in cottages but also, at Barford St Michael, in the vicarage kitchen and scullery; at Bloxham, in the vicar's loft; and at Fritwell, in a stable in the vicarage garden. At Hempton, near Deddington, the north-aisle of the chapel was used as a school room for the hamlet, and in many other parishes up and down the country this sort of make-shift arrangement was made to provide a modicum of education for the country child.[99] Perhaps the worst offenders in this respect were the 'dame schools' which still survived in many localities, where mothers sent their youngsters for a penny or two per week and which were little more than child-minding institutions. In 1858 the Revd W. Warburton, HMI for the Berkshire, Hampshire, Wiltshire and Isle of Wight area, condemned these schools in no uncertain terms: 'The greater part of the private dames' schools are held in dwelling rooms . . . It is one of the many ways of making their bread adopted by people scrambling for a livelihood in no certain or definite calling. The children in such schools frequently spend a great part of the school hours sitting on forms round the kitchen, with dog-eared pages of spelling-books in their hands, from which they are supposed to be learning, while the "schoolmistress" is engaged in sewing, washing or cooking.' He thought that their only merit was that they habituated the children 'to some little restraint for certain hours every day . . .'[7] Eighteen years later one of his colleagues working in the Chester district, likewise condemned them as places 'where a number of children are huddled together, learning almost absolutely nothing except perhaps knitting . . .'[7] Nevertheless, in view of what has been said about the low temperatures in the ordinary day schools, it is perhaps worth noting that this HMI considered one of the reasons for the survival of the dame schools was that parents believed them 'warmer than the school'.

Particularly from the 1870s, however, only a small minority of children attended dame schools. The vast majority in the country areas were educated at schools run in accordance with the principles of the National Society, a Church of England organization. In these circumstances, the local clergy would usually exert a considerable influence over the life of the school and its scholars, and in some cases, the incumbent or his curate would personally conduct the daily prayers which prefaced each morning's lessons. Only when these had come to an end would the general day's work begin.

For much of the Victorian period, this consisted of basic instruction in the three

'Rs' (reading, writing and arithmetic), plus religious instruction, singing, and, for the girls, sewing and knitting. Learning by rote was the usual method adopted, and the standards set were not very high. Anyone passing a school at this period would hear the monontonous sing-song chanting of children's voices as they repeated the sentences learned off by heart:

Ann is ill
Take a pill[112]

and so on.

The reading books chosen were often either very boring or extremely sad and gloomy in content, and sometimes both. It was scarcely surprising if the children's minds wandered as they read or chanted such phrases as:

The gold of a guinea might be drawn out so as to reach nine miles and a half. This property in gold of being capable of extension to so extraordinary degree is owing to its great tenacity or cohesion of particles.

And it seems equally unlikely that the average boy or girl, with a limited vocabulary and restricted reading ability, derived much benefit from such stories as *The Death of Hercules*, which was included in Chambers's *Narrative Series of Standard Reading Books* (Standard IV) and whose opening words were: 'The Eleventh Labour put upon Hercules was to procure the golden apples of the Hesperides. The Twelfth Labour was to bring up from the lower regions the three-headed dog Cerberus.'

It was no doubt with this sort of material in mind that Mr Danby, when reporting on the Suffolk and Essex area in 1875, condemned the 'unsatisfactory nature of a great proportion of the older school reading books. These are in many cases marred by errors in spelling and grammar; and when free from mistakes, are of a dryness so repulsive that the notion of regarding a book as a source of pleasure can never for one moment occur to the readers in class . . .'[7] In the following year, one of his colleagues could remark that while 'there are three or four very good series, there are many others altogether inferior, which have sometimes been selected on account merely of greater cheapness or of the attractive advertisement; (like the certain cures of quack doctors), announcing that no child who reads them can possibly fail . . .'[7]

Other extracts, again, were marred by the sickly 'moral' character of their theme, and Document E provides an example of this particular type. Nevertheless, not all of the books should be condemned, and where the reading books *were* carefully chosen they brought the child into contact with new ideas and with a world outside the narrow confines of his or her own particular community. One labouring child who benefited in this way from an education in late Victorian

Children standing outside Cottisford School, Oxfordshire, in July 1905. Flora Thompson attended the school in the 1880s and descriptions of her education there feature prominently in *Lark Rise to Candleford*. (Oxfordshire Education Committee)

Yorkshire, afterwards wrote: 'One thing I shall always be grateful for is that [the schoolmistress] taught me to love and reverence good literature. Although I have never made much success of life – which was no fault of her teaching – life has been made rich because when ploughing up a nest of field-mice I could recite Robert Burns's *Ode to a Field-mouse* . . . Thus, at an early age I learned of a world beyond the boundary wall of the park, and in fancy I journeyed in Lady Brassey's *Sunbeam*, or got wrecked on *The Coral Island*, or shared *The Adventures of Robinson Crusoe*.'[105] And Flora Thompson remembered with pleasure the *Royal Reader* which had been used at Cottisford School in north Oxfordshire: 'There was plenty there to enthral any child: 'The Skater Chased by Wolves'; 'The Siege of Torquilstone', from *Ivanhoe*; Fenimore Cooper's *Prairie on Fire*; and Washington Irving's *Capture of Wild Horses*.'[144]

But if learning to read was one of the essential three 'Rs', a second was learning to write. Children were initially taught to write on slates, and their first task was normally to make 'pothooks'; from this they went on to practise 'letters with a squeaking slate pencil'.[112] Then, when these basic skills had been acquired, they were set endless copying tasks to improve their facility. A task which was monotonous in itself was sometimes made even more so by the unsuitable material chosen for the purpose. In 1860, even the stern HMI Brodie was moved to complain of the 'old-fashioned copy books, still in use in some places', and which were apparently designed 'to render a dull study duller. For of what use can it be to copy ten or twelve times over such crackjaw words as these: "Zumiologist," "Xenodochium" . . . ? Or such pompous moral phrases as these – "Study universal rectitude" "Wanton actions are very unseemly?" . . . Such words and phrases evoke only dull wonder and a stare, rendering the task more than ever mechanical, and still more perniciously cause inattention, careless blundering, inaccuracies, and bad spelling . . .'[7]

The inevitable companion of 'copying' was dictation. This, too, was normally taken down on slates, rather than on paper – so as to economise in the use of school materials, for the slate could easily be cleaned (usually, as the HMIs disapprovingly observed, by spitting on it and wiping it clean on the sleeve). The occasion when a fresh group of children first began to write on paper was, indeed, often thought sufficiently important to merit mention in the school log book.

Arithmetic, the last of the three 'Rs', was the one which normally gave the most trouble in country schools, even though it was usually confined to such simple rules as addition, subtraction, division and the like. On occasion, however, these rules were incorporated into questions made especially long and tedious, so as to keep the children occupied while the teacher dealt with some of his or her other charges – for in many schools there would only be one teacher, plus perhaps a pupil teacher and a monitress, to cope with all the different age groups in the school. One example of this long-winded type is provided by the surviving arithmetic book of Thomas Cole, who lived at Great Oakley in Essex. Although he went to school in the first half of the century, the same sort of questions were being asked decades later: 'What will the Thatching of the following Stacks cost at 10d per square foot, the first was 36 feet by 27, the second 42 by 34, the third 38 by 24, and the fourth 47 by 39?' A whole page in Thomas' exercise book was needed to work out the answer. And at Blaxhall School, Suffolk, in 1851, children were asked similarly to calculate, 'How many furlongs, rods, yards, feet and inches and Barleycorns will reach round the Earth, supposing it according to the best calculation to be 25,020 miles?' Once again a page of calculations was the result.[81] John Langley of Banbury (born about 1880) recalled the boredom of this work: ' . . . we often spent two solid hours working through sums on a card.'[106]

Yet it was arithmetic which most often proved the Achilles heel in the country child's academic career. Time and again, teachers lamented their charges' inability

to grasp the simple principles or their failure to pass their arithmetic examinations. The master at Cranfield, Bedfordshire, probably expressed the views of
many when he wrote in his log book on 25 March 1870: 'Don't think it possible
to teach children Arithmetic who have nothing to sharpen them in the Village'.
His opinion was certainly echoed by the master at Austrey in north Warwickshire, who lamented the 'low' standard of intelligence of his pupils, and declared
that this constituted 'a teacher's chief difficulty in a village far removed from any
centre of population. Austrey is absolutely without any concurrent aides to the
development of mental capacity.' However, an examination of the Austrey
examination results leads one to believe that in this case at least an over-gloomy
view was being taken.

After the three 'Rs' had been dealt with, some time at least would normally be
devoted to singing. The songs chosen varied according to the taste of the teacher
or the requirements of the HMI, but among the items noted in the Whitchurch
Log Book (Oxfordshire) for 1894 were: 'The Daisy'; 'Fresh Air'; 'It's Never Too
Late to Mend'. At Asthall, in the same county, the songs chosen for 1890
included: 'If I were a Sunbeam'; 'Before all Lands'; and 'Work with Power'. On
the other hand, at Mrs Kate Edward's school in Lotting Fen at around the same
time better-known tunes were selected – like 'The Ash Grove' or 'Home Sweet
Home'. In the more prosperous schools the singing would be accompanied by a
harmonium or perhaps a piano, but in the less fortunate, teachers and pupils were
forced to struggle along without the aid of musical instruments. At Ivinghoe
School, Buckinghamshire, the master reported in 1880 the 'great difficulty' he
had in teaching singing without an instrument. No doubt the sound made in
these circumstances was hardly 'musical', but at least the children enjoyed it. One
Inspector noted of the marching or 'action' type songs chosen for the infants in
his particular area that they were rendered 'with spirit and precision. The bright
faces and sparkling eyes of the little ones [testified] to the interest they [took] in
the exercises.'

However, if these 'basic' subjects (plus religious instruction and needlework)
were the ones most widely taught in country schools during the Victorian period,
increasing efforts were made at least from the late 1860s to widen the curriculum.
This trend was particularly encouraged by the fact that from 1867 such subjects as
history, geography and grammar were made eligible for government grants in
their own right; and from the early 1870s they and other subjects were brought
into general use by a further amendment to the Government code on which
grants were based.[64] Similarly, 'drawing' also became a subject on which grants
could be earned – this time from the Department of Science and Art, rather than
the Education Department – and from 1890 it was compulsory for boys to learn
to draw 'unless [it was] certified impracticable' for them to do so.[133]

Children displaying their slates after a drawing lesson at the Town School, Sheep Street, Devizes, c. 1895. (Dr D. Buxton)

As a result of these changes some – although by no means all – country schools tried to earn higher government grants by preparing students for examination in the additional subjects; for on the results achieved in an annual examination supervised by the local HMI the amount of the grant largely depended, especially for the extra subjects. Thus at Mixbury School in Oxfordshire by the mid-1870s the older children were receiving instruction in history and geography, although the method adopted tended to be dry and uninspiring. On 17 September 1875, the Mixbury children were given 'a Lesson in Geography of Ireland', and the home lesson for that evening was 'to write out what they remember about Ireland'. Again on 22 October of the same year they were set to write out from memory: 'The Geography of England . . . It was fairly done for the first attempt.' The same sort of situation often existed elsewhere, although the more enlightened teachers did in a few cases encourage their pupils to enliven proceedings by, for example, making a plastercine relief map of Britain on which they marked the major industries with appropriate symbols, e.g. small pieces of coal for the coal fields. But in all too many cases the children were merely learning off by heart such statistics as the area of a country; its length and breadth; population per square mile, and so on. As one HMI pointed out: 'A child who had never heard of Paris or Edinburgh, will tell you measurements of England in length and breadth, and square mileages, till his tongue is tired . . .' Another noted with equal gloom that: 'The form and motions of the earth can hardly be comprehended by children (aged perhaps 8 years), though something more could be accomplished if schools were more commonly furnished with a small globe . . .'[28]

History teaching had the same basic flaws, being taught in too many cases 'in a desultory manner and unsatisfactorily, since the hair of Rufus and the legs of Edward I seem still to be of as great historical importance as the Reformation and Rebellion', according to a disillusioned Inspector. One school which prided itself on its history teaching had as its chief boast the fact that the boys were able 'to repeat the names and dates of the kings of England very fast and correctly *backward* from Queen Victoria . . .'[141] Small wonder, in these circumstances, that HMI Currey could write of the schools in Northamptonshire in 1875: 'Geography and history are generally got up in the "cram" system . . . The revision of papers on history is about the most monotonous work that an Inspector has to do . . .'[7] Most of his colleagues – and no doubt the unfortunate pupils, too – would have agreed with this blanket condemnation. Perhaps the best solution, given the limitations under which the schools laboured, with one teacher to instruct all ages and all subjects, was that adopted at Cottisford, where no formal history lessons were given, but instead history readers were in use 'containing such picturesque stories as those of King Alfred and the cakes, King Canute commanding the waves . . . and Raleigh spreading his cloak for Queen Elizabeth'.[144]

Another aspect of the attempts to widen the curriculum, this time for the infants, was the introduction of 'Object Lessons', which became a regular part of the programme in most country schools during the late Victorian period. In 1895, indeed, they were made compulsory for the younger children and Document E provides an example of the Object Lessons taught to both infants and older children at Asthall School, Oxfordshire, during the year 1898.

However, the potential value of these lessons in increasing a child's perception of the world was sadly diminished where lack of equipment meant that no 'objects' were available to illustrate the lessons. Sometimes this was overcome, as at Asthall School, by choosing object lessons which related to the countryside and which were, therefore, familiar to pupils. But this was not always possible, and in 1895 an HMI commented unfavourably on the fact that at Asthall the 'Object Lesson [could] not be given properly because there [were] no pictures for the purpose of illustration'. Less than two months later steps had been taken to rectify

Children carrying out military drill in the school playground, c. 1903. It was a response to the upsurge of patriotic feeling which accompanied the outbreak of the Boer War in 1899. Broom handles were usually pressed into service for these exercises. (Miss D. Marshall)

this, and the school log book recorded that four new pictures had been received: 'viz. Tea, Sugar, and Cotton plants, and a Ship'. In other cases again, of course, the teacher might take matters into her own hands to remedy defects. In October 1897, the mistress at Cublington School in Buckinghamshire recorded that she had 'applied to several manufacturers for specimens for use for object teaching as the school is very bare and nothing is provided to interest the children . . .' Again, at Elmdon in Warwickshire during February 1897, it was noted that: 'In the Upper Division the children set Mustard seed to illustrate their lesson on the "Growth of a seed" and "Leaves". Unfortunately, not all teachers possessed this sort of interest and initiative and object lessons degenerated into a lack-lustre discussion, with the children answering 'in monosyllables and very indistinctly'.

Nevertheless, even in the most boring daily routine there were welcome breaks – either a brief playtime or else, later in the period, the introduction of physical

exercises. At Whitchurch in Oxfordshire, during the 1870s, the master introduced 'military drill' in the playground as a break-time activity for the boys,
while the infants were later set on 'marching' round their classrooms. And at
Wasperton School in Warwickshire, the log book entry for 1 February 1898,
records that 'twenty pairs of "Dumb-bells" ' had been received for the children.
Elsewhere physical exercise and drill along these lines became accepted as part of
the regular routine, and during the South African War at the very end of
Victoria's reign a special impetus was given to this trend in some Devon schools
when servicemen were engaged as drill sergeants. Indeed, at the parish of
Thurlestone the boys were even provided with toy guns, sailor suits and two air
guns 'in the hope of making them good marksmen', under the direction of the
local RNVR coastguard![133] But few schools seem to have taken their military
duties as seriously as this.

Again, in the later years of the century, infants were allowed to spend some
time in non-academic work – at least in the more enlightened schools. At
Matlock Church of England School in Derbyshire a toy train and rails were
apparently provided for 'object and conversation lessons', while at Rowthorne
School in the same county occupations like colour drawing, bead threading,
tablet laying, guessing games, ball making and picture lessons were all considered
suitable for the infants. Mrs Hilda Eriksen has similar recollections of Cropredy
School, Oxfordshire, at the end of the Victorian period. She first attended the
school at the age of three and her 'happiest memory of all' in the infant class was
'of a very understanding teacher, who kept a miniature tea-set in the cupboard; it
was brought out on special occasions together with a sheet of music (a suitable
song to fit the little tea-party). Paper weaving and mosaic "work" [play] were
lovely too.'

Nevertheless, perhaps the most welcome break of all in the school day for older
and younger children alike, was the dinner hour or, more literally, two hours in
the middle of it. During the winter months those children who came from a long
distance would stay inside the school room to eat the bread and lard or treacle
they had brought with them. Very often the biggest children would crowd round
the solitary fire, so that 'the little 'uns and the weakest ones and the shy ones
never got near it at all'. Mrs Kate Edwards, recalled that during her own school
days: 'We were never looked after at all in the dinner times, so nobody knowed or
cared whether we ever felt the fire or not, though I remember envying one little
girl as I used to play with. She were a farmer's child, and I should think the
teacher must a–give orders as she were to have a special place near the fire,
because it were allus left for her. She were the only one of us as had proper
sandwiches with meat in them for her dockey [lunch], and she used to bring a
long knitting needle and hang a sandwich on the end of it and toast it in front o'

the fire, and make all our mouths water so that our own bit o' "bread and seam" [lard] di'n't taste as good as it ought to a-done . . .'[11]

But in a few cases there were exceptions to this rule of official indifference to the children's welfare during the lunch break. Thus at mid-nineteenth century Finmere in Oxfordshire, a hot soup dinner was provided on two days a week by the rector during the winter months. It was made from 'half an ox-head each time. In addition to oatmeal to thicken, and onions to flavour, peas, potatoes, carrots, turnips, artichokes were liberally thrown into the huge boiler . . . This, with bread, fed 120 children.'[35] Again, at Odell in Bedfordshire the master's wife warmed the dinners of some of those who stayed to lunch, during the early 1880s, while at Huccombe in Devon the mistress provided many of the children with a hot drink during the winter months. And at Rousdon in the same county, the new school built in 1876 supplied hot 'Penny Dinners' from the very first.[133] Unfortunately, most schools conformed to a far more Spartan régime than this.

Yet if the winter breaks were not always attractive, in the summer months the situation was very different, for now the time between 12 and 2 p.m. could be spent out of doors, in the fields or under the hedgerows. When their simple meal was eaten the children were free to paddle in the nearest river or stream, or to wander off looking for birds' nests or merely playing games with one another. Some turned their talents to chasing cows in the nearby fields, or to playing fox and hounds among themselves, while certain of the more fortunate who had a ball might play cricket. In June 1866, the boys of Launton School in north Oxfordshire were given a ball for this purpose, but they quickly ran into trouble when they returned for afternoon school with untidy hair and dirty faces. The master sternly warned them 'that for the future they must come tidier or else not play at cricket at dinner-time'. Since no further entries are made in the school log book on the subject, the boys apparently heeded the warning. In addition, other children obtained breaks in the daily routine in perhaps rather less pleasant ways; for example, both boys and girls might help to clean the school or the teacher's house. At Cublington School, Buckinghamshire, in June, 1877, the mistress had eventually to put in a request that 'a woman be allowed to do the sweeping. The mothers of the children dislike their doing it and keep them away in consequence.' Her request was quickly agreed to and a local woman was engaged at 6d per week to do the sweeping and to light fires 'during the winter seasons'.

Again, at her school in the Lotting Fen area, Mrs Edwards was, for several years, expected to wash-up, dust, clean shoes, pare vegetables, and carry out other chores in the schoolmaster's house during the morning. For this she received each week a 'quarter of an orange peel', and an unsatisfactory education.[112] And at Blaxhall in Suffolk during the later 1870s or early 1880s, Katie Ling was employed, ostensibly as a monitress, at a wage of 2d a week to clean the school, lay the fires, ring the school bell before morning school, and at the weekends scrub the school lavatories. In addition, she received 2d a week for fetching the schoolmistress's bread and milk.[81] A number of other schools adopted similar policies and 'helping to clean the school' was a by no means unusual activity, at least for the older girls. Indeed, even if some parents disapproved of their children carrying out these chores, certain outside observers took a different view. Mr Norman, an Assistant Commissioner in connection with the *Royal Commission on the Employment of Children, Young Persons and Women in Agriculture* in 1868–69, reported with regret that 'in many cases a woman is hired to keep the school clean, instead of the girls being employed for that purpose. This seems to me to be a mistake. The girls would probably take more pride in the condition of the school if they were themselves responsible for

A gardening class at Uphill school, Avon, c. 1906. By the beginning of the twentieth century gardening had become an integral part of the curriculum for boys at many country schools.
(Reproduced by courtesy of Woodspring Museum, Weston-super-Mare)

it; and a good opportunity is thus lost of giving the girls instruction in what is a very important operation.'[2] He was not alone in his opinions.

The boys, on the other hand, were more likely to be employed out-of-doors. One such was Andy Smith, who was born in about 1886 in Norfolk, and who later remembered that during his school days in the early 1890s he did not make much progress because he 'used to be out gardening for the schoolmaster'. Similarly, at Austrey in north Warwickshire a log book entry for 21 March 1892, recorded: 'Two boys occupied for one hour in tidying the garden paths, under the direction of master'. However, in a few schools, gardening was taken more seriously and was regarded as an appropriate training for those who were to spend their lives working on the land. Even in the late 1860s, schools at Godstone, in Surrey and Hagley in Worcestershire (to name only two) had 'small gardens attached to the school which the older boys were permitted to cultivate, generally as a reward for good conduct'. At Godstone the pupils were expected to keep a profit and loss account on the enterprise.

Nevertheless for most country children, the daily round lacked these diversions, and was run instead in strict accordance with the school timetable, which had previously been approved by the HMI. Any deviation from this plan was severely frowned upon by the authorities. One such timetable which has survived for Hawkesbury School in north Warwickshire shows that in 1867 the children spent each week five hours five minutes on religion and prayers; fifteen hours five minutes on the three 'Rs' (the girls had two hours less to allow time for sewing lessons); two hours on drawing and free play, etc., and ten minutes on music.[76] The position elsewhere was no doubt much the same. And given that the children were all crammed together into one classroom, it was small wonder that, for example, the young Joseph Ashby of Tysoe in south Warwickshire could recollect of his own schooldays: 'What a noise there used to be! Several children would be reading aloud, teachers scolding, infants reciting, all waxing louder and louder until the master rang the bell on his desk and the noise slid down to a lower note and less volume . . . A specially hard time was the two "sewing afternoons". While the girls were collected together for sewing the boys merely did more sums or an extra dictation, just the sort of thing they had been doing all morning. As they craned their necks to see what sort of garments, what colours, were coming out of the vicarage basket of mending, they were unusually tiresome to the poor pupil-teacher, losing their places over and over again or mis-spelling words they knew perfectly well – forgetting everything . . .'[63]

It was, perhaps, hardly surprising that in this sort of atmosphere some of the schoolmasters degenerated into bullies and tyrants. As the son of a Welsh shoemaker later wrote bitterly of his own village school master in Llangernyw, Denbighshire: 'The cane was in his hand from the opening of the school in the morning to its close at four o'clock in the afternoon; faults, errors, slips, a constant succession of petty nothingnesses led to its use either on the hand or on the back, or on both hands and back. Some child whispers; he cannot find out which. He thrashes the class all round . . . and there was lamentation in the school all day long . . .

'But probably what the boys disliked most in him were his obvious favouritisms. These were shown invariably to the well-dressed children of the well-to-do who attended not the Methodist or Baptist chapel, but the village church. They were hardly ever caned, even lightly. But the chapel-going children, and especially those who were poor or slow, suffered many a blow, and were stung by many a vulgar sarcasm levelled at their "religion".'[90]

On the other hand, some of the wilder children were equally ready to disobey, or even 'bait' the teacher, should the opportunity arise. At Cottisford School (Oxfordshire) in the later 1880s there was a grey-haired, frail, gentle mistress

ARITHMETIC.

Teacher. "How many Commandments are there, Sally?"
Sally. "Please, Teacher, ten."
Teacher. "Suppose you were to break a Commandment . . ." *(impressive pause).*
Sally. "Then there'd be nine."

Biblical arithmetic! (*Punch*, 1906)

who was certainly no strict disciplinarian: 'she ruled, if she can be said to have ruled at all, by love and patience and ready forgiveness. In time, even the blackest of her sheep realized this and kept within certain limits . . .', but this did not prevent a few of them from asking unnecessary questions or misbehaving in other ways.[144] At Launton, in the same county, the master who took up his appointment in November, 1865, likewise discovered that he was 'obliged to use the stick very freely in school today, for without it I could in no way obtain anything like Discipline, as if I simply *spoke* to the children they would stand and laugh at me . . .' A surviving Punishment Book for a south Northamptonshire village school for 1908 records such punishments as 'two stripes' for 'whistling in school', 'two stripes' for 'disobedience' and 'one stripe' for 'tearing book (temper)'.[71]

The views of Captain Vye on the 'bad word(s)' written by children on gate posts, etc., which were quoted at the beginning of the Chapter, equally find confirmation in log book entries. For example, at Shillington School, Bedfordshire, it was noted on 7 July 1876: 'This week the master has again suspended Stephen Flint for writing something most indecent on his slate and showing it to two girls.' And at Clifton School in the same county an entry for 1 December 1863, reads: 'Wm. Dunton birched for writing obscene language upon his slate in school'. These were certainly not isolated transgressors.

Sometimes the discipline problems were posed by offences committed outside the school – such as stealing fruit, chasing cows, etc., or even – as at Odell in Bedfordshire during December, 1884 – by rather more unpleasant pranks. On 12 December, the Odell master recorded that he had given Henry Bradshaw and Alfred Odell a stroke upon the hand and Albert Gills 'a stroke upon each hand, the first two for holding Alfred Osborn and the latter for blacking his face upon passing the blacksmith's shop last night in going home from school'.

Nevertheless, one of the most fruitful sources of conflict between teacher and pupils was provided by Home Lessons, which the youngsters time and time again either refused to do at all, or else did badly. This defiance is perhaps more easily understood when the overcrowded condition of most cottages is remembered. Such circumstances would have made learning difficult at the best of times, while the tedious nature of the Home Lessons usually set reinforced this. One favourite home task was to require the children to learn off by heart such items as the Collect in readiness for the church service on the coming Sunday, or to commit to memory other large chunks of indigestible prose. Many were the struggles waged by school teachers over getting this performed satisfactorily. At Souldern, Oxfordshire, in the late 1860s, the master even tried to 'bribe' pupils into learning the Collect by offering book prizes to those who proved themselves most diligent, while in the autumn of 1876 the mistress at Cublington School,

Buckinghamshire, unsuccessfully tried to follow a similar policy. But most teachers preferred the simpler approach of caning persistent offenders.

On the other hand, in a few communities parental opposition might be strong enough to discourage the setting of the lessons eventually. In one Warwickshire village the schoolmaster admitted that he had been warned by the parents that if he persisted in setting 'home lessons', then 'the books shall be burnt and the slates broken'.[2] At Brailes in the same county the mistress was likewise forced to admit defeat on similar grounds: 'Home lessons suspended to suit parents' views,' reads the log book entry for 30 July 1875. Nevertheless, in most cases parental feeling was not vigorous enough to secure this sort of response, and so the skirmishes over home lessons continued in a desultory fashion in many schools for the remainder of the century.

The school day usually drew to its close at 4 p.m., although during the winter months the dinner hour would often be shortened and school would end at 3.30 p.m. instead, so that the children could walk home in the light. And whether the child had enjoyed its daily schooling or not, at least the restrictions could then be cast aside, as youngsters rushed towards their homes – or, perhaps, in the summer months, played games on the journey instead. Some brought their hoops or tops with them, while others picked wild flowers or played with marbles 'along the sides of the roads when dry'. In the Lotting Fen area during the warmer months of the year the children would play 'down the dyke side getting wild flowers, and reeds and rushes . . . We dug up tansy roots to eat . . . we sucked the taste of honey from the tip ends of the white dead-nettle . . . Then off to gather different sorts of flowers again to dress ourselves up to play "Kings and Queens" – great pink-striped bindweed flowers on trails of green twisty stalks and leaves, as you could bind round your heads and waists and trail about in as if they were royal robes . . .'[112]

When they arrived home, the older children might have chores to perform – water to fetch, younger brothers and sisters to mind, gardening to do – but for a brief period all this could be forgotten. Of course, not all of the youngsters played in such a harmless fashion. There were always a few who would 'fall in a body upon some . . . small girl in a clean frock, and . . . "run her", as they called it. This meant chasing her until they caught her, then dragging her down and sitting upon her, tearing her clothes, smudging her face, and tousling her hair in the process.' The boys would sometimes fight among themselves or, in winter would slide on the ice of the puddles, 'or make snowballs – soft ones for their friends, and hard ones with a stone inside for their enemies'.[144] But an elementary sense of fair play usually prevented any really serious damage.

From time to time, too, the appearance on the road of a carriage belonging to the squire or some other village notable would jerk them back to their best behaviour. As the carriage passed it was customary for the children to draw hastily to one side and to salute the passengers in an appropriate manner. Thus at Langley Burrell in Wiltshire, Miss Constance Pearce, who was the daughter of the local brewer, remembers that at about the turn of the century, the children, who attended the village school were still 'taught to "bob" to the Squire's family, or Sir John Dickson's family, who lived in Pewhill house, when out on the road'. (The Squire was a Mr Ashe, and it is perhaps indicative of the awe in which he was held that, according to an earlier observer – Francis Kilvert – at the beginning of the 1870s, 'One of the Langley Burrell school children being asked, "Who made the World?" replied, "Mr Ashe" '.) Similar attitudes seem to have been displayed in a number of other parishes, and at Helmingham in Suffolk a girl who omitted on one occasion to curtsey to the Squire's lady, was apparently caned in school for this the next day. Even though not all of the local gentry had such rigid standards as that, it appears likely that most village children would be careful to show their respect to any of their 'betters' whom they encountered on their homeward journey.[92]

NOTES ON ADDITIONAL SOURCES USED
Information on Alfred Dodman and Andy Smith of Norfolk obtained via Mrs R. Evans of Culham, Oxfordshire, to whom my thanks are due.
Reminiscences of my mother concerning Austrey, north Warwickshire, early in the present century.
Information on Cropredy and Bourton National School provided by Mrs Hilda Eriksen of Cropredy, in correspondence with the author – November, 1971.
Information on Langley Burrell in the late nineteenth century provided by Miss C. Pearce, of Chippenham, in correspondence with the author – November, 1971.
Thomas Cole's Arithmetic Exercise Book is preserved at the Museum of English Rural Life, Reading, D.60/16.
Chambers's Narrative Series of Standard Reading Books (Standard IV), published in 1863. The price of these Standard Reading Books ranged from 6d for Standard I, to 8d for Standard II, 1s for Standard III, and 1s 2d for Standard IV.

CHAPTER THREE

The Arrival of Her Majesty's Inspector

Would you like to know the reason
Why we all look bright and gay
As we hasten to our places
This is our Inspection Day!
Fie! what is that you say,
You hate Inspection Day?

If we know we've done our duty,
Daily striving with our might,
Teacher says we need not worry
Though our sums will not come right
So we are glad and gay,
Though 'tis Inspection Day.

(The above song was no doubt intended to bolster up the failing spirits of the children on Inspection day; it is quoted in Richard Bourne and Brian MacArthur – *The Struggle for Education* 1870–1970, issued by the National Union of Teachers (1970), p. 36.)

State inspection of elementary schools began with the recruitment of the first two HMIs in December 1839. Their appointment followed approximately six years after the first Government grants had been made towards the education of the poor, and from 1839 acceptance of a grant automatically gave the right of official inspection. Dislike of inspection, however, often made school authorities unwilling to take advantage of the financial help available, and in 1847 there were, for example, in Lincolnshire only forty-three Church Schools under government inspection; ten years later the figure had risen to 124, but even then the local HMI, the Revd J.J. Blandford, was lamenting that 'the managers of the schools connected with the Church at Louth have not put them under inspection in order to avail themselves of the pecuniary assistance afforded . . . At Grimsby there are no schools under inspection . . .'[129] In other counties the position was similar, but as time passed, and as changes were made in the grants available so this reluctance was slowly broken down. Thus from 1853, special capitation grants were made available to schools in agricultural districts. They ranged between 4s and 6s for each boy and 3s and 5s for each girl and were linked to attendance; to qualify for a grant children had to attend school for at least 176 days each year. The idea was both to improve educational facilities and to encourage children to attend school more regularly.

In its early days, state aid was confined to the two voluntary societies which had done the most to build schools and bring education within the reach of the underprivileged. These were the Church of England National Society, founded in 1811, and the British and Foreign School Society, set up shortly afterwards on the basis of non-sectarian education – but having, in practice, a close association with Nonconformity. Nevertheless, in the course of the next two decades, other religious bodies providing elementary education became eligible for assistance, and the amount of Government expenditure on education rose steeply, until by 1853 about £200,000 per annum was being spent in this direction – or roughly ten times the level of twenty years earlier.

The number of Government Inspectors also rose and by 1850 had reached twenty-three.[78] As yet their duties remained extremely wide – they included approving specimen building plans, ascertaining 'means of instruction' (such as inspection of subject-teaching, books and school apparatus), assessing 'organisation and discipline', and inquiring into religious teaching.[78] Most of the HMIs were recruited from a well-to-do background and had enjoyed an education at one of the older universities before they assumed their inspectorial role; they were naturally held in some awe by the humble elementary school teachers whom they visited, and also by the pupils. But as yet they did not inspire the fear and dislike which future generations of teachers and children were to feel towards them.

This transition from respected superior to dreaded ogre took place only in the early 1860s, as a result of a change in Government policy in regard to the distribution of state grants. Instead of these being based very largely upon the principle of self-help, with the Government grant being matched by voluntary effort from the religious bodies concerned, a much more rigid approach was adopted. In part, the change was due to a desire to curb the rise in state expenditure on education and in part to a desire to ensure that the money was spent as 'efficiently' as possible. In addition, as HMI Du Port wrote in 1895, there may also have been the laudable intention of making sure that 'every child, however backward, young, or dull, had . . . its full share of conscientious attention'. Under the new 'Payment by Results' system introduced by the Revised Code of 1862, all future grants, except for building, were to be made on the basis of a capitation payment of 12s per child per annum; 4s of this depended upon the child's regular attendance at school (under a qualified head teacher) and the rest upon his or her performance at an annual examination in the three 'Rs' which was now to be conducted by an HMI Failure in any one of the three subjects examined – reading, writing and arithmetic – meant the loss of 2s 8d from that particular child's grant. The examinations were arranged in a series of Standards and each child was expected to move up a Standard every year. The details of the Standard examinations are given below:

Standard I
Reading: Narrative in monosyllables.
Writing: Form on blackboard or slate, from dictation, letters, capital and small, manuscript.
Arithmetic: Form on blackboard or slate, from dictation, figures up to 20; name at sight figures up to 20; add and subtract figures up to 10, orally, from examples on blackboard.

Standard II
Reading: One of the Narratives next in order after monosyllables in an elementary reading book used in the school.
Writing: Copy in manuscript character a line of print.
Arithmetic: A sum in simple addition or subtraction and the multiplication table.

Standard III
Reading: A short paragraph from an elementary reading book used in the school.
Writing: A sentence from the same paragraph, slowly read once, and then dictated in single words.
Arithmetic: A sum in any simple rule as far as short division (inclusive).

Standard IV
Reading: A short paragraph from a more advanced reading book used in the school.
Writing: A sentence slowly dictated once by a few words at a time, from the same book, but not from the paragraph read.
Arithmetic: A sum in compound rules (money).

Standard V

Reading: A few lines of poetry from a reading book used in the first class of the
school.

Writing: A sentence slowly dictated once, by a few words at a time, from a
reading book used in the first class of the school.

Arithmetic: A sum in compound rules (common weights and measures).

Standard VI

Reading: A short ordinary paragraph in a newspaper, or other modern
narrative.

Writing: Another short ordinary paragraph in a newspaper, or other modern
narrative, slowly dictated once, by a few words at a time.

Arithmetic: A sum in practice or bills of parcels.[28]

In the course of time the Code was amended somewhat, so that writing was
tested in Standard I by a ten-word spelling test, in Standards II, III and IV by a
prescribed number of lines of 'Dictation', and in Standard V by the reproduction
of a short story read twice by the Inspector. In 1882 Standard VII was introduced,
requiring pupils to 'read passage from Shakespeare or Milton, etc., or from a
History of England: write theme or letter: work sums in averages, percentages,
discount of stocks'. But very few country children ever reached the dizzy heights
of Standard VII.

The ordeal of the examination had to be faced by all children, except for the
infants under six. For them a total grant of 10s 6d could be claimed, subject to
adequate attendance and a report by the Inspector that they were being 'instructed
suitably to their age'.[28] The great emphasis now placed on success in the
examination, if a maximum grant were to be earned, quickly had its effect on the
curriculum of elementary schools. It became a steady grind of the three 'Rs', plus
religious instruction and, for the girls, sewing.[133] And although over the years
efforts were made to widen the scope with, for example, the provision of
additional grants for 'specific subjects' (grammar, history, geography) in 1867,
and eight years later the conversion of these latter to 'class subjects', with the
grant earned by the proficiency of the whole class not by the *individual*
examination successes, in general little impact was made in the country areas. The
three-'R' examination, combined with average attendances, formed the basis of
state grants right up to 1890, and the last elements of 'payment by results' did not
disappear until the end of the nineteenth century.[133] However, after 1890 the
three-'R' grant itself was replaced by higher payments for attendance and an
'additional "discipline and organisation" item' – and the change undoubtedly
relieved children of the pressures which had been placed upon them by anxious

teachers at examination time. (See also Document F for variations in the grants over the years.)

Of course, few country children understood all of the finer points of government policy in the matter of examinations and the financing of schools, but even the dullest rapidly came to appreciate that the HMI was a person to be reckoned with – the 'almighty government inspector who seemed to "bestride the narrow world like a colossus". Children in schools were trained to tremble at his name . . .'[78] This sense of alienation was further increased by the continuing practice of recruiting the Inspectors from among middle-class Oxford or Cambridge graduates, who all too often looked with arrogant contempt upon the efforts both of the children they were examining and of the teachers themselves. (This remained true despite the Instructions to Inspectors in 1878 which laid down that 'it is no part of an Inspector's duty either to find fault with or to reprove a teacher'.[148])

For the children, however, the ordeal of the annual examination began well before the arrival of the HMI. For weeks beforehand regular tests were held, in preparation for the great day, and it is possible to trace a note of growing trepidation and even hysteria in the log books of teachers as the inspection date drew nearer. Most were ready to take advantage of any loop-holes in the system which they could discover. For example, the HMIs complained that when it was discovered that two sums correct out of four were sufficient to bring a pass in arithmetic, many teachers did not even attempt to instruct the children in the more difficult problems, but preferred instead to concentrate on those items which would ensure bare examination success.

Again, through the judicious comparison of notes between teachers in a particular district, dictation exercises could be made a simpler proposition – as HMI Kenney-Herbert pointed out in respect of the Aylesbury district of Buckinghamshire in 1887. According to his experience 'spelling proper [was] not taught, but the spelling of particular passages of particular books'. He went on: 'We have now for some time been giving dictation from the books "ordinarily in use at the school", according to the instructions. Now it is a very difficult matter to find passages of a certain length suitable as tests of spelling; they occur, of course, but are few and far between. Teachers naturally observe what pieces are chosen and, when they meet, compare notes. The result is that the passages soon become "stock", and it is not uncommon to see a smile of satisfaction run round a class, on the day of the examination, when one of its oldest of old friends is read out as the exercise selected for it.'[7]

Nevertheless, this alleged self-confidence was little in evidence during the run up to the annual inspection – as a few quotations from school log books will perhaps indicate. Thus at Weston-on-Avon the master noted gloomily in January

"ONE TOUCH OF HUMOUR," &c.

Dignified School-Board Visitor. "NOW, MY BOY, SUPPOSE YOU WERE TO GIVE ME A PENNY, AND I WERE TO GIVE YOU BACK A
HALFPENNY, HOW MUCH SHOULD I OWE YOU?"

[*At this Question a grin of delight lit up the little faces—the Gentleman was at last beginning to "make fun."*

Lowest Boy (quite ready for him). "WHAT YER'D JOLLY WELL STICK TO, IF YER GOT 'OLD OF IT!"

[*A peal of Laughter all round, and Examination breaks up!*

School board visitor questioning the children. (*Punch,* 1882)

1879, 'The Government Inspector has announced his visit to Weston School . . .
Do not expect much success . . .' And at Leckford Board School in Hampshire an
entry for 15 June 1877, reads: 'Received notice of the inspection taking place in
July. Wrote to parents requesting that the children might come as often as
possible.' This policy was continued in the following years, so that an entry for
the week 10–14 July 1882, recorded: 'Received notice that the examination would
take place on Monday, 17th, at ten o'clock. Obliged to send word to all the
parents, asking them to send their children without fail. Examined the children
present in Arithmetic this morning and passed 93 per cent.' Again, at Whitchurch
School in Oxfordshire preparation for the Inspector's visit on 31 January 1870,
had begun as early as the previous December. An entry in the school log book for

THE ARRIVAL OF HER MAJESTY'S INSPECTOR

10 December 1869, noted: 'Examination in dictation very faulty. Must ascertain the number of mistakes allowed by HM Inspector.' Nevertheless, the tests continued until on 21 January a gloomy note was once more sounded: 'Examination not gone as well as last week. Told the children they had only more week to prepare for it.' Nor were the youngsters allowed to relax when the examination had been held, for on 1 February the Whitchurch master recorded that he had spoken to the children 'about yesterday's work, praised their writing and sums and censured their reading'. Unfortunately, the HMI's report provided a dampening confirmation of his fears in regard to reading – although the master himself did not escape criticism either. For while it was agreed that 'good progress' had been made in writing and arithmetic, the Report went on: 'but Reading shows no sign of skill. It is unintelligent and inarticulate. The tone of teaching and prayers is too loud and wants refinement . . . Geography is very fairly started, but the class wants more thoroughness and more intelligence.'

Of course, with the general provisions for compulsory elementary education under the Education Acts of 1876 and 1880, and the introduction of regulations which permitted children who had completed a certain specified number of attendances to go to work for the rest of the year, the teacher's problems were further increased as regards the annual inspection. This was shown by the comments made at Leckford Board School quoted above asking parents to send the children to school, and also by those made at Whitchurch School, Oxfordshire early in January 1876, when the master noted that he had written 'to the employers of children who have boys at work and completed the required number of attendances to send the same boys to school to prepare for HM Inspector's visit on January 26th.' In this case they returned to school as requested and, no doubt with considerable anxiety, were tested, along with the other children, in preparation for the visit. After an absence of several weeks there was always a danger that the young workers would have forgotten almost all they had ever learnt, but at Whitchurch at least there was a happy outcome on this occasion, for the Report stated that 'the general school progress for the year is very satisfactory; and the children are very orderly and interested in their work'.

Elsewhere, the practice of annually hired farm servants and labourers changing their employment at Michaelmas, when the autumn term had just begun, also meant that the education of their children was disrupted, and a change of school made necessary. This was a constant complaint at Weston-on-Avon during the 1880s and 1890s. Thus on 8 October 1897, the mistress reported that nine children had left her small school on that day because their families were leaving the village. As a result, the attendance was 'thin and uncertain'. On 14 October in the following year her concern was obviously still greater: 'Sixteen children have left school this week, and four fresh ones have come. The work of the school is terribly hindered, and upset, by this yearly change. All the children who have left are children who were always at school and would have done the school credit.' Obviously with an exodus on this scale, especially among the better pupils, the achievement of a good standard of work in readiness for the HMI's visit was made very difficult. The same sort of anxiety lay behind an entry at Louth Wesleyan School for 14 November 1879: 'Received notice of alteration of Inspection from February to June. For one reason this change will not be beneficial, viz. in Lincolnshire servants etc. are hired from May to May, hence it not infrequently happens that two or three families leave the town during that Month and children belonging to those families cannot be present at Inspection unless the Committee like to pay Railway fare for those within a reasonable distance.' Shortly afterwards, the master found that his worst fears were to be realized, for on 12 March 1880, came a note: 'As I surmised several families are leaving the neighbourhood, hence some ten or a dozen children who have made up the number of attendances for Examination will be away on the day of Inspection very probably . . .'[129]

Another cause for concern was the extensive use of child labour in agriculture at the busy seasons of the year, despite spasmodic official efforts to prevent it. This problem, as it affected inspection, was pinpointed by HMI Barrington-Ward in 1877 in regard to the Lincolnshire/Nottinghamshire area: 'All agricultural districts present one obstacle to a systematic arrangement of the Inspector's work. The children are pretty regular in winter and early spring, but when summer comes the fields claim their presence, and the schools are half emptied. And so country managers very naturally beg the Inspector to visit them between December and April, and are most unwilling to offer their schools for inspection in June or October . . . A few of [the] occupations are winter excuses, but the great majority of them apply to spring, summer and autumn . . . A country school cannot be inspected at midsummer so as to secure its managers the same amount of grant which they might have earned had the Inspector's annual visit taken place in February or March. When a rural child is made to attend school regularly in every month the case will be materially different, but thanks to prejudice, ignorance, and the desire of gain, the days of regular attendance in country districts seem still far distant . . .'[129]

Of course, the concern of managers and teachers for a good result at the annual inspection arose out of their dependence on the government grant for the continued running of their school. In the average school, the grant formed anything between one-third and one-half of the annual income – depending upon the success of the pupils in the examination, the standard of their attendance, and the availability of other forms of financial help (e.g. the school pence of the children and subscriptions of well-wishers). A series of bad reports could cripple

Drayton School, near Banbury, Oxfordshire on 5 December, 1906; a corner of the room showing the fireplace, the long desks and a picture of a kangaroo on the wall. (Oxfordshire Education Committee).

a school financially, and might also affect the teacher's own salary. For it was not uncommon to link the amount of this to the grant earned – as at Holbeton in Devon, where the salary in 1872 consisted of £60 plus half the amount of the Grant; and at Bovey Tracy British School in the same county, where the 1872 salary comprised £45 and one-third of the Grant.[133] Indeed, as late as 1903 in Devon '31 per cent of headteachers in board schools and 19 per cent in voluntary schools were still being paid on a Grant-share basis'. In the 1870s and 1880s the proportion had certainly been much higher.[133]

In these circumstances, it is easy to understand the despair of teachers when, despite all their efforts, a poor result was obtained. At Holsworthy Wesleyan School, Devon, in 1886, the log book sadly records: 'Have worked harder this year than ever before. *No good.*'[133] The Market Rasen Wesleyan School master was equally forthright – even though his own results were satisfactory ones: 'Teachers are expected to perform miracles and try to do so . . . I have worked hard – labouriously [sic] hard. Throughout the year I have felt underneath my work – I have sought change of air, Medical Advice, etc., but my doctor tells me nothing will do me good but complete rest. Query. How can a teacher obtain rest? I may say that the present system is equally hard for teachers and Inspectors.'[129] Who can doubt that in this tense atmosphere the children's own position would often be extremely uncomfortable.

Then, too, if the teacher fell foul of the Inspector, the pupils might suffer through no fault of their own, since 'even the results of the formal three-'R' examination depended on [an Inspector's] personal definition of "legibility" and "intelligibility"'. And here the mood and personality of the HMI himself was obviously of great importance. Thus at Rattery School in Devon, in 1879, the routine drudgery of his work, or perhaps a sudden outburst of irritability, led HMI to condemn the children as sly and dishonest, during their examination, declaring that, 'There can be no graver offence against good discipline.' Yet the apparently harmless cause of his spleen was the fact that two children 'were using the same ruler, and one asked the other for it'. But, perhaps significantly, relations here between Inspector and teacher were not of the happiest.[133]

In this sort of situation, it is scarcely surprising that as time passed 'examination day became more of a torment in schools, and the inspectors themselves became slaves of the examination machine, filling in forms, visiting schools and writing reports.'[78] The mechanical nature of their work, the large amount of horse-drawn travel over poor roads, and the perhaps over-generous hospitality of school managers anxious to create a good impression, must all have helped to make the most even-tempered HMI adopt a bullying and disagreeable tone on occasion.

And there can be no doubt that some of the HMIs *did* bully from time to time. In North Devon, the Inspector from 1875 until his retirement in 1899 was 'Henry Codd, a tall frock-coated, top-hatted, saturnine-figure'. Even in the 1960s stories were still told 'of his habit of rapping on school windows from horseback, and of his encounters with the bucolic young. Examining a class in geography, he asked which side of a house was the warmest: to which, after a pause for reflection, came the inspired reply "Inzoide, zur." Rounding on one sniveller whom he had already told to blow his nose, he received the answer, "Oi did, zur, but a won't bide blowed." . . . Codd thundered like Jove when faced with gross inefficiency . . .'[133] HMI Brodie who operated in the Worcester district during the 1880s and early 1890s, seems to have been another tyrant and complaints were eventually lodged with the Education Department in London concerning his bad behaviour in a school, with 'the teacher . . . in tears, the children terrified and the chairman of the School Board insulted'.[141]

Again, at Cottisford in north Oxfordshire, the young Flora Thompson remembered with bitterness her own brushes with the HMI. In this particular area in the 1880s the office was held by an elderly clergyman, the Revd H. A.

Pickard, who had 'an immense paunch and tiny grey eyes like gimlets. He had the reputation of being "strict", but that was a mild way of describing his autocratic demeanour and scathing judgement. His voice was an exasperated roar and his criticism was a blend of outraged learning and sarcasm. Fortunately, nine out of ten of his examinees were proof against the latter. He looked at the rows of children as if he hated them and at the mistress as if he despised her . . .' All of the other children shared Flora's apprehension. 'There was no singing or quarrelling on the way to school that morning. The children, in clean pinafores and well blackened boots, walked deep in thought; or, with open spelling or table books in hand, tried to make up in an hour for all their wasted yesterdays . . .' However, 'the very sound of [the Inspector's] voice scattered the few wits of the less gifted, and even those who could have done better were too terrified in his presence to be able to collect their thoughts or keep their hands from trembling.

'But slowly as the hands of the clock seemed to move, the afternoon wore on. Classes came out and toed the chalk line to read; other classes bent over their sums, or wrote letters to grandmothers describing imaginary summer holidays. Some wrote to the great man's dictation pieces full of hard spelling words . . .'[144]

At Tysoe in Warwickshire similar reactions were apparent in the 1860s, when the young Joseph Ashby witnessed the frightened response of his own school fellows to the arrival of the HMI:

'Two inspectors came once a year and carried out a dramatic examination. The schoolmaster came into school in his best suit; all the pupils and teachers would be listening till at ten o'clock a dog-cart would be heard on the road even though it was eighty yards away. In would come two gentlemen with a deportment of high authority, with rich voices. Each would sit at a desk and children would be called in turn to one or other. The master hovered round, calling children out as they were needed. The children could see him start with vexation as a good pupil stuck at a word in the reading book he had been using all the year, or sat motionless with his sum in front of him . . . One year the atmosphere of anxiety so affected the lower standards that, one after another as they were brought to the Inspector, the boys howled and the girls whimpered. It took hours to get through them.'[63] However, here at least there was a compensation once the ordeal was over, for a local benefactor, (the Marquess of Northampton) regularly provided a box of oranges on inspection day, and once the HMIs had departed, each child was given an orange.

Yet the Inspectors had their own problems as well. Although a few may have delighted in humiliating teachers and children, for most the dilemma was a genuine one, especially in those country schools where the standard of education was particularly low. As the Revd C.F. Johnstone pointed out in respect of schools in the South Western Division of England during the year 1886, the

Inspector must 'either refuse the grant and perhaps crush the school, or he must recommend the grant for work which he knows falls infinitely short of the standard laid down for him in the Code. He chooses probably the more merciful part, and from that hour he perpetuates bad teaching by rewarding imperfect effort.'[7] Even the apparently over-strict Brodie welcomed the ending in 1890 of the old 'payment by results' system in its most rigid form, declaring: 'To the Inspector the relief is great. He can gauge the intelligence of a school far more thoroughly and fairly than before, because he has time to prove and examine more searchingly all those subjects which need the most intelligent handling, such as reading, recitation, good methods in arithmetic, class subjects . . .'[7]

The Code of 1890, which brought about this modest improvement in Inspector/school relations, was reinforced in 1895 by a further alteration, which allowed the Inspector to substitute 'two visits without notice, spent simply observing the school in a normal day's work, for the annual pre-arranged examination visit'. Although by no means all schools adopted the new form, many did and the development was widely welcomed. Thus at Holsworthy Wesleyan School, Devon, in 1896, the teacher noted happily: 'First visit of Inspection under the new system. Attended with much less excitement and worry than on the Parade Days of the past.' At Loddiswell National School in 1897, the log book similarly displayed a more cheerful attitude: 'HMI gave us teachers some valuable help, a thing so different from coming and taking the bare results in the old form of Examination'.[133] Similarly at Cheriton in Hampshire, when the Inspector called early in August, 1899, to look at exercise books, etc., the mistress recorded with evident satisfaction his comment that he had had a 'very pleasant visit'. Obviously by the end of the nineteenth century HMI was beginning to lose some at least of the ogre-like qualities which had been attributed to him by more than one generation of elementary school teachers and their pupils.

However, perhaps the most revealing – and humorous – account of the attitude of a typical Inspector towards his elementary school work in the pre-1890 era is provided, appropriately enough, by the autobiography of one of their number, entitled *HMI – Some passages in the Life of One of HM Inspectors of Schools*. The author, E.M. Sneyd-Kynnersley, examined children in rural Wales during the early 1870s and noted that the 'great aim of inspector, teacher, and children was to finish by 12.30 [p.m.] at the latest.

'Our plan of campaign was delightfully simple. Most of the children were in the two lowest standards. These were supplied with slates, pencils, and a reading-book, and were drawn up in two long lines down the middle of the room. They stood back-to-back, to prevent copying, and did dictation, and arithmetic, sometimes dropping their slates, sometimes their pencils, sometimes

Child's arithmetic exercises. The working out of these long sums enabled hard-pressed teachers to attend to other children in the class. (Museum of English Rural Life, Reading)

their books, not infrequently all three, with a crash on the floor. When we had marked the results on the Examination Schedule, all these children were sent home, and the atmosphere was immensely improved. Then we proceeded to examine the rest, the aristocracy, who worked their sums on paper. As a rule, if we began about 10 we finished about 11.45. If the master was a good fellow, and trustworthy, we looked over the few papers in dictation and arithmetic, marked the Examination Schedule, and showed him the whole result before we left . . . But if the man were cross-grained, and likely to complain that the exercises were too hard, the standard of marking too high, and so on, he would be left in merciful ignorance of details.'

While the examination was in progress the school managers – or one of their number – would arrive with the school accounts. At one small Welsh school inspected by Sneyd-Kynnersley, the squire, a Mr Trevor, appeared with the accounts but also brought with him his wife, who announced that she was 'particularly interested in sewing, and [wanted] to have my opinion as an expert.

Horror! Meanwhile Standards III, IV and V are struggling with sums, and, at intervals, with Dictation, given out by the master in a convincing accent. Then they read with a fluency that in those early days used to amaze me, knowing, as I did, that they knew very little English; till I found by greater experience that they knew the two books by heart, and could go on equally well if the book fell on the ground . . .

'Mrs Trevor insists that I shall report on the sewing. There is a table covered with female garments in unbleached calico (which smells like hot glue), linen, and flannel; and I am expected to look as if I knew one stitch from another. By great good luck I drive away both Mrs Squire and [the Master's wife] by picking up, in my ignorance, a garment so shocking to the modest eye that my critics turn hastily away, and are speechless.'[136] Nor was Sneyd-Kynnersley the only Inspector to find difficulty in inspecting needlework, which was, of course, compulsory for the girls. In the year 1887, Mr Milman of the Warwick district, even asked for the appointment of a female superintendent for needlework, so that this particular task could be taken out of his hands, 'if only to be saved the question asked so often with withering scorn, "What can you know about needlework?"'[7]

Despite all these efforts, too, in a few of the more remote areas, village schools could still be found in the 1890s which had somehow escaped the reforming spirit of both Education Department and HMIs. One such was Crosby Garrett Church of England School in Westmorland, which was visited by HMI Fisher in 1890. In a plaintive report to his superiors, Mr Fisher noted that he had visited the school 'after due notice on February 28. On my arrival . . . I found the master and 31 children present, but no preparation whatever had been made for examination; nor did the teacher appear to expect one. I then had an interview with the vicar . . . who is one of the three trustees of the school. I find that the vicar and (I imagine) the body of trustees are on bad terms with the teacher and have no more communication with him than they can help. The teacher had therefore not received the examination schedule . . . I then spent some time in explaining to the teacher – an old and feeble man of eighty – born 1810 – how to fill up the examination schedule . . .

'To summarize as to teacher and management
  (i)   There is no official management, the teacher does just what he pleases
  (ii) The teacher is an old man of 80
  (iii) According to exam. schedule children are only presented as high as
        Standard I – but this is probably an error
  (iv) Needlework is not taught and – as things are at present – cannot be
  (v)   The trustees decline to certify satisfactorily to the character of the master . . .'

THE ARRIVAL OF HER MAJESTY'S INSPECTOR

Fisher also considered that the school building itself, although accepted as adequate in 1874 by a previous Inspector, was not in fact up to standard; it was built 'on a very sloping rocky bank – is unenclosed and on the high side, the vicar tells me, the rock comes some way up the wall – and keeps the rooms damp . . . The school moreover has that abomination – a stone floor – and has no ceiling – the slates of the roof being its only covering . . .'

Needless to say, once these facts had been brought to light, machinery was soon set in motion to bring about changes. In 1891 the school was finally closed, and a school board was elected from among the local ratepayers to run the new school – a school which was now, of course, partly financed out of the rates. However, while such an extreme example as this was rare by the last decade of the nineteenth century, it is true to say that the quality of teaching still left much to be desired in a number of country schools. Obviously this affected the educational prospects of the children.

On the other hand, it must be admitted, that for most of their school life neither the children nor their parents paid much attention to the results of the annual examinations – save only that the children usually endured the ordeal of the inspection itself with sickly apprehension. But for older ones at least this parental indifference was modified following the introduction of compulsory education under the legislation of 1876 and 1880. For although the completion of a specified number of attendances permitted children to work *part-time* once they had passed the minimum school leaving age of ten, a *permanent* severing of the links with school below the age of thirteen depended upon the results of their annual examination. With the 'dunce's pass' they could leave at thirteen if they had made 250 attendances per annum for five years prior to reaching that age. Under local bye-laws, therefore, a minimum level of attainment was laid down – usually Standard IV or Standard V – and only when this had been achieved could the children *legally* leave. Given the economic pressures on labouring parents and the desire of most of them to have their children at work as soon as possible, it comes as no surprise to discover that as the youngsters approached the appropriate age and Standard, their parents began to display interest in their education. Marked improvements in school attendance could be observed, and as Roger Sellman has pointed out in respect of Devon schools: 'There are repeated comments in Log Books on the almost full attendance at, and just before, the inspection, and rueful remarks on how much better results would be if this were normal'.[13]

Yet, against the miserably poor family background of many labourers and their children, this anxiety is understandable. It is touchingly illustrated in a letter written by a labourer's wife (a Mrs Spray) from Magham Down, near Hailsham in Sussex which was sent to the Education Department in 1886. It referred to her

Chadlington National School, Oxfordshire, in the 1890s. (Mrs M. Dring)

twin daughters, aged twelve, who were seeking work as nursemaids and who, presumably, had not passed the appropriate Standard examination:

> I now write a few lines to you to ask you if my daughters can leave school I have sent you there own writeing and there age and figures because we cannot finde them in clothes and food and keep a home for them any longer without there help there Father his sixty years of age and he goes four miles every morning and four miles back that makes eight miles a day and then if it his fine all the week so he can work on the farm he gets 14s but if it his wet he cannot work on the farm and he his paid for the days he does work so his earning never amounts to more than 10s a week and very often under 10s in the winter months . . . and this cruel cruel law of a school board it his too bad . . . just ask yourselves how you could keep a family on 14s a week for six month in a year and 10s the other six and finde everything that his wanted will you please will you let me know because they must go for a nurse maide I know of two places and they would have gone only this school board nucence . . .

THE ARRIVAL OF HER MAJESTY'S INSPECTOR

With Mrs Spray's letter were some simple addition and subtraction sums produced by her daughters, plus quotations carefully copied from the Bible. Unhappily for her, this unusual method of approaching the authorities did not yield the result she was seeking. 'Exemption depended not on poverty but on past attendance and the passing of the appropriate standard.'[79]

Some parents, of course, took the risk of sending their children to work anyway, and of facing such legal repercussions as came along as a result. (See Chapter 4.) But in other cases, the children sought to pass their 'school leaving' examination – or Labour certificate, as it was usually called – at as early an age as possible. Until the 1890s the examination was taken by scholars as part of their ordinary inspection – indeed, it *was* part of the ordinary inspection. But with the abolition of the annual examination in the three 'Rs' and the substitution, in 1895, of the option of 'two unannounced visits' by the HMI for the old formal set up, alternative arrangements had to be made in those schools which changed over to the new system. In the more sparsely populated rural areas this meant that schools had to be specially designated at which the 'labour certificate' examination would be held, on certain dates, for the children of the district. Thus at Cheriton Lane End School, Hampshire, in December, 1898, the mistress was annoyed to discover that there 'would be an Inspection at Old Alresford . . . I immediately wrote to Clerk [of the School Board] saying the distance was too great for children to go there to be examined for Labour Certificate from this school'. But despite her protest no alternative arrangement appears to have been made. Again, at St Giles' School in Stony Stratford, the master noted in May, 1893: 'Two boys . . . were presented at the British School today for examination for labour certificate'. At Whitchurch School in South Oxfordshire, six children were required to attend the Purley schools, on 1 April 1895, so that they could be examined for their labour certificates, while at Asthall School in the same county, during 1898, the mistress recorded that 'an examination for Labour Certificate would be held in Witney on June 1st'. On 9 June she 'received the Examination Schedule . . . showing that the two girls sent in for Labour Certificates had passed.' In the following year, the examination was held on Saturday 3 June, also at Witney, but this time there were three candidates. Unfortunately, only two of them passed, the third (Lizzy Mills) having failed in arithmetic. This was a serious blow for the girl in question, since she would not be able to get a job, and the mistress expressed her surprise at the result, as 'Lizzy was the best of the three in this subject. I can only think it must have been caused by nervousness or sheer carelessness.' However, Lizzy's story had a happy ending (if one can call leaving school with a minimum level of education at the age of eleven or twelve happy), for on 22 June Sub-Inspector Lucas visited Asthall School on one of his random calls. The mistress seized the opportunity to discuss Lizzy's plight with him, and he 'kindly consented to re-examine [her] for a Labour Certificate. She passed obtaining four sums right', according to the log book entry – no doubt to her own satisfaction and that of the mistress.

Indeed, even before this there are examples of children anxious to leave school at the first possible moment being allowed to join in an examination at another school – although they are comparatively rare. One such is provided by Ravenstone School in Buckinghamshire, which permitted children from schools at nearby Stoke Goldington and Weston Underwood to attend the summer inspections held at Ravenstone in July, 1883, 1884 and 1885. But in the latter year the application from Stoke for permission for nine children to attend called forth objections from the Ravenstone master. He considered that this would make the school too full and offered to take 'half the number only'. In the end, four Stoke Goldington children attended.

Of course, Her Majesty's Inspector was not the only person authorized to carry out an inspectorial function – at least in the church schools. For from 1839 onwards a growing number of dioceses began to appoint their own inspectors as well. Nevertheless, even though in the early days, these men examined pupils in the three 'Rs' as well as in religious instruction, by the 1860s, most of them were confining their attention to religious knowledge only.[78] Their reports were, in general, less 'condemning than those of Her Majesty's inspectors; possibly because they accepted lower standards of work and performance,' while, in any case, they did not carry with them the dreaded financial authority of the HMIs. For this reason both teachers and pupils held them in less awe than their government counterparts realizing that in most cases they 'seem[ed] to have come looking for something to praise . . . [while] having little power, [they] escaped the corruption of power, and were able to meet the teacher on less unequal terms.'[133] At Blyborough, in Lincolnshire, where the schoolroom was the parsonage kitchen the incumbent admitted, indeed: 'I think a system of Diocesan Inspection would be very useful to schools like mine. The requirements of governmental inspectors are too much for such schools and discourage both teachers and scholars.' Although by the 1870s most elementary schools were under Government supervision, the situation remained much the same as regards the attitudes of teachers and pupils towards diocesan inspectors. Even for the children themselves there was little nervous tension on the day of 'Scripture Inspector's visit, for he 'beamed upon and encouraged [them], even to the extent of prompting those who were not word-perfect', according to Flora Thompson's recollections from Cottisford School in the 1880s.[144] (For further information on the influence of diocesan inspection upon the country child see Chapter Eight.)

THE ARRIVAL OF HER MAJESTY'S INSPECTOR

NOTES ON ADDITIONAL SOURCES USED

For details of Crosby Garrett school see Educational Parish Records of Westmorland at Public Record Office, Ed. 2.457.

For reports of diocesan inspectors see Oxford Diocese, Deanery of Woodstock. Report of Inspector of Schools, 1854 – MS. Oxf. dioc. Pp. 51, at Oxfordshire Record Office; and Oxford Diocese, Deanery of Reading – Reports of Inspector for 1853 and 1854, MS. Oxf. dioc. Pp. e. 49 and MS. Oxf. dioc. Pp. e. 50 at Oxfordshire Record Office.

CHAPTER FOUR

The School Attendance Laws

'*28th June,* 1900: School breaks up today until July 30th. A very poor school all the week owing to the "pea picking" having begun in several places . . . *24th August,* 1900: Children still absent, wanted to carry food to the Harvest fields. I complained to the Attendance Officer, and he said that magistrates would not convict if a summons were issued, the children really being needed at this time of year.' – Entries made by the mistress in *Weston-on-Avon Board School Log Book,* which is preserved at Warwickshire County Record Office. (Weston-on-Avon has been part of Warwickshire since 1931.)

Throughout the last quarter of the nineteenth century one of the most frequent causes of conflict between the country child and the law arose from the various Education Acts passed during the period 1870–80, with the purpose of enforcing the attendance at school of every child over the age of five. Yet, as the above extract from Weston-on-Avon School log book shows, in some rural areas even in 1900 these regulations were only imperfectly applied. One writer has, in fact, gone so far as to speak of the 'myth of compulsory attendance', during this period.[133] But before the validity of his statement is examined in detail, it is perhaps worthwhile to look again at the education legislation which had attempted to bring about an improvement in attendance levels.

The first move in this direction came as a result of the 1870 Education Act, which laid down that adequate provision for elementary education must be made in all parts of the country. Where existing voluntary schools (usually Church ones) were unable to meet the needs of the locality, then a school board could be established to make good the deficiency. The school board was to be elected from among the ratepayers and had authority both to finance its school partly out of the rates and also to enforce attendance at school by all children over the age of five who lived within its area. However, although in a number of towns, school boards were set up as a result of this Act, in the country districts local voluntary effort normally sufficed to provide any extra accommodation needed. Indeed, many of the country clergy, in particular, resented this attempt to undermine their influence (as they saw it) in the educational life of the community. As the incumbent of Soulbury, Buckinghamshire, wrote to his Bishop in 1872, in his village there was, 'no School Board, nor shall there be with God's help unless some further alteration is made in the law'. And at Fawley in the same county, the incumbent declared, 'No – emphatically no . . .' when asked if there were to be a school board within his parish. Likewise supporters of Ingoldmells National School in Lincolnshire 'unanimously agreed that exertions . . . be used to raise sufficient funds to keep the school under its present voluntary system . . .'[129] In a few parishes, however, the advent of a school board could not be prevented, and it then became the aim of the local clergymen to become an elected member of it; consequently, in such villages as Sutton Courtenay then in Berkshire and Shillington in Bedfordshire, among others, clerical authority continued to be exercised even when school boards were appointed in the mid-1870s. But in most villages, board schools were avoided, and so this first attempt at introducing compulsory school attendance had little general effect in the agricultural areas.

It was in the light of that knowledge that in February, 1873, Mr C.S. Read, a tenant farmer and Conservative Member of Parliament for South Norfolk, decided to put before the Commons a bill specifically to deal with the plight of the rural child. This legislation was approved by Parliament, and under its terms, no child below 'the age of eight years [was to be] employed in the execution of any kind of agricultural work for an employer'. The requirement did not, however, hold good against a father or guardian employing his own child on the land. And between the ages of eight and ten years, a boy or girl could only be employed if a minimum of 250 school attendances had been made and certified by the 'principal teacher' of the local school, while between the ages of ten and twelve, 150 school attendances were required. Once the youngsters had reached the age of twelve, the Act ceased to apply and they were free to seek employment if they wished. But permanent exemption below this age could only be secured if the child had passed an examination which showed he had 'reached the fourth standard of education as prescribed by the Minutes of the Education Department'.

In addition, several short-term exemptions were laid down. For example, during the hay, corn or hop harvests the need to produce a certificate of attendance was waived, while at other times of the year, the restrictions could be suspended if a written application to that end were made by the farmers to their local petty sessions and approved by the magistrates.

Nevertheless, in the period between the passage of this Agricultural Children Act and its implementation on 1 January 1875, hopes were widely expressed that it might effect an improvement in the level of school attendance in the rural areas. The National Agricultural Labourers' Union (the farm workers' trade union, established in 1872), was one organization which saw compulsory education as a step in the right direction. In June, 1873, an Oxfordshire member even went so far as to say that 'the Education Act . . . was the best law which had ever been passed for the agricultural labourer'. And at a conference held in the autumn of 1875, after the Act had come into operation, the Union Treasurer asserted that 'compulsion was needed just as much for the parents as for any other reason'; and he declared that 'better education meant better wages'. Another speaker pointed out that from the Union's point of view more schooling would be extremely beneficial, since 'where ignorance existed the Union had not flourished'. The conference then passed a resolution calling for 'compulsory free attendance, with unsectarian teaching in order that the agricultural classes should enjoy the greatest opportunities to gain a sound elementary education for their children'.

But not all parents shared this enthusiasm. Many, of course, feared the loss of children's earnings and the effect this would have on a precarious family budget. As 1 January 1875 drew near, there is evidence that some of them at least began to encourage their children to make an effort to achieve the educational and attendance standards laid down for exemption. Thus at Brailes in Warwickshire, an entry in the school log book for 9 October 1874 reads: 'Children taking interest in their work. Parents very anxious owing to the Act regulating the labour of children.'

But events were soon to show that these parents had little to worry about, for almost immediately the Act proved totally ineffective. This was partially due to weaknesses in its drafting. For example, the various exemption clauses prevented any uniform observance of its terms, so that at Daventry Petty Sessions in November 1875, an application by a number of farmers for its restrictions to be set aside 'given the special circumstances of the unusually wet weather which had caused great delay in getting in the seed corn' proved successful. On the other hand, a similar request from Warwickshire farmers in the Offchurch area, in April 1876, was firmly rejected.

Yet even more damaging than these inconsistencies in interpretation and the resentment to which they gave rise was the failure of the legislation to specify any agency to see that its provisions were properly carried out. The speedy result of this latter omission in many villages, therefore, was a brazen and widespread disregard of all of its provisions. Indeed, as the Revd G. R. Moncrieff HMI neatly summarized it, in respect of the counties of Gloucestershire and Somerset: 'A very few weeks sufficed to betray the fact that the law was powerless for want of an official machinery to work it. The lesson was soon learnt; hardly anyone would undertake the invidious duty of prosecutor. I know of one or two instances in which the clergymen were prepared to do so, but these were naturally isolated cases; and as the matter now stands I imagine the law is regarded as a dead letter . . .'[7]

His colleagues agreed with him. Mr Danby, reporting on Suffolk and Essex, considered the Act 'wholly inoperative', and a similar conclusion was reached by the Revd R.L. Koe in Sussex. Outside observers were equally alive to the Act's failures. Thus, at the quarterly meeting of Norfolk magistrates in April, 1875, the position was deplored by a Mr Jex-Blake 'who pointed out that the underlying difficulty was the absence of an informer against employers of small boys. The Chief Constable said it had been resolved, unless otherwise ordered by the court, not to employ the police in the matter.' Jex-Blake declared that he personally had seen 'very small boys employed in crow keeping' (i.e. bird scaring) while a fellow magistrate noted that 'in his neighbourhood the Act was openly set at defiance'.

Although not all counties had quite such abysmal records as these – the Chief Constable of Leicestershire, for example, claimed considerable success in securing observance of the Act – nevertheless further Government intervention was obviously essential if the law were not to fall into utter disrepute. It was, therefore, only following this earlier failure that in 1876 a second general Education Act was passed, calling for the appointment of school attendance committees in all districts where there were no school boards. These committees were given powers to make bye-laws demanding compulsory attendance, but were not forced to use their powers. Consequently, given that a number of the school attendance committees had little enthusiasm for education anyway, in several areas the framing of compulsory education regulations continued to be neglected. It was only in 1880 that legislation was finally passed which unequivocally imposed compulsory school attendance on a national scale for children between the ages of five and fourteen. This meant, in practice, that for boys and girls aged between five and ten, full-time attendance was required and in 1893, the upper limit was raised to eleven.[135] For those aged between ten and twelve, a minimum of 250 attendances per annum had to be made, while for the over-twelves the figure was 150. Legal exemption from school could thus only be granted on a part-time basis if the child had passed the age of ten (or eleven after 1893) and if the specified number of attendances had been made. Complete exemption below the age of fourteen depended either upon the child passing his 'Labour certificate' at the standard laid down by the education bye-laws in his own school district (usually either Standard IV or Standard V), or upon his having reached the age of thirteen and having made at least 250 attendances per annum for the previous five years. This latter means of exit was known as the 'dunce's leaving certificate' (See Chapter Three). However, for those comparatively few children who lived more than *two* miles from a school, a loophole still

July 14   Scripture Examination. Registers not marked. Average for week 68. 6

17   Childrens treat, whole holiday given

19   Mr Howlett visited the School

26   Half holiday given

28   Another case of Scarletina. Three children sent home

August 1st   Children have been very irregular during the week. Average 67.4

7   Opened School in the morning only 11 children present so closed the School until after harvest

Sept 18   Reopened School 37 children present in the morning 32 in the afternoon   Average for week 42.

26   Mr Howlett visited the School. Elder Scholars very irregular. Average for whole School 52.4. On the Registers 99

October 6   Average for this week 71.5

" 11   Thame fair several children have taken a holiday

16   Very wet many of the children away

20   The children are very irregular. Have sent in the names of 21 to the Attendance committee.

Extracts from Sydenham National School log book, Oxfordshire, showing attendance problems in the 1880s. (Oxfordshire Record Office)

remained – for most bye-laws exempted them from compulsory attendance.

In order to try to ensure that the provisions of the various Education Acts were observed, both school boards and attendance committees were required to appoint attendance officers. Frequently the local sanitary or relieving officer was appointed to this position by school attendance committees, receiving a 'miserable' increase of perhaps £5 per annum to his existing salary for the extra work. School boards were likewise expected to supply their own attendance officer, but here again in the rural areas, the appointment was 'always a very part-time one', and a small salary only was paid. 'At South Brent [in Devon] for some years a postman was employed, on the assumption that he would know everybody and could make enquiries on his rounds; . . . The Okehampton Board tried to employ a policeman in his spare time, but the chief constable objected. At Ermington the clerk to the school board was also the village shopkeeper and would take no steps to enforce attendance "as there is a fear that compulsory measures might injure the custom".'[133] At Inkpen, in Berkshire, a local grocer and draper, named William Homer, was similarly employed, carrying out the tasks not only of attendance officer but also of collector of poor rates and clerk to the school board. He, too, appears to have displayed little enthusiasm for his 'educational' calling.

In the circumstances of low pay and a complete lack of training it is scarcely surprising that few school attendance officers felt spurred on 'to much activity' when carrying out their duties, especially when these led – as they often did – to abuse from parents who resented interference with their freedom to dispose of their children's time and labour as they thought fit. On the part of a number of employers, too, there was annoyance that a source of cheap casual labour was apparently being restricted, and as early as 1880 some farmers were declaring that the loss of children's labour 'had adversely affected their farming as they were unable to pay men's wages for the work the children had been accustomed to do'. Indeed, in 1901 people in Suffolk were still making it a scapegoat by complaining that: 'The primary cause of . . . [the unsatisfactory condition of the roads] . . . is the doing away with the system of picking stones in the fields due to the advance of education.'[81]

It was, therefore, in this sort of situation that the master or mistress at a school might feel it a duty to intervene to check illegal employment, if attendance officers were thought to be taking no action. For example, at Mixbury School, Oxfordshire, in March 1875, the master recorded in his log book that he had 'sent a note to Mr Watts [a local farmer] for employing a boy in Agricultural labour without a certificate, telling him of the risk he was incurring'. Hardly surprisingly most agriculturists did not take kindly to this interference – as pained entries in log books bear witness. Thus at Westleigh in Devon in 1880 the teacher

Children helping their mothers to pick hops near Sittingbourne in Kent, 1896–1900. Their earnings were a valuable supplement to family income. (Mr E. Swain)

recorded that he had 'sent to one farmer for six boys employed in mangel picking. Received a message to the effect that when he wanted boys he should have them, and that I was not to enquire for them again.' Smallholder parents likewise took a dim view of attempts to remove their children's labour. At Thornbury one small Devon farmer admitted that 'he could not afford to pay a man 2s a day to do work the boy could do'. He preferred to risk the 'remote possibility' of prosecution for breaking the attendance laws and perhaps a 5s fine which 'could not weigh against an immediate 2s a day'.[133]

In these conditions, whatever the intentions of successive Governments may have been, many teething troubles were to be encountered before the majority of youngsters in the rural areas were at last brought safely within the school walls for the prescribed period. Persistent breaches of the Education Acts were especially common during the later 1870s and the 1880s, and it was only following the virtual abolition of school fees for elementary education in 1891, plus a general decline in the farmer's use of child labour, that the breaches were slowly reduced. Yet, even at the end of the nineteenth century widespread disregard of the law could be reported – as at Weston-on-Avon school in 1900, in the quotation at the head of this chapter.

The HMIs, for their part, were fully aware of the situation. Thus in 1898, it was claimed in their official reports that in the rural areas around Exeter 'very little evidence' could be found of 'any systematic or serious efforts on the part of rural school boards or school attendance committees to enforce regularity [of attendance]'. At about the same time, Cornwall was condemned as having the 'unenviable distinction of being the worst county in England in this matter . . . It is a commonplace now that many members of School Boards and attendance committees are among the worst offenders in employing children illegally. It is to be feared that many School Boards are not merely negatively uneducational but positively anti-educational . . .' Elsewhere, in spite of the undoubted – and acknowledged – improvement in the level of school attendance as compared with earlier years, much still remained to be done. In Lincolnshire, there were areas where 'local authorities and magistrates . . . combine to make Bye-laws and Education Acts dead letters', while in the York district, HMI Howard frankly admitted: 'So long as certain farming operations can be performed by children, and so long as we hear of agricultural depression, it appears that employers and parents will continue to break the law, magistrates will be slow to convict, school attendance committees will not press cases against employers and parents, managers will not furnish names of offenders for fear of losing subscriptions or making the school unpopular, and teachers will not make enemies by furnishing information.' In an obvious attempt to make the best of a bad job, he continued: 'Something, however, might be done by arranging the school holidays for those times when children are most likely to be kept from school. The bye-laws should be explained to the parents and the facilities for obtaining labour certificates should be made known.'[7] As examination of school log books shows that his advice about the timing of holidays to coincide with the busy agricultural seasons had already been widely implemented. (See Chapter Five for a discussion of this.)

Nor was it only the Inspectors who were unhappy about the situation. In 1894 the Clerk to the Hevingham School Board in Norfolk wrote to the Education Department in London about the Board's inability to obtain convictions because of local magisterial indifference to breaches of education bye-laws. And despite intervention by the Department, the situation remained unsatisfactory.

Of course, not all magistrates were as lax as this, and as HMI Oliver pointed out in 1898, 'resort to the law is required for only a small percentage of cases . . . when the attendance officer is zealous and offenders know the local authority is determined to fulfil its duty. Under these conditions warning and persuasion will, in most cases, suffice.'[7]

Many teachers, however, were convinced (and as we have seen sometimes with justification) that the attendance officers were not 'zealous' in the pursuit of the persistent offender. Log books abound with complaints as to their failures, and certainly it does seem that while timid and blameless children like the young George Sturt of Farnham in Surrey were frightened of them,[139] youngsters of a rougher temperament took little notice. One typical example of the dissatisfaction of teachers with school attendance officers can be taken from the pages of Ivinghoe Log Book in Buckinghamshire, where the children were widely employed in a local cottage industry – straw plaiting – as well as in agriculture. Here the master recorded sourly in January, 1878: 'The attendance officer has done little in this parish towards filling the school and securing the regular attendance of the children'. Just over a year later his impatience had grown still further: 'I wrote to the Attendance Officer but as yet he has taken no notice of my letter not so much as to acknowledge it. He has as yet caused more to stay from school than to come.' Again, in August, 1880, came the complaint: 'Nothing done by the Attendance Officer in working up irregular pupils'. Yet, an examination of the local petty sessions records indicates that his complaints were exaggerated; indeed, in the year 1879 over one-third of all cases heard before the Ivinghoe Petty Sessions (not all relating to Ivinghoe village, of course) were school attendance cases (thirty-three out of ninety-one cases), and in 1880 the proportion was slightly higher (thirty-two out of eighty-eight cases). Not until the mid-1880s did the attendance position finally improve, and prosecutions for breaches of the legislation dwindle.

Elsewhere, too, there are signs that a number of attendance officers and local authorities took their duties seriously. At Henley Petty Sessions, in Oxfordshire, where the legislation only seems to have begun to 'bite' in 1878, there were in October of that year four cases heard, all from the Whitchurch area, and one of them involving the village blacksmith. In each case an order was made for the children concerned to attend Whitchurch school. In March, 1879, further cases were heard and this time the district involved was wider and the numbers greater, fifteen offending parents being brought before the court in that month. Furthermore, those who had failed to comply with the earlier court orders were now fined 5s per child. And although labourers' children were the most numerous of the truants since in their homes economic pressures were likely to be the most severe, by no means all offending parents came into this category. The case of the Whitchurch blacksmith has been mentioned already, and in the years that followed offenders included a baker, a painter, a fly driver, a carpenter, a woodman and a wood dealer. Altogether, in the twelve months ending 20 November 1879, about twenty school attendance cases were brought before this particular petty sessions. In the following twelve months, there were eighteen (or roughly one-eighth of all cases heard). Fines varied, but 2s 6d per

RURAL SIMPLICITY.

"BEEN TO SCHOOL, LITTLE LASSIE?"   "AYE, SIR."   "GOOD GIRL—THERE'S A PENNY FOR YOU."
"THANK YOU, SIR. I'LL HAE TO BE STEPPIN'—BUT AWM GAUN TO SKEULL I' THE MORNIN'—WULL YE BE THIS WAY I' THE EFTERNEUN?!"

Encouragement to good school attendance! (*Punch*, 1877)

child was fairly common when a parent failed to comply with the order to send his children to school. More rarely, employers were also charged with breaches of the legislation – as in January, 1880, when the Henley magistrates fined a farmer from Caversham 1s with 14s costs for employing a child under legal age.

By the end of the century, however, the number of attendance cases had declined sharply, so that in the twelve months ending 8 December 1898, there were only seven such heard at Henley. A similar trend emerged at Watlington Petty Sessions, also in Oxfordshire: 'In 1880–81 breaches of the comparatively new-fangled school attendance rules gave rise to 22 per cent of the cases [heard], a class of offence which in the 1900s hardly ever counted for more than 5 per cent.'[114] In other words, rural families were probably learning to avoid the blatant breaches of the law which brought penalties with them, but were perhaps doing little more than that. Certainly there is little evidence that labouring families felt *guilty* at ignoring the restrictions – and some of the children, especially the older boys, on the contrary, felt ashamed when they were forced to go to school, instead of being allowed to work and to contribute to the family income.

One unwilling pupil from the Huntingdonshire fen country, made this very clear as regards the later 1870s: '. . . nobody who lived more than two mile away from the school were compelled to attend, and this applied to a good many children in our district. But I had to go . . . Arter I were about nine year old, I got real ashamed o' going to school when other folks went to work. One morning some men were working in a field as I passed on my way to school, and I 'eard one on 'em say "Look at that bloody grut ol" bor still a-gooing to school. Oughta be getting 'is own living'. After that I used to get into the dykes and slink along out o' sight in case anybody should see me and laugh at me.'[112] This boy eventually left school at the age of twelve.

Similar sentiments were expressed by a Yorkshire lad who lost his father when he was only eleven and whose family was often very short of money: '. . . now at times we didn't know where the next meal was coming from, [but] it somehow came, through mother's wonderful management. I was now twelve years old, with still another year to put in at school. Folk said "it wer' a shame a gurt lad like he bein' kep' at school," and "it wer' a scandless shame as a lad couldn't leave school afore he wer' thirteen to help his mither." But to school I had to go, though I grumbled at being held back from helping to keep the house . . .'[105]

However, some of the less law-abiding sent their children to work and risked the consequences. For instance, at Austrey School in Warwickshire, the master complained in 1890 that average attendances were pulled down 'by a few bad cases, thus George Rowland, during the last twenty-two weeks, has attended 69 times only whereas the school was open 206 times. Esther Godfrey has made only 243 times during the year, school open, 418 times.' At Odell School in Bedfordshire, an entry for 25 July 1884, revealed that 'Charles Ashton [had] refused [to take his leaving certificate examination] and is still at work though he has been warned . . .' Six years later the situation here was apparently much the same: 'The Bye Laws are simply laughed at and ignored by many of the parents.'

Of course, while much of the absenteeism was caused by parents either sending the children to work in the fields or in a cottage industry, or else keeping them at home to look after younger brothers and sisters or assist around the house, these were not the only reasons. Until the virtual abolition of fees for elementary education in 1891, many youngsters were periodically forced to remain at home by lack of school pence. At Hibaldstow Board School in Lincolnshire, an entry for 8 March 1889, regretted the decline in average levels of attendance: 'Some parents could not afford school fees'. Similarly at Barrow on Humber Church School in the same county, the teacher noted on 4 February 1878: 'Four different families sent word that their children were kept at home because they were unable to pay the school fees'.[139] For although the fees were normally very small – only 1d or 2d per child per week in most cases – this could represent a major outlay where there were several children of school age, or where the father of the family was unemployed or working on short-time in the winter months. It is significant, therefore, that at Steeple Aston School, Oxfordshire, during the severe snow of February 1865, when agricultural work would be short and unemployment widespread, at least two children were reported as absent 'for want of money'. Again, at Ivinghoe school, Buckinghamshire, in April, 1881, four children were sent home to fetch their school fees 'in the early part of the week', and according to the master, they had 'not been to this school since . . .' For the poor but sensitive child this singling out for non-payment must have been especially hard to bear.

Sometimes the children were allowed to have their education 'on credit' for a week or two – as at Grimsbury Wesleyan School, Banbury, where an entry in the school log book during February 1882, noted that the school fees of some of the children were 'in arrears, the reason being the fathers out of work'. Again, a few mothers faced with the fee problem would decide that defiance was the best policy. When, in 1888, a small boy from Farringdon, Hampshire, was sent home for his fees, 'as he was four or five weeks in arrears', he quickly returned with a message from his mother that she 'was not going to pay any money', and the teacher 'might do what [she] liked'. But most women lacked the courage to respond in this way and, in any case, teachers grew tired of their reluctant feepayers, and as at Horkstow School, Lincolnshire, 'Cautioned the children against coming to School more than a fortnight without the School fee'.[129] In this school – as in many others – children were excluded for non-payment of fees, despite the compulsory clauses of the Education Acts.

Equally damaging in certain schools were the payments required for the use of books or to purchase slates and pencils, etc. At Bloxham in north Oxfordshire, rules issued in January 1855, required the children to buy books, which 'could be obtained at reduced prices or on hire purchase if necessary. They could be re-sold to the master if, when the children left school, they were clean and whole.' At Leckford Board School in March, 1876, the mistress admitted that she found 'a great difficulty in getting [her pupils] to buy a spelling or geography book'. Even the simple process of writing might be limited by the availability of materials; as one Derbyshire teacher noted, 'Standard II [had] to write on slates because of the difficulty of getting parents to buy books.'[113] Where this sort of situation prevailed, it was not uncommon for 'several children, even in the higher classes [to be] without books altogether . . . .' As Matthew Arnold, HMI, pointed out, such a policy could not fail to be detrimental to the children's education: 'I think that in all schools there should be a public stock of books, from which those who cannot beyond a doubt afford to buy for themselves should be supplied.'[28] In fact, not only was the children's schooling hampered by this lack of funds to buy books, pencils, etc., but their attendance also. As one Victorian child who attended school at Blaxhall, Suffolk, in the late 1880s recalled, he was required to pay fees of 'twopence a week, and a penny for the slate and a halfpenny for a pencil: "When my mother had got the money we went, and when she hadn't we didn't go".'[37]

On the other hand, if a family were completely destitute and in receipt of poor law relief, then the local poor law guardians might agree to pay the school pence of the children. One who benefitted in this way was James William Seely, who was born near Lowestoft in 1894, the eldest of five children. James lost his father at around the turn of the century and his mother was allowed 3s 6d a week by the board of guardians, who also paid the fees of the three children old enough to attend school: ' . . . we had a mile-and-a-half to walk to Loddon school. Then every Saturday morning us three children who were old enough to go to school had to take attendance cards they'd given us to the Relieving Officer to show him we'd been attending school all the week. If we'd been absent it would be marked on the card, he wanted to know exactly what we'd been doing on that day. I suppose it was to see that us children didn't earn any more money working out of school.'[85] At Grimsbury School, Banbury, on the other hand, representatives of the board of guardians themselves visited the school from time to time to check up on the pupils for whom they were responsible. For example, an entry for 1 May 1883, reads: 'Mr Johnson – Mayor – and Mr Shepherd visited the school this morning and took attendances of those children paid for by the Guardians.'

Nevertheless, not all of the guardians were as cooperative as this, even though from 1876 they were explicitly authorized to pay the fees of children who were poor and not merely those who were destitute. At South Ferriby in Lincolnshire the teacher complained on 22 January 1886, that the 'Relieving Officer called on me respecting fees for poor children. The Guardians will not allow the fees except on parents promising to repay.' And on 19 February, of the same year, the subject was taken up again: 'I have a poor attendance . . . I cannot receive school fees from several parents as they are unemployed. I have repeatedly asked the Guardians but to no effect.'[129] Similarly, at Cropredy and Bourton School, Oxfordshire, the master sadly recorded on 25 April 1880: 'Of those receiving Parish payment benefit, application was made for Labour certificates because the Board of Guardians decided not to allow payment of school fees of any scholar who had passed the third standard.'[130]

Of course, for those children whose parents *could* afford the school fees the weekly possession of a few pennies on the journey to school might prove an overpowering temptation – especially if they had to pass a sweetshop. For labouring children rarely had pocket money of their own to spend. One who offended in this way at Steeple Aston School, Oxfordshire, was the young Amelia Cross, who, on 30 November 1864, was found to have been 'robbing her father and spending the money in sweets &c. M. Durran received 3d from her knowing her to have stolen it.' The master's reaction was to lock them both up 'the whole day after mak[ing] their parents acquainted with the circumstances'. Similarly, Andy Smith, who was born in Norfolk, in 1886, remembered transgressing on one occasion when taking his penny to school. He went into the local shop 'and bought a pennorth of mixed sweets. When I went to the school the old woman [the mistress] stood there. She said, "Where's your penny, boy?" I said "I went and bought some sweets." She said, "What have you done with them?" I said, "We've ate them." Her hand was like a bull's foot and she had a great old thimble on there as big as an eggcup and she hit me on top of the skull and there was a bump as big as a hen's egg.' Nor did Andy's troubles end there. He was sent home with a note to his mother explaining his misdemeanour, and as soon as his father returned in the evening he was ordered upstairs in disgrace. Nearly eighty years later Andy remembered: 'I only got up in time or he would have kicked me up.' There was no question of spare the rod and spoil the child in his home.

Some children took days off, unbeknown to their parents, merely for their own pleasure. The temptation to play truant must have been especially strong in the spring time and early summer, when the brightening sunshine, the green grass, the song of the birds and the ripple of the streams presented such an attractive contrast to the tedium of school life, where so much time was devoted to mechanical learning by heart. Thus, an entry at Henley-in-Arden British School Log Book on 26 May 1863, noted: 'Very poor attendance owing, I expect to a picnic to be held in the fields'. At Steeple Aston School in Oxfordshire during November of the same year, sixteen boys were severely censured for coming late in the afternoon 'having been after the hounds', and the whole school was warned against 'doing the same again'. A similar cause for displeasure was the lateness of boys who had 'stopped to see soldiers pass', or had been 'to see steam ploughing machine at work'.[99]

At Odell in Bedfordshire, on the other hand, on 30 September 1878, the excuse was, 'Sale at the Bell Inn p.m. Several children away from school. I sent after [them] and the parents refused to let them come.' And at the same school on 3 July 1882: 'A great many away from school this morning. I sent after some of them, but many refused to come, as it is Harrold Feast.'

Truancy in direct *defiance* of parents likewise occurred. There was a notable example of this at Ipplepen in Devon during 1886, when the master on arrival 'found J— O— strapped up to the gallery. His mother had fastened him there on her road to work, as she could not depend on his attending without such means.' Next day the culprit was 'again brought to school by his mother, and strapped up during the dinner hour, but succeeded in biting the rope through and freeing himself'.[133] Although few pupils went as far as this, as Joseph Ashby of Tysoe in Warwickshire remembered, 'they absented themselves . . . for every sort of reason . . . boys would go to every flower-show, every meet of the hunt within seven miles. When the cowslips bloomed both boys and girls would be taken out by their mothers to pick the flowers for wine and for a cowslip pudding.'[63]

The teachers, for their part, regarded these frivolous absences with a rather more jaundiced eye than they turned to non-attendance for seasonal employment on the land, for they realized that these occasional earnings were probably, if regrettably, a vital part of the family income. Their concern about absenteeism was, of course, based partly on the effect it had upon educational achievement, but also on the link between the level of average attendance at their school, and the size of the Government financial grant. In these circumstances, they – and the school managers – sometimes offered inducements to the pupils in order to secure good attendances, while at the same time severely punishing (usually by beating) those who offended by playing truant for no particular reason. In some schools, as at Odell in Bedfordshire during the 1890s, the rewards took the form of attendance certificates issued to those who 'had made every attendance during . . . four weeks'. Again, at Long Compton Church School, Warwickshire, the master apparently took photographs of groups of children during 'recreation time' for future display. Since all the children wanted to make sure they appeared on the photographs, attendances were boosted.[121] Simiarly, at Melbourne National School in Derbyshire an 'Order of Regularity and Good Conduct' was established in January, 1899. 'By May thirty-three girls had been admitted to the order.'[113] But perhaps one of the most dramatic examples of this type was provided by Bodmin National School during the 1890s, where the bait was an attendance banner, which was kept for a week by the class whose attendance had been the highest in the preceding week. In 1898: 'The contest for this banner [was] extremely keen and on one occasion on Friday morning Standard II and Standard IV were within a decimal point of each other in the percentage of attendance, Standard IV being slightly ahead. On Friday afternoon Standard II attended in full strength, but one boy in Standard IV was absent, and this was just sufficient to put Standard II ahead and to gain them the banner for the following week. The point of this story [lay] in the sequel – for it is recorded that the Fourth Standard boys, being wroth at losing the banner, waylaid their truant comrade and gave him a sound thrashing.'[7]

In other cases, the prizes were rather more useful than the mere right to display a banner. At Cholsey in Berkshire annual gifts of 'petticoats [for] the girls . . . most regular in attendance' were provided, while at Darley Abbey in Derbyshire the local landowner's wife supplied the girls with cotton dresses as prizes for good attendance.[113] Similarly, the Tollemache family at Helmingham in Suffolk gave shirts and underclothing to regular attenders during the 1880s, and there are many other examples of clothes being presented in an effort to raise attendance levels.

Much less common was the giving of money. Nevertheless, at East Prawle in Devon, 'at the turn of the century, [the board] was giving crown pieces for a full, and double-florins for a nearly full, attendance'. A similar financial inducement was offered at Kentisbeare in the same county – namely the offer of a farthing 'for every attendance over 300', with a maximum outlay of about 2s 6d, 'halved for failure to pass the 3 'R' examination'.[133] At Brailes in Warwickshire, on the other hand, the payment was made indirectly, in so far as Mrs Sheldon, the wife of the lord of the manor, provided the school fees of a number of labouring children, but apparently withdrew the privilege if they did not attend regularly. Thus a log book entry for 29 October 1863, reads: 'Sarah Ann Bailey punished for irregular attendances, Mrs Sheldon said she would not pay her schooling unless she came regularly.' Yet, as Roger Sellman points out, whatever the intention may have been, these various rewards probably did little to encourage the worst truants to raise their standards. They merely inspired 'the already good attender' to still greater heights.[133]

NOTES ON ADDITIONAL SOURCES USED
Clergy Visitation Returns, Oxford diocese, Bucks. Archdeaconry, 1872 – MS. Oxf. Dioc. Pp. c. 337, for clerical comments on Soulbury and Fawley in Buckinghamshire.
For details of Hevingham attendance cases see correspondence between the Clerk to the Hevingham School Board in Norfolk and the Education Department in Parish Files: Norfolk – Ed. 2/318 at Public Record Office.
Information on Andy Smith obtained via Mrs R. Evans of Culham, Oxfordshire.
For School Attendance cases see Petty Session Minute Books: Hungerford (1877–79), D/Ph. Vol. 8 at Berkshire County Record Office: Ivinghoe (1878–92), PS/1/M1 at Buckinghamshire County Record Office; Henley (1862–1881 and 1898–1903), MS. Dep. Deeds, Henley A XVI (10) and (11), at Oxfordshire Record Office; Wallingford (1900–2), P/W/2/2, at Berkshire County Record Office.

CHAPTER FIVE

At Work on the Land

The sheep get up and make their many tracks
And bear a load of snow upon their backs,
And gnaw the frozen turnip to the ground
With sharp quick bite, and then go noising round
The boy that pecks the turnips all the day
And knocks his hands to keep the cold away
And laps his legs in straw to keep them warm
And hides behind the hedges from the storm.

(From 'Sheep in Winter' by John Clare – 1793–1864)

Despite both changes in the law governing school attendance and the accompanying restrictions on the use of child labour, as Chapter Four demonstrated, even in the last quarter of the nineteenth century the employment of young boys and girls in agriculture was a matter of some significance. Nevertheless the greater use of farm machinery, the conversion of land from labour-intensive arable to pastoral purposes, and the influence of the education legislation of the 1870s, had effected *some* reduction in the size of the juvenile work force as compared with earlier decades. This was especially true of those employed on a permanent, full-time basis, and whereas in 1861 about 11 per cent of all boys in England and Wales aged ten–fourteen inclusive had been engaged in agricultural labouring, by 1891, less than 4 per cent in the same age group were so occupied. However, the process of reform in regard to casual employment was much less impressive, and improvement here often seemed to come with painful slowness.

For their part, most teachers accepted the absences of children for seasonal employment with wry philosophy, appreciating that against the background of family poverty which existed, they were probably inevitable. As the master of Ermington School in Devon noted, for example: 'It is no uncommon thing to find boys absent during the whole or part of the day apple-picking. I earnestly want their attendance, but it is very hard to snatch a few pence from a parent's weekly income when such an opportunity offers. Many boys have earned their parents many shillings in this and similar ways during the present autumn.'[133] Similar understanding was displayed at Cheriton Lane End School in Hampshire, when boys were required to help with covert-beating for local shooting parties, and in numerous other places as well.

In this situation, therefore, the tendency was for children to attend school when work on the farms was slack, and then to stay away when opportunities for employment offered themselves. If the school authorities took exception to this – well, the children had normally earned their pennies and were back at their desks again before the official machinery of the law had creaked into action.

Usually the first of the part-time tasks became available in the spring, during March, when extra, unskilled labour was required for weeding, stone-picking, or, in potato-growing districts, for setting potatoes. Quite young children were, often illegally, employed for all of these tasks, and Alfred Williams of South Marston recalled that he had been only eight years of age when in the 1880s, he 'took his place in the fields amongst the men and women and other young children. [He] was first employed at crawling on his hands and knees between drills of peas and wheat nearly a foot high, and methodically pulling out charlock by the roots.'[70] Stone-picking was a similarly common occupation, and some-times a whole family would be engaged upon it. This was the custom at Blaxhall in Suffolk, in the late nineteenth century, when each family was allocated a field. 'Stones were taken off the fields when the corn was about two inches high. The men raked some of the land overnight in order to loosen the stones so that the women and children could pick them the more easily the next day.'[81] They used a small wooden rake with six inch nails, closely set together, to help them, and each picker 'took an ordinary two-gallon pail which could hold about a peck of stones'. The family was paid by the load, and approximately eighty pails of stones were needed to make up every load. The stones were later used for repairs to the local roads.

In other parishes, however, it was not customary for families to work together in this way; instead several groups of children were employed under the direction of one or more of the full-time adult labourers. Each youngster was, in this case, paid a daily wage of perhaps 4d or 6d, depending upon his or her age and energy. And it is perhaps a tribute to the importance attached by some farmers to stone-picking that at Helmingham School in Suffolk as late as March 1899, a fortnight's holiday was declared by the managers (against the wishes of the master) 'so as to give the children an opportunity of stone-picking'.[84]

Among other spring-time tasks performed by the younger children there was, of course, bird-scaring, when the corn had been newly sown. This was a lonely

AN ENGLISH GOLD FIELD.

Bird scaring was a major occupation for country boys in the early and mid-Victorian years. (*Punch*, 1852)

job, for the children were required to go out to the fields on their own as soon as it was light and remain there until the birds had gone to roost. It was also a seven-days-a-week task, for since the birds did not take a Sunday holiday, then neither could the young scarer – even when, as in the Exning area of Suffolk during the 1860s, Sabbath day working was apparently unpaid. According to Elizabeth Wilson, a labourer's wife from Exning, her son received '5d a day for six days, or 2s 6d a week', but 'nothing for Sundays'. Yet, despite this and the long hours involved, bird scaring was often welcomed because of the plentiful opportunities for employment which it afforded. As Mrs Wilson noted, it lasted 'many weeks in the year altogether. The chief times are when the corn is sown and when it is getting ripe, but sometimes birds are kept from the stacks too. One of my boys had to do this all through the winter. The crows come and pull the straws out and litter them all over the field, so that they have to be picked up.'[5]

But perhaps, as with the young Jude Fawley in Thomas Hardy's novel, *Jude the Obscure*, a fellow feeling with the birds would well up in the solitary scarer, until 'at length his heart grew sympathetic with the birds' thwarted desires . . . Why should he frighten them away? They took upon them more and more the aspect of gentle friends and pensioners . . . They stayed and ate, inky spots on the nut-brown soil, and Jude enjoyed their appetite. A magic thread of fellow-feeling united his own life with theirs. Puny and sorry as those lives were, they much resembled his own.' Yet few *farmers* had sympathy with such daydreams, and Jude was soon brought back to reality with 'a smart blow upon his buttock' – the first of many inflicted by his furious employer. Most other scarers who failed to live up to expectations received similar treatment.[160]

There could be little doubt regarding the long hours worked, as an inspection of evidence collected in 1866 in connection with the *Children's Employment Commission* soon reveals. One typical boy interviewed – George Moore of Friston in Suffolk – declared that 'at bird keeping I had to stay from 6 till 6, except at barley, and then from 5 a.m. till 8 p.m., because the sun rised early and was down late. Sunday was the same as other days. Got $3\frac{1}{2}$d a day.'[5]

Usually the children went to work armed with a wooden rattle or an old pail and stick, which they beat in order to drive the birds off. But some – like the young Joseph Ashby of Tysoe – preferred to shout, at least part of the time, in order to hear the sound of a human voice. 'This method had another convenience; you couldn't cry while you shouted.'[63] Others attempted to pass the time by cutting 'labyrinths . . . in turf, or carving on gates, trees, or sticks', while, as one well-to-do clergyman from Dorset noted, 'their inquiries of passers-by as to "what o'clock it is", prove how gladly they watch for the hour that is to release them from their day's labour.' Yet few of the children would have agreed with his complacent conclusion: 'for my own part, I think the importance of their trust, and the knowledge that they are earning wages, goes far to lighten the effect of the monotony of their employment',[1] even though most *did* feel gratification at contributing to the family income. One five-year-old later confessed that he was 'as proud as a duke' at his first pay day.[80] (See also Document G.)

A third common spring-time and autumn task for the youngsters was 'minding' sheep or pigs in the fields and at the sides of the roads. Where children were employed in this fashion in the fields it was presumably cheaper to pay their wage of 4d or 6d per day than to make the fences secure. Yet, as a young 'tenter' recalled, you had to be very vigilant if you were to keep the animals in the field. On one occasion, during the autumn, she was severely reprimanded by the farmer for allowing the pigs to stampede in search of acorns; no doubt if she had been a boy she would also have been whipped. But as she humbly admitted, 'they were after the acorns and I just couldn't stop them'.[85] John Purser of Ilmington in Warwickshire was another minder, who was responsible for watching the pigs as they fed on the ears of corn left behind after the harvest fields had been cleared. 'I was not sorry, then, when school started, for it was a dreary job if the weather were cold. I liked the pigs all right, and used to give them names . . . One season, an older brother took the pigs out, and with a long pole shook the trees. The pigs, he said, soon knew the oak trees as well as he did. Acorns were good food, and the pigs liked them.'[119]

Nevertheless, if the period from March to May were a busy one for child workers, it fell far below the level of hectic activity which characterized the months from June to September. It was at this latter time that the juvenile labour force reached its peak. First came haysel, when boys and girls helped as the mowing got under way. As one Suffolk man recollected, even in the 1890s children of ten or eleven were regularly expected to assist in the work. On the farm where he was employed the custom was to have 'a boy and a girl behind each man as they *mew* the grass; and you used to pick it up as they mew it. You'd keep about a yard or two behind, and you used to take up the grass and sprinkle it all down the middle, kinda make a grass floor.'[85] Later, when dry, it would have to be raked together and pitched into haycocks.

But in other localities, the child's haymaking activities took a different form. In many areas, mowing machinery was in use by the later nineteenth century – as at South Marston in Wiltshire, where the young Alfred Williams took part in his first haysel at the age of eight. On this occasion he was required 'to lead the horses, carry the wooden bottles of ale to and from the farm, or rake up the hay with the girls; but I felt very important, especially when the time came round to receive my wages for the task – a bright two-shilling piece every weekend.'[150]

The commencement of haymaking in any parish was soon reflected in a much diminished school attendance. This can be seen by the following random extracts from school log books during the last quarter of the nineteenth century. Thus at Ivinghoe School, Buckinghamshire, on 21 June 1875: 'The attendance of the school diminished on account of several of the children being employed at the "hay harvest".' And at Cublington in the same county, on 17 July, 1891: 'Children kept away to work in the hay-fields'. At Cholsey School, Berkshire, on 7 June, 1878; 'Attendance this week rather irregular owing to children tending their fathers who are mowing'. However, few school authorities went as far as Great Gaddesden School Board in Hertfordshire, which issued a circular letter to local farmers, requesting that: ' . . . in case you should require any Boys for Hay-making during the present season – upon filling up and signing the Form

Girls helping their mothers to harvest lavender near Hitchin, Herts., c. 1900. This was one of the many seasonal agricultural tasks undertaken by children. Lavender was grown on the south-west facing slopes less than half a mile from Hitchin town centre. Two local firms processed it. (Hitchin Museum)

enclosed herewith, and sending it to either of the Teachers of the Gaddesden Row Board School – the Great Gaddesden National School – or the Potten End School; leave will be given to such Boys as you may require, for a period of 4 weeks.'[92]

Even when children – especially the older girls – were not directly employed in the fields themselves, they very often had to remain at home to look after younger brothers and sisters, while their mothers lent a hand with the hay-making. Or else those who did attend school frequently had to leave early so that they could carry tea to their parents in the fields. In cases like these, the more down-to-earth teachers adjusted the luncheon break so as to permit the children to put in their full two-hours attendance and still be free to carry out their tea-carrying duties. For example at Leckford Board School in Hampshire the mistress noted in June, 1882, that she had taken 'the children in at one o'clock as a number of them would otherwise have lost their attendance'. Other masters and mistresses curtailed the mid-day break by half-an-hour and commenced afternoon school at 1.30 p.m.

In the horticultural areas of the country there were, of course, special labour requirements at this time which affected school attendance. Fruit picking, pea pulling and other similar operations all exerted an influence. At the small parish of Weston-on-Avon the children were regularly granted a holiday in June and July to allow them to help with the local pea pulling and currant gathering. On 23 June 1899, for example, the mistress recorded: 'Pea picking has begun and some of the children are wanted. The attendance officer came this morning and said he would suggest that the school break up for the holiday.' Seven years earlier the holiday had proved too short, and so on that occasion 'an extra week' had been given by the School Board to allow the picking to be completed – yet another indication of the order of priority of farm work and education in many rural districts. In counties like Kent and Worcestershire the labour requirements of horticulture and of fruit growing were much greater. In Kent the fruit picking began in early June and from then on boys and girls of about twelve years of age and over were regularly employed alongside the women. In the middle of the nineteenth century they were paid about 6d a day for gathering gooseberries and currants, and later cherries, filberts and plums. September was apple-picking time.[1] (See also Document H.)

But in most counties after haymaking had been completed and the first specialized horticultural crops gathered, there came a brief lull before the arrival of what was regarded as the most important event of the farming year – the corn harvest. And if the school ranks had been thinned by the demands of the hayfield, how much more was this the case when the wheat had to be cut and carried. Normally the school summer holidays – significantly always called the 'harvest holiday' in the school log books – were timed to coincide with the commencement of these operations. Indeed, the exact starting date was often varied according to the ripeness – or otherwise – of the corn. Thus at Launton in Oxfordshire during 1867, the beginning of the holidays was delayed to 16 August, the master noting: 'This is later than usual as the corn is backward this year owing to the wetness of the season'. At Souldern in the same county two years later, it was likewise observed: 'The harvest seems to be forward and we shall most likely have holidays soon'. This entry was made on 5 July and the school actually broke up on 6 August – although it had been reported as early as 2 August that there were 'very few present as the harvest work is begun'. Again, the very wet summer of 1879, with its disastrous effect on grain yields, also influenced the start of the 'harvest holiday'. At Weston-on-Avon Board School it was postponed to 5 September, which, as the teacher remarked, was 'something like a month later

Children helping in the hayfields near Oxford, c. 1900. (Oxfordshire County Council, Department of Leisure and Arts)

than usual'. But, the customary attitude was probably best summarized by the vicar of Wasperton in Warwickshire, who was also the correspondent for the school managers; on 3 September, 1898, he wrote firmly in the log book: 'The Autumn holidays of this School should in future be regulated by the commencement of Harvest.'

On the other hand, a prolongation of the harvest through bad weather could equally affect the date of the return to school. For if the harvest were not finished then the children simply stayed away, no matter what date had been fixed for the beginning of the new term. In some cases school managers decided to persevere with 'very thin' attendances until harvest operations were over; others, as at Cholsey National School in Berkshire, decided to bow to the inevitable. A note in the Cholsey log book for 9 September 1878, reads: 'Harvest not yet completed. Only 28 scholars assembled this morning. As the attendance was so small it was decided to give another week's holiday.' But even that proved scarcely sufficient, for the entry a week later referred to only 'moderate' attendance among the school's hundred or so pupils, the explanation for this being 'a good number of the older scholars away minding the baby, the pigs, or assisting to get up the potatoes'. This latter excuse referred to another common autumn employment, either on the land of a local farmer in a potato growing area, or, more frequently, on behalf of the family itself on the allotment. Home-grown potatoes were rightly valued as a vital part of the diet of labouring people and children had to play their part in picking them.

Similar postponements of the return to school on account of harvest operations are provided by Childrey Wesleyan School in Berkshire and Helmingham School in Suffolk – to name but two examples out of the hundreds which could be quoted. At Childrey, even on 1 October 1888, the master noted: 'Late harvest. Last week very wet; operations stopped so that harvest is not finished. According to announcement I opened school, only nine scholars came, the other (Church) schools closed for another week, so we closed for the week.' But as at Cholsey in the previous example, despite the concession, the pace of return proved to be slow. As late as 12 October, the log book records: 'Several still in the harvest fields'. At Helmingham, too, right at the end of the century (16 September 1898), the master noted in his log book: 'Owing to the operations in the harvest being greatly hindered by the laid condition of the crops and consequently gleaning being behind, the Managers decided to extend the holiday another week; and the Clergy were asked to give notice to that effect in the churches.'[84]

All rural areas during the Victorian period were profoundly influenced by the annual demand for child labour on the land, and in a number of cases – especially during the 1850s and 1860s – children would cease school attendance entirely in the early summer and would not resume until all the autumn work had ended. Naturally their education suffered, and the heartfelt cry of the Cublington School mistress in Buckinghamshire during November 1877, was echoed by many of her colleagues from the country districts: 'James Elmer and William Carter returned after nearly three months' absence, gone back terribly in their reading and writing . . .' At places like Weston-on-Avon, in fact, where pea pulling and harvesting followed closely on one another, the whole school's attendance was sometimes disrupted for almost three months every year. Not surprisingly it was reported when they returned that 'the children seem to have forgotten a good deal'.

While the harvest was in progress some of the children were employed in leading the horses or carrying refreshments to the men at work in the fields; occasionally, too, while the last of the corn was being cut, the older boys would stand alongside the men, armed with sticks, ready to knock down and kill any rabbits or other vermin which had been hiding in the thick cover. A rabbit killed in that way meant meat for the pot.

AT WORK ON THE LAND

But the majority of youngsters played no part in this. Their concern was with making bands to tie the corn. Where a reaping-machine was employed (and by 1871 about 25 per cent of the total corn area was cut by machinery) it was quite customary for there to be five men, five women and five boys or girls to work with each machine. Often the older girls, already sensitive to the effect of sunshine on their complexion, 'wore drawn cotton bonnets with great flapping curtains to keep off the sun, and gloves to prevent their hands being wounded by the stubble'.[159] Many of the children, were extremely young when they started work. George Edwards, who later became the founding father of the National Union of Agricultural and Allied Workers, recollected that he entered his first harvest in 1856, before he had reached the age of six. In those days in his home parish of Marsham in Norfolk, there were no reaping machines in use, 'the corn all having to be cut by the scythe. Women were engaged to tie up the corn, and the little boys made bands with which to tie the corn. For this work I received 3d per day, or at the rate of 1s 6d per week.'[80]

So great was the pressure to bring in the harvest as quickly as possible that the hours of work were desperately long – especially for the younger children. A Suffolk mother remembered in the mid-1860s that her ten-year-old son was 'hired by a man at 6d a day to make bands for sheaves for him, and afterwards led carts for the carrying; he had to start at 4 a.m., and was not back till towards 9 p.m., or sometimes later; . . . he used to be very tired when he came home; . . . I was obliged to wake him up in the morning, but had not a great deal of trouble with him . . .'[5]

John Purser of Ilmington in Warwickshire had similar memories at the very end of the century, 'working from six in the morning till seven, or later, in the evening. It was a weary tramp home at night, but there was a feeling of happiness as the families called to one another across the widening distance.' John also remembered with nostalgia the midday meal eaten out-of-doors while the work was temporarily halted. He and his brothers and father had a basket of food which Mrs Purser brought to the field – 'broiled bacon, new potatoes, currant roly poly pudding, and a large can of tea. No king ever enjoyed his table as we did on those days, sitting in the open, or under the shade of a hedge.'[119]

But if the earnings of children during the harvest provided one vital contribution to the family budget, that was not the only benefit derived, for most families would also go out gleaning – or leazing, as it was known in some areas. In those days of crude or non-existent harvesting machinery, a worthwhile quantity of grain was left behind in the fields when the corn had been carried, and this was carefully collected by a mother and her children, for eventual grinding into flour.

Very often elaborate gleaning rules were developed, to prevent any family

Children bringing home corn they had gleaned. The grain thus gathered could either be ground into flour or used to feed the family's livestock. It was a valuable addition to household resources. (Blockley Antiquarian Society)

from taking an unfair advantage of the rest. Thus at Marsham in Norfolk and Blaxhall and Tunstall in Suffolk as well as elsewhere in East Anglia 'no one was allowed in the field while there was a sheaf of corn there, and at a given hour the farmer would open the gate and remove the [last] sheaf, and shout "All on." If anyone went into the field before this was done the rest would "shake" the corn she had gleaned.' The sheaf which was left behind 'on guard' was appropriately known as the 'Policeman'.[84] At Tysoe in Warwickshire, the gleaners had to wait until the parish clock had struck eight o'clock in the morning. For 'until the first stroke of this bell . . . no one of the company, woman or child, must pick an ear of corn from the stubbles. This is the most strictly observed unwritten law . . . a breach of which is punished by forms of lynching, which tax and do credit to female ingenuity . . .'[33]

But, once freedom to work had been secured, the gleaners were quickly engrossed in their labours. At Juniper Hill in north Oxfordshire during the 1880s

At Work on the Land

Flora Thompson remembered the busy women and children 'picking up the ears of wheat the horse-rake had missed . . . Up and down and over and over the stubble they hurried, backs bent, eyes on the ground, one hand outstretched to pick up the ears, the other resting on the small of the back with the "handful". When this had been completed, it was bound round with a wisp of straw and erected with others in a double rank, like the harvesters erected their sheaves in shocks, beside the leazer's water-can and dinner-basket.'[144] At Tysoe the gleaners also wore 'a linsey-woolsey bag' hanging from the waist to collect the broken-off ears, and even the smallest child would have his or her own little bag. At the end of the day all of the family's gleanings would be carefully laid on a sheet, which they had brought with them for the purpose, and would then be bundled up for carrying home.[63]

Gleaning usually lasted about two or three weeks and at the end of it the most active families had obtained a goodly supply; after the corn had been threshed at home by the father of the family (using a flail), together with any wheat grown on the allotment, the grain would be sent to the miller for grinding. He usually 'paid himself for grinding by taking toll of the flour', although some families, like the Pursers of Ilmington, perferred to keep all the flour for themselves and to pay whatever charge was required out of their earnings. 'Great was the excitement in a good year when the flour came home – one bushel, two bushels, or even more in large industrious families. The mealy-white sack with its contents was often kept for a time on show on a chair in the living-room and it was a common thing for a passer-by to be invited to "step inside an' see our little bit o' leazings". They liked to have the product of their labour before their own eyes and to let others admire it . . .'[144] It was also a comforting sign of future security, for at least the flour for bread and puddings was now assured for several weeks to come.

Meanwhile, the children, having played their part in the harvest and its aftermath, were now free to return to school for the autumn and winter months – although, even then, not always without interruptions. Very often, as we have seen, potatoes had to be gathered, while other opportunities for earning a few shillings included collecting acorns to feed to the pigs or gathering mangold wurzel. At Leckford in Hampshire, 'sedge picking' was noted as another cause of autumn absences, while – in admittedly rare cases – a child might even be employed to guard mushrooms. In evidence before Henley-in-Arden Petty Sessions, Warwickshire, in 1893, a local farmer claimed that he spent 'a considerable sum in cultivating and watching' mushrooms. This was said to be common practice in his area, and young boys were employed to fill the role of 'watcher'.

Sometimes a strong wind would loosen branches and twigs, and children would be kept from school to collect this additional winter firing, while on

A REMINISCENCE OF THE FIRST.

Small Rustic (to tall London Visitor, who, being considered dangerous by the other guns, has been asked to beat).

"NOW, ZURR, YEAU HEV DUN THEY THREE FIELDS VERY WELL, NOW DO'E CRAWL IN THER AND WORK ROUND THE

NEXT TWO, AN' I'LL STAY HERE AN' MARK!"

Not all child labourers were expected to offer advice as well! (*Punch*, 1880)

estates where the landowner preserved game, a number of the older boys earned extra money as beaters for the shooting parties. At Elmdon School in north Warwickshire, there were several absences on this account in the late nineteenth and early twentieth centuries. For example, on 26 January 1900, an entry in the school log book reads: 'Attendance very poor this week, owing to the boys being away on Thursday and Friday bush-beating', while three days later came the note: 'Boys away again bush beating'. On 28 November of the same year: 'The scholars had a holiday as the Squire needed all the boys for bush beating'. Similar entries appeared on 4 December and 17 December of that year – as they did during the shooting season of both the preceding and succeeding years. At Cheriton in Hampshire the same pattern was followed, with such entries as that

AT WORK ON THE LAND

for 16 December, 1898: 'A few boys were required for covert breaking for two days.'

Elsewhere children supplemented the family income by catching sparrows or vermin for a small payment. Thus Gaius Carley, (born 1888) of Upper Dicker, Arlington, Sussex, remembered catching sparrows in a 'framed net . . . Sometimes two or three dozen were caught at once.' He and his friends were paid one penny for four sparrows' heads and a penny for a rat's tail. 'We became experts catching the rats with a hazel bender stick and a wire noose.'[67] Similarly, estate records for Mapledurham in south Oxfordshire reveal payments to 'boys' for killing rats – on 14 March 1873, for example, 5s 6d was paid 'for killing thirty-three rats,' and in July of the following year 2s 10d for seventeen rats.

Again, with the autumn sowing of crops, there might be employment for bird-scarers, while a number of children were always occupied – as was the shepherd boy in Clare's poem quoted at the beginning of the chapter – in looking after stock or in cleaning turnips to feed to them.

Work on the land in the winter months was an especially bleak and bitter prospect for the often ill-fed and poorly clothed child workers. The young George Edwards remembered being set to work in the winter of 1856–57 'cleaning turnips, and what cold I had when the snow was on the ground! And what suffering from backache!'[80] About fifty years later another young worker – this time in Yorkshire – recalled the misery endured in preparing fodder for stock during the winter months. 'After breakfast I helped the cowman to feed the stock, staggering along under heavy skeps of meal and turnips to some dozen fat bullocks. I was too small to keep out of the muck, and waded through slop and cow-muck until I became absolutely lost. My breeches became so caked in pig-swill, calf-porridge, and meal I believe they could have stood upright without me inside them. My hands, by the same process, aided by the raw winds, became so swollen and cracked it was purgatory to wash them. And often I didn't.'[115]

As the above paragraphs perhaps make clear, therefore, most country children – or at least those who were the offspring of the smaller farmers and labourers – would expect to spend some part of every year at work on the land. In many cases, they were employed by a local farmer for wages, but sometimes they worked on their own family's holding. In this respect it was believed by contemporaries that the children of smallholders fared much worse in the matter of education, school attendance, etc. than did those of the labourers. This point was made, for instance, by the Assistant Commissioner who visited Cumberland and Westmorland in connection with the *Royal Commission on the Employment of Children, Young Persons and Women in Agriculture, 1867–69.* He noted of the small proprietors (or 'statesmen' as they were known) in these counties: 'The effect of these small properties on the children of their owners is not favourable for they are often kept from school for months to assist in the work of the farm. On inquiring of one at what age his children began to assist in farm work, "as soon as they can crawl", was the reply; and I believe I am correct in stating that as a rule the children of the smaller proprietors . . . do not prosper in the world as well as those of agricultural labourers.'

Similar conclusions were reached concerning the children of smallholders in the south of Durham, where the land was also much subdivided; indeed it was reported that the smallholders 'have a struggle to live, and take their children away from school to help "at a very early age"'.[2] The small farmers in the Isle of Axholme and the Marshes of Lincolnshire normally kept their children away from school to help with potato setting and other farm tasks. Here, too, it was concluded that, 'Their children . . . worked earlier and as a consequence [had] less schooling than those of hired labourers'.[2] Comments in respect of the smallholders of Cambridgeshire and the North and West Ridings of Yorkshire were along the same lines. Yet, as one Assistant Commissioner declared: 'To these men, the loss of their children's aid (under ten years of age) would be fatal; they are too poor to hire labour and the assistance rendered by a child of eight or nine years of age is of great value'.[2] Indeed, in the depressed years of the 1880s, when arable farmers were hit by the slump in grain prices, even the more substantial agriculturists had to call upon their children's labour. One such was the Lincolnshire Wold tenant farmer, Cornelius Stovin of Binbrook, who worked 500 acres with a labour force of seven men, two lads and three boys in the more prosperous days of the early 1870s. But, as his son remembered, during the difficult 'eighties and nineties . . . the labour force on his father's farm was cut to the bone, and all the children in the family lent a hand with the work before and after school. In this way they kept going, making a bare living until the first years of the present century when conditions slowly improved . . .'[143]

Nevertheless, if the need for child labour was tacitly accepted in almost all rural areas during the Victorian era, it perhaps reached its highest level of exploitation on the large arable holdings of East Anglia during the 1850s and 1860s, when the notorious 'gang system' was in operation. Thanks to the sparse population and the labour–intensive methods of cultivation then in vogue, numerous public gangs of children, youths and women were regularly employed under a gangmaster, to carry out weeding, stone–picking, and other activities, first on one farm and then on another.[143] Needless to say, the gangmaster's own remuneration depended on the amount of labour which he could extract from his workers, and few concessions were therefore made to the age or strength of the children involved.

Public disquiet at this state of affairs began to increase sharply as the result of a

AT WORK ON THE LAND

Report by the *Children's Employment Commission* in 1866 on conditions in 'ganging' areas of East Anglia. Statistics were produced which revealed, for example, that at Binbrook in Lincolnshire there were no less than 203 members of a local gang – 81 of them being between the ages of seven and thirteen, while at March in Cambridgeshire, 388 people were so employed – 183 of them being children aged between seven and thirteen; at Stilton in Huntingdonshire, 40 workers were involved – 22 of them between the ages of seven and thirteen, plus 5 *under* the age of seven; and at Grimston in Norfolk, out of a gang of about 60 persons, 30 were aged between seven and thirteen. These random examples, taken from the many figures quoted in the Report, perhaps indicate the essentially juvenile character of the gangs – for about half of their number comprised youngsters 'from the age of six to that of eighteen.' In addition, the hours of work were extremely long, lasting 'in some places from 8 a.m. to 6 p.m. in summer, and to 5 p.m. in autumn; in others from 5 a.m. to 7 p.m., including the time occupied in going and returning. The distances to which the young children, together with the rest of the gang [went] to their work, sometimes [amounted] to five, six, or even seven miles. In such cases the journey to and from must [have entailed] on the children three or four hours additional labour, even supposing the time spent in the field to be reduced by one or two hours. In very rare instances they [received] assistance in the way of conveyance, for either a part or the whole of those distances, from carts or waggons sent for them, or donkeys provided by the gangmaster, on which the smaller ones [might] ride by turns'. In one case, '*A boy 5 years old* used to be carried home from his work by the others. And elsewhere, "You see the big ones come dragging the little ones home, and sometimes taking them on their backs when they are overtired".'[5]

Once they had arrived at their place of work, the gangs immediately commenced whatever task was required – picking twitch, singling turnips, setting potatoes, topping and tailing mangolds and turnips, etc., according to the season. Although naturally their main employment was during the late spring, summer and early autumn when agricultral activity was at its height, even in November it was reported that 'gathering potatoes, mangold wurzel, turnips and carrots still [occupied] a great number of children in many districts' during the mid-1860s.

No attempt was made to segregate young from old, or male from female, and where the gang was employed on a farm a long way from home all of the members might sleep together in a barn at their place of work. This might last for several days or weeks, with one of the party being sent home 'from time to time to bring back food for the rest'.[143] To the Victorian mind, and not altogether unjustifiably, the moral danger thus posed to the children was immense – especially when it was reinforced by the lewd conversation of many of the youths and women. For this reason, some mothers refused to let their daughters work in a gang. As a labourer's wife from Billingborough in Lincolnshire declared: 'I don't believe in girls going out at all to work. I'd sooner let mine go on 'taters and salt'.[128] Outsiders were equally shocked at conditions in the gangs; as one such observer said of the youngsters at Binbrook, 'The language used by children . . . in my hearing, surpassed anything of the sort I could have believed'.[2]

There was also much concern at the 'demoralization' of young girls which resulted from the ganging system. Thus the Revd T. Hutton, Vicar of Stilton, Huntingdonshire, declared: 'Instances of juvenile prostitution and immorality occur in connexion with the gangs that are a scandal and disgrace to a Christian country', while his colleague, the Revd J. Rumph, rector of Bluntisham and Earith, Huntingdonshire, stated that he had himself 'traced the ruin of girls of thirteen and fourteen to the mixture of the sexes in gang work'. Mr George Craven, master of the Spalding Union Workhouse in Lincolnshire similarly observed: 'We have now in this house twenty-eight illegitimate children, whose mothers were in the habit of going out to field work in the gangs at the time they were born. Many of these children were born here; others have been brought here, having been deserted by their mothers, or from their mothers having died . . .' Most of the witnesses agreed that it was on the homeward journey that the greatest problem was likely to arise, but court cases were quoted of young girls indecently assaulted by older members of the gang, or even by the gangmaster himself, during the midday break – and sometimes in view of other workers.[5] Although certain of the fears expressed may have been exaggerated, there seems little doubt that for girls of about twelve or thirteen and above ganging could present a moral hazard.

Still more did it hamper the schooling of children. This situation was made absolutely clear by such local teachers as Mr Fletcher of North and South Kime in Lincolnshire, who declared: 'From June to October the school is almost deserted for work: some go as young as six . . . Many come to school only two months in the year.'[128] Charles Winter, schoolmaster, of Caistor in Lincolnshire, was equally forthright: 'The children from 8 to 12 years old all leave the school here in March, and don't come back till November, except for an odd day or two sometimes . . . But there are lots of families here who never send their children at all.'[128]

These complaints were born out by interviews with some of the young workers themselves – boys like George Brodell from Potter Hanworth, Lincolnshire, who in the autumn of 1866 admitted to beginning work in May 'picking ketlucks [and] singling turnips', while 'since harvest [he had been] picking potatoes'. Girls were not exempt either – save in the few cases where mothers were concerned about the moral welfare of their daughters. Thus one

Cherry picking in an orchard at Sittingbourne, c. 1900. Nine children are shown in the photograph. Most had clearly been brought along to be under the eye of their mother while she worked, for they were far too young to take part in the picking. (Mr E. Swain)

eight-year-old girl from Coningsby in Lincolnshire pointed out that the previous winter she had gone out with her father 'getting up turnips for the sheep . . . I was at school regularly all the spring to gleaning time. After gleaning I went to pick potatoes for four weeks . . .'[5] And at Amcotts in Lincolnshire, a parish overseer admitted that 'Girls of seven or eight and little boys are used to gather potatoes. Boys of eight sometimes drive carts on the farms.'[128]

It was, therefore, in an attempt to eradicate some of these evils that the 1867 Gangs Act was passed. It prohibited the employment of any child under the age of eight in a public agricultural gang, and provided that all gangmasters must for the future be duly licensed by the local magistrates; in addition, public gangs of *mixed* sex were prohibited, and where women or girls were employed there had to be a licensed gangmistress present as well.

Perhaps not unexpectedly, in the immediately post-1867 period attempts were

99

made to evade the spirit of the law by farmers who decided, instead, to employ their own *private* gangs – since these were not covered by the Act. And in some cases there were, as we shall see, clear breaches of the legislation, as well. But, despite all this, reform was slowly achieved and in those districts where the public gangs did continue to operate there was a general raising of standards. In particular, 'the worst characters among the gangmasters (were) unable to obtain a licence'.[2] Then, too, the women and girls now worked in their own gangs – as at Swaffham in the early 1890s, where a local labourer named William Bensley (born 1871) reported three gangs at work; two for males and one for females. He himself had joined the gang for three years when he left school at the age of thirteen, and had started off with a wage of 8d a day.[84]

Yet possibly the most blatant early evasion of the Gangs Act occurred not in East Anglia, as might have been expected, but in Cumberland. The Assistant Commissioner who visited that county in connection with the Royal Commission on the Employment of Children, etc. in Agriculture, 1867–68, was amazed to discover when he arrived at Penrith that there were no less than eight public gangs of *mixed* sex at work, affording employment to about 300 women, young persons and children. They were employed 'from March to the end of November', and as he later reported: 'The Act of Parliament passed in 1867 for the regulation of agricultural gangs seems not to have been known in this district, and I availed myself of the opportunity . . . of pointing out to them the consequences to which they had exposed themselves by violating the law, and of explaining its provisions . . . I also considered it my duty to call the attention of the magistrates of the district to the Act . . . and I received assurances that its enactment should henceforth be strictly enforced.' It is interesting to note that communication with the local police on the subject likewise revealed ignorance on their part concerning the provisions of the Act.

So far attention has been primarily devoted to the children who were employed on a part-time or seasonal basis only – even if part-time in this connection meant that they were absent from school for over six months in the year (at least up to the 1870s, and in limited cases even after that date). Nevertheless, during the 1850s and 1860s especially, many children began *full-time* employment at an early age. As we have seen, George Edwards, the future agricultural trade union leader, (born 1850) began full-time employment before he had reached the age of six. He was by no means unique.

In the main, these full-time child workers were engaged upon the same sort of tasks as the part-timers already discussed, and many of them continued to live at home with their families. Nevertheless, as permanent employees they were very much more under the control of their master and of his senior workers than were their temporary counterparts. This often led to harsh treatment and to a consequent coarsening of character. Many of the children were required to work on their own, too, for farmers said, 'One boy is a boy, two boys is half a boy, and three boys is no boy at all'. The constant solitude tended to make the young worker slow of speech and dull witted.[137]

Sometimes, a father would take his son to work with him, as in Kent, where it was noted that waggoners very often took their youngsters to work alongside them as a 'mate' before they had reached the age of ten. They – and all other carter boys – were then required to work such desperately long hours that all other opportunities for self-improvement were lost. One Assistant Commissioner noted in the late 1860s: 'A boy works from 6 a.m. till 8 or 9 p.m., and is entirely under the control of the waggoner, almost invariably an utterly ignorant man. Very few farmers will interfere to make it possible for the mate to go to a night school, if he would . . . Often the hours for feeding horses are so arranged that it is quite impossible for the lads to get away to either school or church.'[2]

John Purser, too, remembered that it was common for a boy to become 'a ploughboy on first leaving school. It was a leg-aching job, trudging along beside the horses, the boy doing his best to keep them going, cracking his whip and talking encouragingly. "Gee up, my lads" . . . He got two or three pounds of dirt to his boots, all thrown in for sixpence a day, with only a short stop to eat his bread and cheese, or bacon, with a bottle of cold tea. Then shut off at three o'clock, attend to his horses, and home for his dinner, so hungry that nothing came amiss.'[119]

But perhaps the most vulnerable of the young workers were those who were hired not on a weekly basis but annually, from Michaelmas to Michaelmas, as farm servants. In East Anglia many of these youthful helpers, who also assisted with household chores, were known as 'back-house boys'. Usually the lads were completely at the mercy of their employer, and their fate therefore depended on his or her good nature. A large variety of odd jobs had normally to be carried out, and as a young Yorkshire hireling recollected of his servant days in the early twentieth century, he was kept running about by his mistress 'from morning to night . . . so that during mealtimes I was running in and out like a dog in a fair . . . We got up at five o'clock every morning, excepting Sunday, when we laid in an hour longer. I cleaned out the stable . . . . Then I went to the cowshed and milked four cows – dairying was only a sideline in those days, beef and barley being the main products – and took the milk into the house on the stroke of six. Breakfast was at six prompt. If I went in at three minutes past, the missus would say: "Tha wants ta sharpen thi sen up in a mornin'; 'ere tha's bin an hour a milkin' four cows, an' corves awaiting for their parridge."

'I learned to have my breakfast with one eye on that calf-porridge. I had fat boiled bacon, with a basin of milk, for breakfast, and had never got very far into it before the missus would jerk the calf-porridge off the fire, saying "'Ere, ma lad, jist nip wi' this afore it gets cowd. Ye can finish ateing when ye come back."' And so the day went on. After helping the cowman in the yard and perhaps carting turnips, there were the afternoon chores to be performed, such as 'chopping kindling, riddling cinders, carrying straw for bedding-down at night . . . filling the chop-bin for the horses, and then, in my spare time, hunt the eggs up'.[105]

In parts of Berkshire during the late 1860s it was the practice to hire carters' boys by the year as farm servants. As a contemporary pointed out, these young workers were required to arrive at the stables soon after 4 a.m., 'when they bait their horses, at 6 they are allowed an hour for breakfast, from 7 a.m. till 3 p.m. they drive the team in the field, having a rest of from 15 to 30 minutes for luncheon at 12 o'clock, after putting in the horses at 3 they are allowed till 4 o'clock for dinner, and are in the stables again baiting and doing up their horses till about 6 p.m., they therefore have 11 or 12 hours work, less the 15 or 30 minutes for luncheon, according as they are in the stables at 4 or 5 a.m . . . . The long hours of the carter boy are by several witnesses considered to be injurious to his health, and it is said that where such boys are hired by the year, and lodged either with the carter or in the farmer's house (a very common custom in Berks.) they are often subject to rough usage at the hands of the carter.' All too often, severe beatings were administered, and for this labour, the lads only received pay at the rate of between 3s a week (with 20s at Michaelmas) and 5s a week (with 50s at Michaelmas), according to their age and experience. The age range involved was normally between ten and fifteen, for it was only rarely that children under ten were hired annually, even before the 1880 Education Act made it illegal for children under the age of ten to be employed full-time. However, from the 1860s onwards the number of young farm servants fell (see Table 1), as, except in the north of England, farmers preferred to rid themselves of the responsibility of feeding and housing the boys and instead to employ only those who would cater for themselves, as day labourers.

Of course, some of the young servants were much better treated than the examples quoted so far perhaps indicate. One East Anglian lad who professed himself well satisfied had answered an advertisement for 'a young boy to live in the house, to look after two ponies, exercise four greyhounds, sweep and clean the yards up, chop sticks, get coal in, and keep the harness clean'.[85] Another fairly contented boy recollected that he had been concerned with cleaning boots, collecting vegetables for dinner, taking letters to the post office, and carrying out the usual chores of wood chopping, feeding fowls, cleaning knives and, occasionally, churning the butter. For this he received his board (including a nauseating breakfast of herrings and salt pork) and a wage of £1 per quarter. But there were some perquisites as well. 'He received a penny a score for the eggs he picked up about the farm [and] a penny for plucking each fowl that was sold from the farm. The plucking of fowls that were consumed in the household was considered as part of his duty and there was no extra payment for these.'[81]

Very often the full-time child workers, especially those concerned with feeding the stock, were expected to work on Sundays as well as during the week. They thus lost all opportunity to attend church or Sunday school, even if they had been so inclined, and many clergymen lamented this as a 'great evil,' and as 'brutalizing. The boy never cleans himself, never puts on his best clothes, loses all reverence for the Sabbath, severs a link that attached him to his teachers and

GOLFING AMENITIES.

*Major Brummel (comparing the length of his and his opponent's " drives "). "*I think I'm shorter than Mr. Simkins?"
Small Caddie (a new hand, greatly flattered at being asked, as he thinks, to judge of their personal appearance). "Yes, Sir, and
fatterer too, Sir!" *[Delight of the gallant Major.*

In the early twentieth century the growing interest in golf led to the employment of boys as caddies –
to the strong disapproval of teachers and HM Inspectors. (*Punch*, 1903)

school-fellows, and misses the chance that the Sunday school would have given him of having a little intellectual movement imparted at least once a week to the stagnant faculties of his mind.'[2]

Village night schools often languished for this same reason, with children either being kept at work late 'suppering up' the horses, etc., or else being too tired after the day's labours to resume a battle with the three 'Rs' which they had often found too much even at the day-school. Yet a few did persevere. Alfred Dodman of East Rudham, in Norfolk, who left school in about 1889, when he was aged ten, later recalled going to the local village school in the evening for instruction. In particular, he remembered learning to measure – to work out, for example, how many bricks were required to pave a piece of road, or the 'size of squares of glass' required for windows. For this he paid 2d a week.

The incidence of night school provision varied considerably from one county to another. In Northamptonshire, for example, during the later 1860s they were widely available, while in Oxfordshire by the year 1862 all but 49 of the county's 208 villages and market towns had evening classes, meeting once, twice and sometimes even three times per week during the autumn and winter months. Usually the classes lasted for two hours at each session – from 6 p.m. to 8 p.m., and the main emphasis was on the three 'Rs'. Nevertheless, some were rather more ambitious, so that at Cottisford, lectures and singing classes were also laid on, while the vicar of North Stoke emphasized the wider aims of *his* lectures, when he wrote: 'We wish not only to teach our scholars reading and writing but also, as far as we are able, to lead them into the habit of thinking and reflecting.'[113] In a number of villages up and down the country this effort was supported by the setting up of reading-rooms, stocked with such periodicals as the *British Workman*, the *Illustrated Times*, the *Churchmen's Magazine*, and the *Sunday at Home*. At one stage around the middle of the nineteenth century, over two thousand of these periodicals were circulated in forty Norfolk parishes 'in the course of one winter'.[137]

Usually the instruction at the night schools was given by the incumbent and his curate or by the teacher in the day school, but sometimes members of the clergyman's family would lend a hand. In this connection perhaps the work of Mary Simpson, in her father's parish of Boynton and Carnaby with Fraisthorpe, in Yorkshire was the 'most remarkable . . . In the course of the eighteen-fifties and sixties she gradually elaborated her own peculiar technique of education. The organization of her work fell into three main parts – pioneer work in the fields, evening classes during the week, and Sunday evening Bible classes, with attendance at church if possible . . . The system of annual Martinmas hirings meant that the farm servants seldom remained in the parish above a year, so that each November she had to make the acquaintance, and win the confidence, of some fifty or so farm workers who had just come to live in the farm houses at Carnaby and Boynton . . . With some of them she formed friendships which lasted long after they had left the district.'[95] Although the standard of care shown by Mary Simpson was unlikely to be achieved in most Yorkshire villages, it is worth noting that by the later 1860s nearly 60 per cent of the county's rural parishes had night schools of some kind. Yet, here as elsewhere, many failed to retain the support of the young labourers they were seeking to help. The tiring nature of field work – 'writing only will keep them from falling asleep' – was blamed by certain incumbents for the inattention of those who did appear, but sometimes the school failed for other, less excusable reasons. From Acaster Selby in Yorkshire 'came the simple statement: "I did have evening schools for adults, but found the farmers opposed to them."' And from Aughton in the same county came the comment: 'An attempt was made to establish an evening school for the farm servants, but unsuccessfully, as some of the farmers declined either to support it or allow their servants to attend'.[95] The incumbent of Whitwell, Yorkshire, made the same complaint: 'I find an unwillingness on the part of employers . . . to allow their servants to come under instruction in their brief hours of leisure, a jealousy perhaps lest too much learning should spoil the machine. The only time when a night school in my district can meet is from half-past six to eight, and then there are constantly errands to run, "odd jobs to be done," or "master's boots to clean," or these masters don't like to trust them into the village . . . for fear they should not come back in time for the eight o'clock "suppering up," i.e. the last feeding of the horses, which is a perfectly immovable feast apparently, one which never can be infringed upon or altered by half-an-hour on either side.'[51]

These latter excuses were also brought forward in respect of other counties where the level of general provision was well below that of Yorkshire. Thus in both Nottinghamshire and Lincolnshire only about one-quarter of the parishes had any night school in the later 1860s, and in Lincolnshire their failure was directly attributed in a number of cases to the opposition of employers, who had 'a dislike of the farm lads being off the premises'. This dislike could equally apply to purely leisure activities as well, and there are even examples of legal action being taken by employers against their servants for leaving the premises in the evening without permission. For instance, at Lutterworth Petty Sessions in August 1869, two young farm servants from Great Ashby, Leicestershire, were charged by their employer 'with going out at night for a short time, after they had done work for the day. The complainant said the lads were good servants, and he had no other fault to find with them . . .' The magistrates then asked the young men to apologize and to pay the costs of 7s each; at the same time an order was made out that unless the money was paid within a month, the defendants were to be committed to gaol for fourteen days.[98] Such overbearing strictness as this was little short of tyranny.

For girls, of course, the position was rather different, for only a few of them went to work full-time on the land or on a farm, as opposed to ordinary domestic service. Indeed, at the time of the 1861 Census of Population there were only about 6,000 female farm servants and labourers in the age range five to fourteen inclusive in the whole of England and Wales, and the trend was sharply down thereafter. (See Table 1.) For those who did become farm servants, work around the house and dairy was the usual pattern. As one Lincolnshire witness interviewed in 1866 declared, in his area (around Glentworth), 'Girls go out to service at 11 years of age. Many farmers who have 11 or 12 acres of land have a little girl of 11 to help the wife. A girl can milk at 11 . . . I should think there [are] a dozen girls of 11 or 12 in service with small farmers within four miles around here. They get their victuals and £1 or £1 10s for the year.'[5] Similarly, the incumbent of Kirkby Stephen in Westmorland noted in March, 1869, that: 'The situation of a servant girl at a large farmhouse is no sinecure. She has to rise early to prepare breakfast for the men before they go out to work, and she is often the last of the household to bed, because she has to "wash up" and "side away" the supper things; and her only holidays are a few days at each of the terms' – this latter comment relating to the practice of hiring the servants on a six-monthly rather than an annual basis.[2] In Somerset at around the same time it was noted that 'the greater part' of the village girls went into service in farm houses. They were said to 'begin service at twelve or fourteen years of age, as soon as they [were] old enough to look after a child; for their keep first, and then with wages gradually increasing. As they become older they are given dairy work; they milk the cows, making the cream, &c., and probably end by marrying one of the farm labourers.'

But if parents in the north of England, Somerset and Lincolnshire were prepared to allow their daughters to enter farm service, their fellows elsewhere proved more reluctant. The customary attitude was described by Flora Thompson in respect of Juniper Hill, Oxfordshire; 'After the girls left school at ten or eleven they were usually kept at home for a year to help with the younger children, then places were found for them locally in the households of tradesmen, schoolmasters, stud grooms or farm bailiffs. Employment in a public house was looked upon with horror by the hamlet mothers, and farm-house servants were a class apart. "Once a farm-house servant, always a farm-house servant," they used to say, and they were more ambitious for their daughters.'[144]

This trend away from farm service was encouraged by the modest increase in educational opportunities which became apparent during the last quarter of the nineteenth century, although even in the 1860s some Hampshire farmers were

At Work on the Land

TABLE 1

PERMANENT CHILD WORKERS IN AGRICULTURE – ENGLAND AND WALES
1851–1881
(Seasonal and part-time workers are, of course, not included.)

	MALE			FEMALE	
Age groups	Agricultural Labourers	Shepherds	Farm Servants	Agricultural Labourers	Farm Servants
	(a)	(b)	(c)	(d)	(e)
1851 CENSUS					
Total – all ages	908,678	12,517	189,116	44,319	99,156
5–9 inclusive	5,463	53	451	261	193
10–14	73,054	1,020	25,667	2,703	10,085
1861 CENSUS					
Total – all ages	914,301	25,559	158,401	43,964	46,561
5–9 inclusive	6,996	207	477	256	20
10–14	81,434	2,060	27,853	3,161	2,645
1871 CENSUS					
Total – all ages	764,574	23,323	134,157	33,513	24,599
5–9 inclusive	3,212	31	144	107	17
10–14	71,417	1,271	21,942	2,069	1,984
1881 CENSUS*					
Total – all ages	807,608**	22,844	(included in (a))	40,346**	(included in (d))
5–14 inclusive	67,054**	941	(included in (a))	2,054**	(included in (d))

Sources: 1851 Census – Parliamentary Papers, 1852–53, Vol. LXXXVIII, Pt. I; 1861 Census – Parliamentary Papers, 1863, Vol. LIII, Pt. I; 1871 Census – Parliamentary Papers, 1873, Vol. LXXI, Pt. I; 1881 Census – Parliamentary Papers, 1883, Vol. LXXX.

* After the 1881 Census no category was provided for the employment of children under ten, as this was illegal, following the 1880 Education Act. In the 1881 Census the age grouping was five to fourteen only. At the 1891 Census there were 63,268 boys employed between the ages of ten to fourteen inclusive as agricultural labourers and farm servants, plus 886 as shepherds and 1,455 as horse-keepers – 1891 Census, Parliamentary Papers, 1893–94, Vol. CVI. At the 1891 Census there were 709,283 male agricultural labourers and farm servants; 21,573 shepherds and 25,701 horse-keepers of all ages. The total number of female agricultural labourers and farm servants was 24,150 – of whom, 1,340 were aged ten to fourteen inclusive.

** Includes farm servants.

complaining that 'the best educated lads go into the police, to the railways, and into the towns where they can command a higher price for the services which their education makes them capable of rendering'. One of them, a Mr Parsons of Abbot's Ann, declared that 'a certificate showing too much knowledge on the part of the lad would be rather an objection than an inducement to the farmer to employ him'. Perhaps significantly, he also noted that in his parish the farmers could not recruit carter boys locally but were 'forced to seek them elsewhere, as those in Abbot's Ann are too highly educated for agricultural labour, and go away from the parish'.

Indeed, on the eve of the First World War at least one writer could conclude that: 'The farmers are almost solidly opposed to any extension of the school age, and many go so far as to distrust education altogether. Compulsory schooling is held by many to be responsible for restlessness and the willingness to listen to "agitators . . . Over-education of the labourers' children," is a phrase constantly on the lips of rural employers.'[65] Support for this contention is provided by the comments of a Northamptonshire landowner, Sir Herewald Wake, made in about 1911 or 1912. Sir Herewald deplored the reluctance of girls to work on the land, as they had once done: 'Nowadays, with their high heels and pretty hats and hobble skirts . . . they are not at all anxious to do any manual labour in the fields, or their own allotment gardens, for that matter . . . I think we have to thank the Education Acts for this alteration in the character of the rising generation of our rustic females. The teachers are town and city bred for the most part, and look upon manual labour, any work in fact which causes the worker to perspire, as beneath the dignity of a twentieth century "laidy" . . .' In Lincolnshire an ex-schoolmaster also remembered that: 'When the children got a little education they began to look down on their parents' condition, and I have often heard boys say: "I'll never be a farmer's drudge if I can help it".' In this man's experience, 'the smartest and best of the young men found employment upon the Railways; a few in the Post Office; and many in the Rural Police . . . I taught a village school myself several years and nearly all the boys passing through that school were lost to agriculture.'[143]

Yet perhaps the most telling response is that of a young farm lad, Richard Hillyer, who managed to escape from the 'lifting, hauling, shoving, trudging about from day to day' which was what he considered agricultural labouring to be. Thanks to coaching from his local rector, Hillyer won a scholarship to Durham University during World War I and in his autobiography, *Country Boy* (1966), p. 194, he describes his feelings when he learnt of his success: 'I had done it! I had broken out of Byfield, the narrowness, the drudgery and all the rest. I was free.'

The gradual elimination of very young full-time workers from the land was

Hop-picking in Sussex, *c*. 1900. Hop-picking employed large numbers of women and children for between four and six weeks each year, from August to October. The youngsters shown are a reminder of the hop-picking holiday which was given at schools in areas where hops were grown. With the cash thus earned a mother and children could purchase boots or clothes for the winter. (Winchelsea Museum).

certainly welcomed by those who had the long-term interests of the labourers at heart – and by none more than the agricultural trade unions. Significantly these had always been hostile to the use of child workers and had steadfastly refused to recruit them to membership, even where they were employed. Thus the leaders of the Oxford district of the National Agricultural Labourers' Union (the largest of them) had decided in January, 1873, less than a year after the union's formation that they would exclude 'all boys under the age of thirteen from membership' – between the ages of thirteen and seventeen they were to be admitted 'at half price'. The Rule Book of the NALU itself was even more explicit; according to its 1879 edition, the would-be entrant had to be at least sixteen years of age. Joseph Arch, the Union President, made clear the general attitude when he told the Trades Union Congress in January, 1873, that 'child labour meant neither more nor less than the perpetuation of pauperism, crime, ignorance, immorality, and every evil . . .' A colleague, Benjamin Taylor, the leader of the small Peterborough Union, agreed with him and complained that 'the children of working men were driven about like sheep or beasts'; he claimed that if child labour were withdrawn from the fields this 'would certainly have the effect of leading to the parents' earnings being improved'.

This approach may be contrasted with what was to prove the obsolete attitude of the various agricultural societies which offered prizes at their annual shows to youths under the ages of eighteen or twenty 'who had worked the greatest number of years for the same master or mistress, or on the same farm'. Among the winners at Stow-on-the-Wold and Chipping Norton Agricultural Society Show and Thame Agricultural and Horticultural Society Show – to name but two – as late as 1870 were those who had started full-time work at the age of eight or nine. Thanks to the reforms of the next ten or so years, this situation was at last to change – for ever.

NOTES ON ADDITIONAL SOURCES USED
Henley-in-Arden Petty Sessions Minute Book at Warwickshire County Record Office, CR. 1085.
For the views of Sir Herewald Wake see draft article on 'Agricultural Wages' in the Wake Collection at Northamptonshire County Record Office.
Mapledurham Estate Records have been consulted by kind permission of Mr J.J. Eyston.

CHAPTER SIX

Cottage Industries

A lthough agriculture remained a major source of employment for village children throughout the second half of the nineteenth century, there were parts of the country to which this did not wholly apply – because of the existence of competing outlets in local factories and cottage industries. Factory work, however, was more characteristic of the industrial areas than of the rural, and so falls outside the scope of this study. But a very different story applies to the cottage industries which survived, with varying degrees of prosperity, at least to the end of the third quarter of the nineteenth century, and in some instances beyond that date. To some extent they all had common characteristics with, in particular, a sad history of exploitation of the children engaged upon them. But they had their individual peculiarities as well. For this reason, therefore, it is proposed to examine in detail the lives of children employed in three of them – namely pillow lacemaking, straw plaiting to supply the hat and bonnet trade, and glovemaking. Obviously these three do not exhaust the trades which could have been investigated (nailmaking and button-making are but two possibilities which spring to mind), but the three have been selected largely because they were essentially *rural* industries and because they were major employers of child labour in the areas in which they were found.

The first – pillow lacemaking – was carried on principally in two country districts of England. The first was the Honiton area of Devon, 'running along the eastern portion of the south coast . . . and including a few places in North Devon'; the second covered the 'greater parts of the counties of Buckingham, Bedford, and Northampton, and the adjoining parts of Oxfordshire and Huntingdonshire'.[4] Although by the middle of the nineteenth century pillow-lace was already facing severe competition from its cheaper machine-made counterpart, it yet continued to occupy many women and children for a number of years to come. In the county of Buckingham alone there were 10,487 female lace workers officially recorded at the time of the 1851 Census, and of these 621 were girls aged from five to nine years of age inclusive, and 1,424 aged ten to fourteen inclusive; by comparison the permanent five to fourteen-year-old female workers

111

in agriculture in the county at that date numbered a derisory 44. (See Table 2.) In Northamptonshire, too, there were in 1851, 10,322 female lacemakers, of whom 754 were aged five to nine years inclusive and 2,124 aged ten to fourteen. The position in some of the other counties mentioned can be seen in Table 2, but it must always be remembered that these figures probably underestimate the size of the work force, since in home industries of this type many of those who worked on a part-time basis only did not bother to declare their occupation to the Census Enumerator.

Furthermore, during the course of the next decade fresh impetus was given to the Midland industry, in particular, by a revival of demand for the Buckinghamshire point lace, which was characteristic of most of these counties, and secondly by the success of Maltese lace at the Great Exhibition of 1851. This latter turned the attention of lacemakers towards a different line – namely the production of the 'showy and comparatively cheap' Maltese guipures and the 'plaited laces', which were quicker and easier to make than the Buckinghamshire point.[55] For 'fifteen years [the guipures] could not be imitated by machine', and so the 1850s saw an Indian summer of the cottage lacemaking industry in the Midlands. But then came further improvements in the production of machine-made lace, plus changes in fashion, and to a small degree the restrictions of the Factory and Workshop legislation of 1867. These led to new difficulties for the domestic industry and, in particular, to a sharp fall in the employment of children.

Although in Devon, too, various sorts of lace were produced, one of the specialities was Honiton lace, whose main characteristics was 'its sprig, which, be it flower, leaf, or other device, forms as it were the unit of each piece, and is made separately . . .'; the Honiton industry made use of machine net on which to apply its bobbin-made sprigs.[8] During the 1860s, however, the production of cheaper tape or braid laces became increasingly common, and in 1865 the shops of the county were said to be 'inundated with their production in the form of collars and cuffs'.[55]

It is against this general background of economic fluctuation in the lacemaking trade, therefore, that the role of the child worker has to be seen. One of the main problems was the fact that most lace experts agreed that children should begin to learn the craft at as early an age as possible – certainly by the time they had reached six, 'though many [began] at five and even younger'.[4] Only so, it was believed, could they acquire the dexterity which was essential for the execution of the best work in later life.

In order to learn the rudiments of the craft, therefore, children went at an early age to one of the many lace schools which flourished in the lacemaking districts – at Newport Pagnell in Buckinghamshire in 1835 there were no less than fifteen

COTTAGE INDUSTRIES

Late-Victorian lacemaker at Olney, Bucks., demonstrating her skills to a young admirer, who would perhaps learn to make lace in her own right later on. (Cowper and Newton Museum, Olney)

small schools 'teaching 210 children', and virtually every lacemaking community would have at least one.[89] However, a few children might receive their first lessons on their mother's pillow at home. Mrs Turney, who was born at the end of the nineteenth century at Great Horwood in Buckinghamshire, remembered receiving instruction in this way from her mother when she was about five. The mother 'put a pin on the end of her pillow and put four bobbins for me to make a leg', i.e. a strap used in connecting the various parts of a piece of Maltese-style lace. The child was then expected to progress from there, and each evening, when she had eaten her tea, she was set to work. 'Mother would always stand guard.'

But most parents, especially in the middle of the century, preferred to send their children to the schools, since the strict discipline imposed there ensured that the maximum work was extracted from the young learners. Prior to their going to the lace classes they may or may not have attended an ordinary school to receive instruction in the three 'Rs', but the early age at which they left meant that even if they had attended, their education was likely to be of only an extremely modest standard. Thus at Radclive cum Checkmore in Buckinghamshire the incumbent complained in 1857 to the Bishop of Oxford that 'few children [attended] daily school after eight or nine – boys being taken away for work – and girls for lace'. And at Marsh Gibbon in the same county the rector lamented: 'My chief difficulty arises from lace making, which draws away the girls from school before they are six years of age; and makes it impossible for me to have a girls' school'. To add to the problem, in a number of villages in the middle of the nineteenth century the lace 'schools' were the only so-called 'educational establishments' within the parish.

Yet in almost every respect these lace making schools were unsatisfactory. They were usually kept by 'a woman in her cottage', whose only justification for acting as a teacher was her skill in her craft, and perhaps her iron discipline. A few teachers did make half-hearted attempts to teach the children to read as well, but most would probably have agreed with Mrs Sarah Mitchell of Oakley in Bedfordshire, who frankly admitted in the late 1860s: 'I can't learn them much, I can't read much myself, but I do the best I can'. At that time she had twelve pupils working with her, eight of them under the age of eight years.[2]

But neglect of formal education was only one of the many disadvantages suffered by children attending the lace schools. Since they were normally held in a small cottage living room or kitchen, often 'with the fireplace stopped up to prevent draught', and with perhaps twenty or thirty children crammed inside, the atmosphere quickly became extremely unpleasant and unhealthy. The problem was aggravated by the fact that there was no other ventilation, 'beyond the door and the window, the latter not always made to open, or, if it [would] open, not opened'. In these circumstances it is not surprising that when an Assistant Commissioner in connection with the Children's Employment Commission of 1863 visited a lace school belonging to Mrs Woodleigh in Newton Poppleford, Devon, he found 'the smell from the crowded state of the room . . . almost unbearable, even without the full number present'.[4] Similarly, at Mrs Harris' lace school at Newport Pagnell in Buckinghamshire, he found the room 'crowded and hot', while, to add to the health hazard, in all too many cases 'the inmates [were] also often exposed to the injurious effects of imperfect drains, sinks, smells, &c.'

Yet there was at least the consolation during the summer months that the children could move outside to work, if the weather were fine. In the winter this was impossible. It was then that the lack of ventilation became particularly noticeable. Normally there were so many children in the room that they had to encroach upon the fireplace in order to fit themselves in, so no fires could be lit. In any case fires were frowned upon because the smoke and dust they emitted might sully the lace. In some schools, therefore, 'the animal heat of the inmates' was thought sufficient for warmth – when combined with a determined exclusion of all air from the outside. But more commonly each worker brought with her a small earthenware pot, shaped rather like a chamber pot, which was filled with hot charcoal or ashes.[4] This pot – often called a dicky pot – was then placed near the feet of the worker, under the hem of her skirt. Needless to say, even if the child's feet were warmed thereby, the acrid smoke emitted by the pots added to the generally foetid atmosphere and irritated the children's throats and lungs.

Child lacemakers in Buckinghamshire, c. 1900. The girls were obviously dressed in their best pinafores for the occasion. (Buckinghamshire County Museum)

Nor was this the only difficulty. The hours of labour were often desperately long, children as young as five or six working 'from four and six to eight hours per day', while from the age of twelve to fifteen years, they worked 'sometimes from 6 a.m. to 10 p.m., although in most places work ceased at 8 p.m.'[4] Above the age of fifteen they were considered mature enough to work either at home or with other adult lacemakers in their cottages. But for the youngest workers at least the confined conditions in which they laboured were a cruel restraint for growing limbs. Indeed, one visitor to Devon lace schools in 1875 expressed the wish 'that some philanthropist would introduce the infant school system of allowing the pupils to march and stretch their limbs at the expiration of every hour'.[55] Her suggestion was not adopted.

Yet to the hardships of confinement for long hours there had also to be added the problems of the work itself. Each young lacemaker was provided with a pillow, which was 'a hard round cushion, stuffed with straw and well hammered to make it hard for the bobbins to rattle on'. It was supported either upon the knees of the worker, or partly upon her knees and partly upon a three-legged pillow-horse, often known as the 'lady'.[156] On to this pillow the stiff parchment pattern was fixed by special brass pins, while other pins picked out the design shown on the pattern. The threads with which the lace was formed were wound on bobbins, made either of bone or of wood, and something of the size and shape of a pencil. The ground of the lace was formed by 'twisting and crossing the threads', while the pattern was 'made by interweaving a thread much thicker than that forming the groundwork, according to the design pricked out on the parchment'.[55]

Given the bulky nature of the pillow and the small size of many of the workers, however, most had to adopt a very awkward bent posture whilst making their lace, thereby causing their neck and shoulders to ache. But perhaps most harmful of all was the practice adopted by some of wearing a 'strong wooden busk in their stays to support them when stooping over their pillow-laces; this, being worn when young, while the bones [were] yet soft, [acted] very injuriously to the sternum and ribs causing great contraction of the chest', and permanent damage to the health and physique of the child concerned.

Most of the lace school pupils paid a small fee each week to cover the cost of their instruction; in some cases this might amount to about 1s per week for the first three months, 6d per week for the second six months, and after this initial period 6d a week or less, 'according to the amount of teaching required'.[8] In this case the child's mother would be given the completed lace and would be at liberty to sell it; but some mistresses charged a lower fee and kept the lace themselves, for eventual sale. In addition, in certain of the Devon lace schools it was the custom formally to apprentice children for a period of about eighteen months to two years, with the mistress taking the children's lace in return for the instruction given, and at first paying the children no wage at all. Then, as they became able to 'improve themselves', the children would receive a few pence per week from the sale of their lace. When the apprenticeship had expired, they paid for any further instruction required with the usual small weekly fee, fixed according to the amount of attention they still needed.

While work was in progress, discipline was very strictly maintained. Some mistresses insisted upon necks and arms being kept bare so that the children could be 'slapped the more easily', while hair had to be plaited neatly out of the way, in case 'a stray hair should fall and get worked up with the lace'.[156] A flour bag was also occasionally used for 'drying the hands or even to disguise soiling of the lace', but the best workers disdained such subterfuges.[89] If the girls and more rarely boys did not progress as well as was expected, then they could expect a sharp blow on the shoulders as punishment, administered while they were bending over their pillow. Another device was to push the child's head roughly down on to the pillow, so that she scratched her nose on the pins, while at a Riseley, Bedfordshire, lace school in the early nineteenth century, where boys were also instructed, any boy who transgressed was apparently 'hung up to a beam by a cord under [his] arms' to teach him to do better in future.[89]

Nevertheless, if the lace schools had much to condemn them, there were at least a few bright spots in the long days of work. In order to while away the tedious hours of practice, the children were often encouraged to recite 'lace tells' to one another. Some of these were macabre tales of violent death or supernatural happenings, but many were simply rhymes about the number of pins which had to be done to finish a certain piece of work. In other cases again, races would be held to see who would be the first to stick in a certain quantity of pins.[156] But whatever the form adopted, the main idea was to encourage the children to work quickly and thereby to increase their dexterity.

Then, too, there were the annual feast days traditionally celebrated by lacemakers – young and old – namely 25 November (St Catherine's Day) and 30 November (St Andrew's Day). Special cakes were made and also other sweet meats; at Bozeat in Northamptonshire a toffee was made to eat on 30 November and was known as 'Tandrew Toffee', while at Olney in Buckinghamshire frumenty was eaten.[111] Games were played and at Spratton, Northamptonshire, 'the children of the lace school used to seize the opportunity, when the mistress left the room, to lock her out. On her return they would sing:

> *Pardon mistress, pardon, master,*
> *Pardon for a pin*
> *If you won't give us a holiday,*
> *We won't let you in.*

117

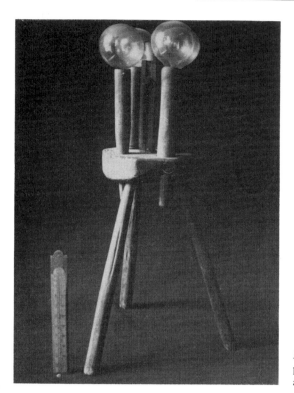

A lacemakers' candlestick – used to provide illumination when girls worked at night. (The author)

After a brief display of counterfeited anger the mistress yielded to their demands.[156]

During the winter months the older children who had to return to the lace school in the evenings were expected to work by candlelight, and in order to economize in the use of candles and at the same time to make the best use of such light as was available, it was customary for them to have a special candle stool. This was shaped rather like a small round table, with four or six holes drilled through the top and near the edge and one in the middle. 'In the centre hole was a long stick with a socket for the candle at one end . . . In the other . . . holes were placed pieces of wood hollowed out like a cup, and into each of these was placed a bottle made of very thin glass and filled with water. These bottles [called flashes] acted as strong condensers or lenses, and the . . . girls sat round the table, three to each bottle, their stools being upon different levels, the highest nearest the bottle, which threw light down upon the work like a burning glass.'[55] Because the bottles were so frail the children were often expected to provide their own, and at Bozeat it was customary to see them carefully carried to the lace school 'in a straw "hutch"', which the child hung by a handle over her arm.[111] Nevertheless, even if

118

the children positioned themselves so as to get the maximum benefit from the beam of light, their eyes were often badly strained as they sought in the dimness to produce their intricate lace.

Occasionally, too, if special orders had to be completed, workers would sit up all night to finish them. One such small group of lacemakers at Great Horwood, Buckinghamshire, at around the end of the nineteenth century, tried 'to pass their time and to keep themselves awake' by singing in turn the song *Excelsior* all through the night.

But if life was hard for the young workers, there was rarely any doubt in the minds of parents that they should encourage their children to earn what they could as quickly as possible. In the later 1860s it was noted of the Buckinghamshire and Bedfordshire lace industry that 'a farm labourer treats it as a matter of course that his daughters will be sent to a lace school at four or five years of age, and that from the time of their leaving the school to the time when they leave his house for good, it is his wife's business to see that they stick to their lace pillow, and work at least as many hours as he does himself'.[2] Nearly a decade later, in 1876, an Assistant Factory Inspector said of Devon parents that there were still some who thought that 'they [had] brought children into the world to no purpose, if they [did] not become contributors to the family purse, as soon as they [could] hold a lace pillow, or shuffle a lace stick'.[8] Nor was it only the labourers' children who were affected; in lacemaking districts, the daughters of small country craftsmen would equally be involved – as an investigation of mid-nineteenth-century Census returns make clear.

Of course, the level of earnings actually received varied with the skill and age of the worker, and with the overall state of the trade. But by the beginning of the 1860s it was noted that a fairly skilled girl of eight in the Buckinghamshire/ Oxfordshire lacemaking area might secure 1s 6d to 2s 6d a week, for a nine-hour day, while a girl aged thirteen, of moderate ability and working ten hours a day, might earn 2s 6d or 3s per week.

Yet if parents remained anxious for children to seize every chance to add to their earnings, elsewhere public concern was increasing, especially as it was realized that many girls were growing up without any formal education at all. The position was underlined, in particular, by the findings of the Children's Employment Commission during 1863–64 and by the interviews with child workers which its Assistant Commissioner carried out. There were, for example, youngsters like seven-year-old Agnes Perryman, interviewed at Otterton in Devon during 1863. She had been 'at lace a year. Comes at 9 or 10 a.m., and stays till 4 p.m., or, if she has not finished her work, till 4½. Pays 2d a week. Learned reading at an old lady's school, but nothing else.' The interviewer tested her and found she could read 'one syllable words' only. Or Leonora Chant, aged nine, of

119

Beer, who 'came . . . as apprentice when seven . . . Does not sit by candle yet, but will next winter. Can make 1s 6d a week. Was at the endowed school four years, and learned to read, knit and sew, not to write. Does not know any figures.' She, too, could only read very short words. These random examples were typical of the children from lacemaking districts who gave evidence in connection with the Children's Employment Commission.[4]

Up to this date home workers had been excluded from the protection afforded by earlier government legislation covering Factories and Workshops, partly because of the obvious difficulty for effective control which they presented. However, in 1867, the situation was changed by a Workshops Regulation Act which not only widened the definition of a workshop but also laid down that no child below the age of eight was to be employed in any handicraft. Between the ages of eight and thirteen, he or she could be employed only in accordance with the half-time system already used in factories and workshops; in other words, each child must attend an approved elementary school for at least ten hours per week, between the hours of 8 a.m. and 6 p.m. and must obtain a certificate from the teacher stating that this had been done. Although difficult to implement in its early days, it was soon reinforced by the general education legislation of the 1870–80 period, which further raised the minimum age for employment to ten and sought to enforce compulsory elementary education for all children. Nevertheless, as with the early attempts to control the employment of children in agriculture, there was a good deal of initial evasion. Even in 1876, Assistant Inspector Whymper complained of this in Devon, saying of the child lacemakers: 'Ignorant they have entered the lace schools, and ignorant they have at present remained'. But he did add that, 'Parents are gradually getting into their heads that the children must be got to school somehow.'[8] Similarly, Sub-Inspector Striedinger, who investigated lacemaking in Oxfordshire, spoke of the continued existence in 1876 of 'those abominations, the . . . pillow-lace schools (a few of which, despite the Workshops Acts still linger about the country . . .)'[8] Indeed, in February of that year Striedinger visited Mixbury School, in the North Oxfordshire lacemaking district, to caution 'the children against lacemaking'. A little earlier than this entries in the school log book show that the master himself had experienced difficulties in enforcing attendance. For example, in July, 1870, he recorded that he had kept 'the Half-Timers after the others went home 20 minutes for coming in late'. A few days earlier he had noted their absence when they had gone to sell lace in the nearby market town of Brackley.

But in the major centres of Buckinghamshire and Bedfordshire the situation was still more difficult. The log book of Odell School in Bedfordshire provides numerous examples both of poor attendance by the half-timers and of their low level of educational attainment. An entry for 12 July 1872, for instance, recorded:

'I find the Halftimers to be a drag upon the others', while about three weeks later the master noted that, 'The Factory Inspector visited the school today in reference to the Halftimers'. On 5 February 1875, came the lament: 'The halftimers are a source of much anxiety', and so it continued until at last on 11 November 1880, a happier report appeared: 'Factory Inspector visited the School today to enquire about the halftimers. I am thankful to say I have very few now.'

Clearly, then, if the passage of the regulatory legislation eventually played some part in bringing to an end the exploitation of child labour in the cottage lacemaking industry, it was not the only factor. For all too often parents were prepared to risk breaking the law if the opportunity for earning extra money presented itself. Probably most significant of all, therefore, in the drop in the employment of half-timers – at Odell as elsewhere – was the difficult position of the lace industry itself in the final decades of the nineteenth century, when changes in fashion and competition from cheap machine-made lace caused prices to slump. This interpretation is supported by evidence collected in 1887 for an official report on the Honiton lace industry, for a number of the older lacemakers and dealers revealed that the 'lace schools' had closed primarily 'because the demand for lace fell off so much . . .' At Exmouth, a lace-dealer reported that 'formerly there were twenty lace schools in the town. Now there are none . . .' while the failure of what had once been 'the staple industry of the district' was said to have caused the 'bitterest distress' among the adult workers. At Otterton in the same county the collapse in demand was likewise blamed for the distress in the local lace industry and for the ending of the lace schools. A lacemaker here declared that a few children were 'taught by their parents, but with no such regularity as at the old lace-schools' – and without constant practice the achievement of the highest level of skill was considered impossible.[10] Consequently, although children continued to learn the rudiments of the trade long after this, either at home (like Mrs Turney in Buckinghamshire) or in a local elementary school, few were either willing or able to make it their career. In addition, it was generally agreed that yet another enemy of the cottage lacemaking industry was 'book-learning' for children who had received even a modest level of education were unwilling to settle down to the drudgery of a lacemaker's life, at starvation wages.[10]

Yet if lacemaking formed one significant domestic industry, a second was that of straw-plaiting – which was particularly characteristic of those areas of Buckinghamshire and Bedfordshire which were not devoted to lacemaking, plus parts of Hertfordshire, Essex and Suffolk. Indeed, by 1851, 80 per cent of the total workers in the trade lived in the south-east Midlands.[88] Once again, the numbers involved even in the third quarter of the century were substantial and Bedfordshire alone at the time of the 1871 Census of Population could boast

20,701 female plaiters, of whom 837 were children aged five to nine inclusive, and 2,535 aged ten to fourteen inclusive. Details of other counties where the trade was carried on can be found in Table 2, while there were also a number of youths and boys employed. In 1861 male workers numbered 2,128 on a national basis, while the comparable female figure was 27,739; 1,561 of the males were under twenty years of age. But these figures, like the lace ones quoted earlier, probably underestimate the real numbers involved, because of the under-recording of part-time workers. In addition, the size of the straw plaiting work force kept up rather longer than in lace, for despite earlier ups and downs the final collapse was delayed to the 1870s and beyond, when cheap Italian, Chinese and later Japanese plait entered the market and irrevocably undermined price levels. From then on, most of the English producers were starved out.[77]

Straw-plaiting was, in essence, a far less skilled occupation than lacemaking, even though a number of specialized plaits were made and individual output – and consequently earnings – depended very much upon the achieving of a high level of dexterity through constant practice. Unlike lace, too, the child worker normally learnt the rudiments of the trade at home from his or her mother, before being sent 'usually at 4 years old, some at 3½' to a plait school. This was often little more than a child-minding institution held in a local cottage, for although most of the 'mistresses' could teach plaiting, some could not and the sole function of these latter was to keep the children working as hard as possible on a task assigned them by their parents. As one mistress admitted: 'The children have so many yards to do, and then their mothers sell the plait. Though my place is called a school, I do not teach plaiting, but merely keep the children to their work, and see that they do the number of yards set to them by their parents, which is according to their age and the kind of plait they are taught by their friends before they come to me. I used to teach them some reading, too, but found that too much, and do not do it now.' It was also reported that 'about thirty yards seem counted the most proper day's work, to take the bigger ones [while] the straw cuts their fingers and their mouths, too, as they draw it through their mouths because it breaks off if it is not damp.' Yet perhaps most ominous of all, from the point of view of the children's overall welfare was the claim of a critic from Toddington in Bedfordshire during the mid-1860s that: 'The mistresses who get the most work out of [the children] are most patronized.' In these circumstances it was scarcely surprising that many plait schools were noted as having 'formidable looking sticks', which the mistresses were more than ready to use if they thought the children were not working hard enough.[4]

Further, if the children did not complete their allotted task at school, they would be expected to finish it at home anyway. For while straw plaiting had the advantage of not confining the children indoors quite as much as did lacemaking,

A woman and perhaps her two daughters plaiting at Charlton Hill Pond near Hitchin, Hertfordshire. (Hitchin Museum)

with its use of the bulky pillow, it also had the disadvantage that children could be kept almost constantly employed upon it, carrying their stock of straws under their arms as they walked around. In the 1860s one observer complained that children were occupied on their plait 'as much on the way to and from school or meals, as when at school. In passing through the country villages, whether about mealtimes or in the evening it is rare to see a girl out-of-doors without her plait in her hand, and working away busily as she walks, no doubt to get on with the task set by her mother. Young boys, too, may be seen plaiting out-of-doors, but not to the same extent.' This generalization was born out by interviews carried out by the Assistant Commissioner in connection with the Children's Employment Commission. For example, in 1864 he met Sarah Ann Meagher, aged seven, of Berkhampsted and a companion 'on their way from school at tea time', plaiting

123

as they walked along. Sarah said she had five yards of plait to do at each session of school, plus 'one yard at dinner and one at tea time'. 'Often I have to get up in the morning at 7 or 6½ and begin work, because I have so much to do . . . If I do "five" mother says I'm [a] good girl; she doesn't hit me, the mistress does sometimes.'[4]

Similarly in Essex during October, 1867, the Revd J. Fraser, an Assistant Commissioner in connection with the *Royal Commission on the Employment of Children, Young Persons and Women in Agriculture*, reported meeting seven 'plaiting girls' in the vicinity of Great Yeldham. 'Four could not read; three thought they could, but on being tried with a very simple passage, could not get on without spelling. Their ages ranged from seven to fifteen. One of them told me she could plait three yards of braid in an hour, and get 4d for 20 yards. A finer sort is paid 11d for 20 yards and the girl said she could do three yards in an hour. They were all coming from a plaiting school, in which there were forty children . . . The school hours are from 9 to 5, and they go home to dinner. They read twice in the course of the day. The girls were walking home from school in a party, gossiping and plaiting as they went.'[2] As regards the level of output claimed by the girls, however, Fraser added a footnote that he found their figures impossible to reconcile with evidence he had obtained elsewhere and he thought it probable that they had 'exaggerated their earnings or their rate of work . . .'

Some of the very youngest children, who were too small to plait, might be employed in other ways. In certain of the plait schools 'infants of two, three and four years old' were employed in clipping off the loose ends of straw from the plait, 'with their scissors tied to their bodies'.[4] Many plait schools openly provided a baby-minding service as well as taking the older children, in order to free mothers from the burden of looking after their infants. They could then get on with their own plaiting. And given this basic preoccupation with their work, it was small wonder if plaiting families had precious little comfort in their home life. Female plaiters were frequently condemned as poor housewives, utterly ignorant of such common things as 'keeping their houses clean, mending their own or their children's clothes, and cooking their husbands' dinners'.[2]

This neglect naturally served to weaken family ties and when coupled with the early financial independence of many young workers, it proved a cause for concern – especially among clergymen in parishes where straw plaiting flourished. This was particularly true of villages where young men were also engaged in plaiting, since many of the women and older girls were regarded as of 'very low moral' condition, with 'fornication lamentably frequent' among them.[3] One observer, for example, condemned the tendency for young 'male and female plaiters to go about the lanes in summer engaged in work which has not even the wholesome corrective of more or less physical exhaustion'.[2] And certainly an inspection of the Census records shows that quite young children left home to

live as lodgers with their neighbours, in order to be free from parental restraint –
and perhaps the discomfort of an overcrowded cottage. Illegitimacy rates were
high in the plaiting communities, so that whereas in 1865 the rate of illegitimate
births in the country as a whole was 62 per 1,000, in the Ampthill, Biggleswade
and Woburn poor-law union areas of Bedfordshire the figures were 70, 83 and
100 respectively. 'In one plaiting village, apparently near Toddington, five out of
twelve births were said to be illegitimate.'[77]

Nor was this the only possible cause of tension within families. According to
the vicar of Ivinghoe, a Buckinghamshire plaiting centre, in 1854, the willingness
of children to leave home in order to assert their independence, made 'parents
afraid of offending [them]', and youngsters 'thus [became] hardened and intract-
able'. Similarly, twelve years later at Aston Clinton, also in Buckinghamshire,
the incumbent felt one of the main hindrances to his priestly mission was 'the
premature withdrawal of the children from the Natl. [school] to their plaiting
schools, and their early independence of their parents, leading to very early
marriages, and worse . . .'

In addition, given the lack of interest in housework and cleanliness among
wives and mothers, it is not surprising that hygiene in the plaiting schools was at
a very low ebb. Of Mrs Wimbush's plait school at Northchurch in Hertfordshire
it was reported by the *Children's Employment Commission* in 1864: 'The window in
this school was shut on a hot summer day, but the door open. The air was of
course close and heavy, with a strong smell.' In the winter, draughts had to be
excluded from the work rooms, 'as the children cannot work if they are cold, and
in some places they have to sit so close into the fireplace that the fire cannot be
lighted, so that they have coal or wood in earthen or even tin pots. These make a
disagreeable smell . . . The straw plait schools are more crowded and afford
much less space per child in ordinary cases than the lace schools . . .'[4]

Educational standards were poor, for at very few plait schools was any attempt
made to give instruction beyond that relating to the trade itself. For instance, at
Chesham in Buckinghamshire, where there were twenty-one plaiting schools in
the mid-1860s, at only two were reading and writing even *claimed* to be taught. In
any case, in most plait schools this sort of 'education' degenerated into the mere
repetition of a few verses from the Bible, which 'they all [knew] by heart'.[2] As
with the children met by the Revd J. Fraser in Essex, there was no true ability to
read. In other cases children might attend the ordinary village school for one or
two days per week, to learn reading and writing, and then spend the rest of the
week at the plaiting school. But so great was the poverty of many labouring
families that they were reluctant to sacrifice even part of the child's day to the
cause of formal education. As late as 1872 the incumbent of Edlesborough in
Buckinghamshire blamed, 'The miserable results of plait schools in keeping up

125

gross ignorance', while at the parish of Ivinghoe the vicar regretfully recorded in 1854 that even his attempts to set up evening classes had been thwarted by straw plait. 'Straw-plaiting occupies too much of the people's time to allow them to come, and in fact forms a principal part of the occupation at our day school. Without offering it we should not have any scholars come.' Likewise at the nearby parish of Cheddington the rector supervised a 'plaiting school' as well as 'daily mixed school for boys and girls and one Sunday school'. Similar complaints were made in Essex. At Little Maplestead an attempt to set up a day school in one of the cottages had failed and there was only a plaiting school in the village, 'kept by an old man, where the children are taught to plait straw, and read two or three times a day, paying 1½d or 2d a week.' In a note the Assistant Commissioner observed: 'Throughout this neighbourhood, from sordid, selfish motives, as enabling them to turn their children's labour to account at the earliest moment, the straw-plaiting, or as it is otherwise called, the "braiding" school, is preferred by the parents to the public school.'[2] At nearby Great Maplestead the local clergyman refused to allow plait to be taught in the daily school but admitted that 'the attendance could be immediately increased were plaiting allowed: but I consider the whole character of the school would be lowered by it'.[77]

It was to combat this sort of neglect that the 1867 Workshops Regulation Act was passed. However, as in the lace industry, in the early days success fell far short of what had been hoped. Indeed, even more than in lace, large scale evasions were at first apparent, as the continued buoyancy of the market for plait encouraged parents and plaiting school mistresses and masters to go on in their old ways as far as possible. Repeated efforts at enforcement were made by the police and Factory Inspectors during the late 1860s and early 1870s, but all too often the 'children would slip out through the back door when anyone in authority called at the [plaiting] school, while the number plaiting at home was too great to be dealt with by the factory inspectorate or the police'.[77] Parents were all too often quite ready to break the law and even incur the 20s fine provided for breaches of the legislation in order to reap the short-term advantages of their children's earnings, while the straw plait teachers 'who relied on the children's pence to keep them from destitution, in many cases' were equally prepared to take risks, until they were directly warned. Thus at Cheddington, Mrs Tooley confessed that 'before the policeman came [she] had five or six [children] under eight' – despite the prohibitions of the 1867 Act. She was certainly not alone in this.[2] Indeed, in 1874, Mr Woods, a Factory Inspector, noted that in the Bedfordshire villages of Tilsworth, Stanbridge and Eggington 'there was no [day] school . . . only seven plait schools, with 85 children under thirteen in them . . . Of the 85 children seen in straw plait schools 31 were infants who ought not to work at all . . .'

COTTAGE INDUSTRIES

As might be expected, elementary schoolmasters and attendance officers often found it difficult to ensure that the children who were employed legally as half-timers in fact made their requisite number of appearances at the ordinary day school. This is revealed, for example, in Ivinghoe school log book, where in November, 1876, it was recorded that the factory inspector had been to the school to check up on attendances. But the master's hope that this would 'do good' was soon shattered; six months later it was necessary for the inspector to come again to visit 'the homes of the irregular ones'. Once more, he had little success. Similarly, at Drayton Parslow school in the same county, the teacher reported in February, 1879: 'Many of the girls absent this week – kept home to plait straw, there being a slight improvement in the plait trade.' In Bedfordshire the problem was equally serious. At Shillington School the Report of the HMI for 1870 gloomily noted: 'Irregular attendance and straw plaiting combine to lower . . . efficiency'. And on 6 July of the following year the mistress recorded, 'Several girls absent plaiting'. The existence of plaiting schools in the parish was also blamed for the fact that 'very few girls' attended the school 'in proportion to [the] numbers of boys.' As late as 1875 there were five plaiting schools in Shillington, and children were kept away from the day school not only to attend them but also to take the plait to be sold at Hitchin market. At Clifton in the same county the head teacher likewise mentioned the problems associated with plaiting, as on 29 September 1873: 'Very small attendance of half-day girls.'

Despite all efforts, including more determined attempts by the education authorities to secure proper standards of elementary school attendance, it was only the collapse of the plait trade itself which eventually brought this particular abuse to an end.

The third example of a cottage industry to be considered is the gloving trade, which mainly concerned children in the Yeovil area of Somerset, the Woodstock district of Oxfordshire and parts of the counties of Worcestershire and Here-fordshire. In many cases glovemaking bore strong resemblances to the other cottage industries which have been discussed, although in the Woodstock and Worcester areas at least it was more common for the children to work with their mother at home rather than to attend a formal gloving school. Thus E. Pinchin, a fourteen-year-old girl from Evesham interviewed by the Assistant Commissioner in connection with the Children's Employment Commission in 1864, declared that she had been 'at gloving for six years and a little more . . . I work at home with mother; some here learn three or four girls together; we have had two besides ourselves working for us in this room; but most work at home. We usually work till dusk from 8 a.m . . . We never work by candle light; that hurts the eyes very much.'[4] At another house in Evesham a mother and two daughters were similarly working together, the younger girl having commenced work at the age of eight. As a group these three workers reckoned to make 'six pair a day of "best men's" . . . and were paid 3s 6d or 3s 9d a dozen pair, with 7d a dozen if they did the pointing as well . . .'[4] In the Woodstock area of Oxfordshire this type of home production, or else work in a local glove factory, was the normal pattern, with factory children in the late nineteenth century working on simple routine tasks from the age of about ten; their hours were from 8 a.m. to 8 p.m. and the weekly wage about 2s 6d.[132]

Still less satisfactory conditions existed in Somerset, where children commenced work in the mid-Victorian period at the age of seven or eight – and a few even earlier. Furthermore, many of the children who did attend the ordinary day school and were not full-time glovers, yet were regularly employed in the evening. In the late 1860s Mr R.F. Boyle visited the county in connection with the Royal Commission on the Employment of Children, etc. in Agriculture and was surprised to discover at the school at Shepton Beauchamp that when the 'mistress who was teaching the first class said "All those who glove in the evening to hold up their hands" . . . every girl, even a little thing of eight, held up her hand. She worked every evening from 5 p.m. to 9 p.m.'[2]

But even more disastrous for both health and education was the position of children who did not attend a day school at all, and who – despite the Workshops Regulation Act of 1867 – were often occupied at the age of six or seven. The girls normally worked in the cottage of 'some agent or overlooker', and for the first three months of their training received no pay; then their earnings commenced in accordance with their skill and level of output. They normally remained at work in one of these gloving establishments until they reached the age of fourteen or fifteen, when like their lacemaker and straw-plait fellows, they were deemed mature enough to work on their own. In order to keep their sewing neat and even many of the girls used 'a brass machine which holds the glove in a vice, and has a row of little holes close together, through which the needle passes, and which keeps the stitches regular.' Boyle then stated: 'We visited several cottages in East Chinnock, where the younger ones were working; in one there were 11 girls at work . . . All were sitting in rows at their machines. The atmosphere was very stuffy . . . but it was a clean cottage, and belonged to a respectable woman. Not all of the employers, however, treat the children well. A girl in Ilchester complained that her eyes had suffered, that she could see well at the beginning of the week, but at the end all the holes seemed to run into one. When her eyes felt bad the woman would not let her look up, and thought it was laziness, so used often to bang her on the head as a hint to go on.'[2]

Not surprisingly, a number of children longed for the day when they would be grown up sufficiently to leave this behind them. One such unwilling glovemaker was eight-year-old Emmeline Cox of Somerton, who had begun to make gloves at the age of five. 'When [she] began [she] could make one pair a day, now can make two . . . Lives with grandmother . . . When older would like to go to service.'[2]

During the course of the next eight or ten years the pressure for reform increased. Nevertheless in 1876 many of the evils of Somerset gloving still survived, if on a diminished scale. According to one critic, at that date the young workers suffered particularly during the winter months: 'The cost of firing being heavy, there is not much kept in, so that in cold weather, notwithstanding all ventilation is prevented in order to keep out the cold air, their feet are numbed by the cold, and their hands rendered incapable of working from time to time by contact with the brass work of the gloving machines . . . The hours of working are unusually severe.'[8] Even at the end of the century it was possible to find whole families engaged in glovemaking in Somerset, 'the father being perhaps a cutter, the mother and daughters sewers', but as with the other cottage trades the competition of foreign producers and of machine-made goods, plus the stricter interpretation of the education and workshops legislation had at least eliminated the worst aspects of the system. At the time of the 1851 Census of Population there had been 1,683 female glovemakers at work full-time in the age range five to fourteen inclusive; by 1871 their numbers had already shrunk to 764, and the trend was downward thereafter. (See Table 2.)

The three domestic industries have been dealt with at such length because they show clearly that even under *non-factory* conditions the plight of the child worker was often an unhappy one – indeed perhaps harsher than in most factories by the 1860s. In this respect, parents and the craft 'teachers' proved themselves as stern disciplinarians as all but the worst factory masters. In addition, the existence of a flourishing cottage industry within a county at least up to the 1870s meant an almost total neglect of the education of large numbers of young girls. For although children might leave off their glovemaking, straw plaiting and lace-making to help in seasonal agricultural activities, only a few parents were prepared to encourage them to do the same in order to attend school. Finally, the labour demands of a cottage industry could interfere even with the number of *young* girls going into domestic service – that major employer of female labour in the later nineteenth century. Thus at the time of the 1871 Census of Population, Bedfordshire with its flourishing straw plait and rather less successful lacemaking trade, could only muster just over 400 female domestic servants in the age group five to fourteen inclusive. Buckinghamshire, another centre of cottage industries, could claim 588 domestic servants in the same age group; on the other hand, Norfolk, without any such competition, had nearly 2,000 female domestic servants in the five to fourteen age group at that date, and Somerset, with its minor glovemaking industry, over 3,000.[69] It is to employment in domestic service and the rural crafts that attention must now be turned.

TABLE 2

FEMALE EMPLOYMENT IN CERTAIN SELECTED COUNTIES
From 1851–1871 Census Returns

County	Agricultural Labourers	Farm Servants	Glovers	Straw Plaiters	Pillow Lacemakers
DEVON					
1851*Census*					
Total all ages	1,189	7,479	3,103	9	5,478
5–9 inclusive	3	22	37	–	259
10–14 inclusive	54	1,449	392	–	968
1861 *Census*					
Total all ages	780	1,576	2,289	5	4,841
5–9 inclusive	2	1	12	–	107
10–14 inclusive	44	182	210	1	561
1871 *Census*					
Total all ages	474	997	2,015	84	4,342
5–9 inclusive	–	1	10	–	64
10–14 inclusive	18	186	193	2	502
BUCKINGHAMSHIRE					
1851 *Census*					
Total all ages	106	1,066	12	2,922	10,487
5–9 inclusive	1	1	–	321	621
10–14 inclusive	1	41	–	669	1,424
1861 *Census*					
Total all ages	131	711	3	2,976	8,459
5–9 inclusive	–	–	–	220	351
10–14 inclusive	4	40	–	538	1,070
1871 *Census*					
Total all ages	160	99	–	3,412	8,077
5–9 inclusive	–	–	–	133	178
10–14 inclusive	8	8	–	580	957
ESSEX					
1851 *Census*					
Total all ages	566	2,343	52	3,058	382
5–9 inclusive	3	2	–	265	23
10–14 inclusive	34	241	2	581	104
1861 *Census*					
Total all ages	770	525	56	2,444	122
5–9 inclusive	15	–	–	78	1
10–14 inclusive	50	59	12	281	15

1871 *Census*					
Total all ages	327	693	27	2,839	441
5–9 inclusive	–	–	–	49	–
10–14 inclusive	14	83	–	332	35
BEDFORDSHIRE					
1851 *Census*					
Total all ages	36	800	6	10,054	5,734
5–9 inclusive	–	–	–	1,282	354
10–14 inclusive	4	29	–	1,899	893
1861 *Census*					
Total all ages	30	137	4	11,476	6,714
5–9 inclusive	–	–	–	705	379
10–14 inclusive	6	4	–	1,888	958
1871 *Census*					
Total all ages	26	34	1	20,701	6,051
5–9 inclusive	–	–	–	837	143
10–14 inclusive	5	–	–	2,535	875
SOMERSET					
1851 *Census*					
Total all ages	2,501	4,533	8,050	25	417
5–9 inclusive	10	7	242	–	10
10–14 inclusive	147	503	1,441	1	77
1861 *Census*					
Total all ages	1,723	1,646	7,748	13	302
5–9 inclusive	4	2	144	–	8
10–14 inclusive	72	130	1,081	–	55
1871 *Census*					
Total all ages	1,455	1,562	6,400	180	343
5–9 inclusive	10	–	52	1	3
10–14 inclusive	66	192	712	1	44

Sources: 1851 Census, Parliamentary Papers, 1852–53, Vol. LXXXVIII, Pt. 1; *1861 Census*, Parliamentary Papers, 1863, Vol. LIII; *1871 Census*, Parliamentary Papers, 1873, Vol. LXXI, Pt. I.

(NB: By 1881 the number of female straw plaiters, bonnet and hat-makers *together* in Bedfordshire had shrunk to 15,058; in this Census the number of straw plaiters alone cannot be isolated. The same drop is apparent elsewhere, and by 1901 Bedfordshire had only 485 female straw plaiters of all ages and Buckinghamshire 173.)

NOTES ON ADDITIONAL SOURCES USED
Reminiscences of the late Mrs E. Turney of Buckinghamshire. I am indebted to my

sister-in-law, Mrs I. Horn, for her help in obtaining the reminiscences shortly before Mrs Turney's death.

The views of clergymen in Buckinghamshire on the effects of lacemaking and straw-plaiting on the home life and education of child workers have been obtained from the Oxford Diocesan Visitation Returns preserved at the Oxfordshire Record Office; 1854 – MS. OXf. Dioc. Pp. d. 701; 1857 – MS. Oxf. Dioc. Pp. d. 179; 1866 – MS. Oxf. Dioc. Pp. d. 331.

CHAPTER SEVEN

Domestic Service and Rural Crafts

'The best thing a cottager's daughter could hope for was to go into service in a good family, and when she was between ten and fifteen years old her parents would try to place her.' – W.J. Reader – *Life in Victorian England* (1964).

Throughout the period 1850–1900 domestic service employed more women and girls than any other single occupation, and at the time of the 1891 Census of Population there were in England and Wales alone nearly 1.4 million female servants – of whom 107,167 were in the age range of ten to fourteen inclusive. By contrast, male servants numbered only a little over 58,500 – 6,891 of them being under the age of fifteen. Admittedly many of these young workers had been born in the towns but there can be no doubt that domestic service provided the main employment outlet for country girls, too, once they had reached the age of eleven or thereabouts. The 1891 Census Report commented on the 'fewness of women, in country districts, at all ages from ten upwards. It also said that almost one-third of all girls in the country, between the ages of fifteen and twenty, were in service, and about one in every eight over the age of ten.'[121] Only in areas affected by cottage industries or factories might this preoccupation with domestic service not apply – although the very last years of the nineteenth century *did* see a decline, especially in the youngest group – those aged ten to fourteen inclusive. By 1901, they numbered only 63,795 as compared to 107,167 ten years earlier. Presumably improvements in education, the raising of the school leaving age and widening opportunities for employment elsewhere had all helped to bring about the change.

Once a girl came to the end of her school career her mother began to look around for what was known as a 'petty place' for her. Occasionally this process might be delayed if the mother had a large number of children and her daughter's presence was required at home to help look after them, but within a few months of leaving the search would certainly be under way. These 'petty places' were usually found in the households of local tradesmen, schoolmasters, clergy, farm bailiffs and the like, and as Flora Thompson has pointed out, they were regarded as 'stepping stones to better things. It was considered unwise to allow a girl to remain in her petty place more than a year; but a year she must stay whether she liked it or not, for that was the custom.' Wages were low – perhaps only one or two shillings per week – but food was also provided, and since in many households this was 'good and abundant', it was possible for a girl of twelve or thirteen to grow within a year sufficiently tall and strong to be placed in 'the desired "gentleman's service"'.[144]

However, not all of the servants were so fortunate. One unlucky youngster was Annie Langdown (born 1873) of Bere Regis in Dorset who went at the age of thirteen to work as a servant in the local manse. 'She arrived before breakfast and left in the evening after a day of heavy work on light meals.' It was this sort of experience that often made mothers unwilling to let their daughters go to work in 'houses where only one servant was kept as the most grinding tasks, such as scouring floors and kitchen furniture with sand, often fell on those least able to sustain the toil'. In Annie's case her mother eventually became worried 'by the exhaustion of her daughter and harassed by family cares . . . recalled Annie from service to resume her home tasks.' But this too, was no easy option with a large family of young children to look after.[104] An inspection of advertisements for young servants in the local press also leads one to the view that Annie's experience of hard work was not unique. Such requirements as: 'Wanted – A strong active Girl, as general servant, age about seventeen, from the country preferred'; or 'Wanted – A strong active girl about fifteen or sixteen', which appeared in the *Oxford Times* of 24 April 1880 and the *Hampshire Chronicle* of 10 May 1890, respectively, are typical of the hundreds of such advertisements published. In almost all, there is a mention that the successful applicant should be 'strong' or 'active'.

Nevertheless despite this, many of the young girls *were* treated as members of the family by their employers. A Christmas present of a frock or winter coat was common for servants in 'petty places', while material was provided for underwear. And if formal caps and aprons and print dresses for mornings had to be worn, they were often provided by the employer. 'She shan't want for anything while she is with me' was a promise frequently made by a shopkeeper's wife when engaging a girl, and many were even better than their word in that respect. They worked with the girls themselves and trained them; then as they said, just as they were becoming useful they left to 'better themselves'.[144]

Most small households operated along similar lines. Thus at West Malvern in Worcestershire during the 1880s and 1890s the curate's family regularly had two young servant girls, aged about thirteen or fourteen years, working for them. One acted as the nurse and the other helped in the kitchen; neither was expected to wear any very formal uniform – just a cap and apron and usually a black dress in the afternoons. The nurse took the children out for walks in the mornings and afternoons, and superintended their games and amusements. At night both of the maids slept in the night nursery with the current baby, while the rest of the children slept in the nursery itself. One of the curate's daughters, Mrs Lane Anderson of Abingdon, to whom I am indebted for these reminiscences, also recalls that the maids normally stayed with her family for about two years before moving on to a larger establishment.

Frequently the change meant employment in a country house or in a prosperous town household, with a consequent severing of the links with home, since such positions could only be obtained by travelling some distance away. Nevertheless it must not be forgotten that many hundreds even of mature servants continued to work in small households as general maids, carrying out all the domestic duties on their own. This is borne out by a random examination of the Census Returns; thus of one hundred and sixty households of mixed-income families in the Bridge Street/Horse Fair area of Banbury at the time of the 1861 Census of Population, around fifty had female servants – about half of them being one-servant households only. These included a coal merchant, who had a house servant of twenty-four, a retired ironmonger, who employed a girl of twenty, and an innkeeper, with a servant of twenty-nine. As Flora Thompson has written, indeed: "Everybody who was anything" as they used to say, kept a maid in those days . . . Even the wives of carpenters and masons paid a girl sixpence to clean the knives and boots and take out the children on Saturday.'[144] But most girls would at least *aim* for something better than this.

Often the first step towards securing a new situation would be taken when a girl's mother approached the local clergyman's family for help or advice. At Juniper Hill, in Oxfordshire the clergyman's daughter was consulted in this way, and if she did not know of any immediate vacancies 'she would wait until she had two or three such candidates for promotion on her list, then advertise in the *Morning Post* or the *Church Times* for situations for them'. But in other instances, where an older sister or cousin was already in service, the family network itself would probably suffice to obtain information of the requisite post. Some girls would perhaps pluck up sufficient courage to answer one of the many adver-tisements for maids which appeared in the local press, or they might approach one of the servant registry offices which flourished in most market towns.

Yet by whatever means the situation was secured, once the decision had been taken, many were the tears shed by the girls as they made ready to depart. But they appreciated the importance of earning their own living and realised that there could be no turning back.

In preparation for their new employment they would probably have to be fitted out with a quantity of underwear, some shoes and even their uniforms, for

Servant training school for young girls (mainly orphans) at Headington Hill Hall, Oxford, August 1913. In Victorian and Edwardian times, domestic service was the main employment for village girls. Only a minority, who perhaps hoped to enter 'superior' households, attended training schools.
(Oxfordshire County Council, Department of Leisure and Arts)

by no means all employers provided working clothes. As Margaret Powell recollects, in Hove even after the First World War she was expected to supply herself with 'three print dresses, blue or green; four white aprons with bibs, and four caps; stockings, and black strapped shoes'.[118] And at a north Oxfordshire country house during the 1880s a tongue-tied twelve-year-old girl of Flora Thompson's acquaintance was informed that she must be fully fitted out with caps and aprons, if she were to be employed. 'Plenty of changes' were required as there was a washing day only every six weeks. But the girl's family had no money to spare for such things and so the position was turned down. Mrs Beeton was equally clear on the subject. In her advice to 'cooks, kitchen-maids, &c.' she declared: 'Provide yourself with at least a dozen good-sized, serviceable cooking-aprons, made with bibs . . . Have them made large enough round so as to nearly meet behind.' Another essential was a pair of 'good, well-fitting boots. You will find them less fatiguing in a warm kitchen than loose untidy slippers.'[31]

Although some of the girls might have saved up enough to buy the necessary items out of their wages while they were at their 'petty place', quite often parents also had to scrape round to cover the greater part of the expenditure. For example, in post-1918 Hove Mrs Powell's mother had to borrow the two pounds required to cover the cost of her daughter's uniform.[118] In some families, too, there was a business-like understanding that the girls would refund the money to their parents on an instalment plan once they were in their new situation. This was the case, with the family of Amos Lelliot, a mid-Victorian small holder, pig meal dealer and carrier from West Sussex. By this means Lelliot managed, despite his low income, to equip all of his daughters suitably for service, and although the reimbursements they made 'had to come from pitifully low wages . . . Amos insisted "It's all to their good; you're never too young to start larnin' independence." Not one of the daughters defaulted on her instalments . . .'

Orphan or illegitimate children who had spent their early years as inmates of a workhouse were, of course, normally provided with clothing by the Poor Law Guardians when *they* went into service – as an investigation of the relevant minute books make clear. Thus, to take one example, at Banbury in north Oxfordshire during the year 1890, boys and girls of thirteen and fourteen were supplied with clothes to the value of two or three pounds before going into service with local tradesmen or clergy.

When the day at last arrived for a girl to leave home, she was normally taken in the local carrier's cart – along with the tin trunk or wooden box which contained her worldly possessions – to the nearest railway station. Very often, as Flora Thompson described, she would leave early in the morning, 'with her yellow tin trunk tied up with thick cord, her bunch of flowers [provided by the family] and brown paper parcel bursting with left-overs'. Perhaps it was the first time she had ever been on a train journey alone, while in any case, there would be a natural anxiety as she thought about the future in as yet unfamiliar surroundings.

Nor would this anxiety easily melt away when the girl at last arrived at her destination. For the work often proved hard and tiring, and despite any 'petty place' experience she may have had, the young servant moving into a large establishment would be bewildered by the unfamiliar complexity of life 'below stairs'. Discipline was strict and even in the late Victorian period might involve a beating or two for the younger girls. For, as a contemporary pointed out: 'No servant would have thought of giving up a place which was essentially a good one, because they were a little roughly handled by their mistress. In those days servants were as liable to personal chastisement as the children of the house and would as little have thought of resenting it.'[72] Occasionally the punishment went too far, however, as in the case of Emily Jane Popejoy, a sixteen-year-old carpenter's daughter from Bagshot in Surrey who was beaten and starved to death by her mistress in fashionable Kensington during the very last years of the nineteenth century. The mistress was eventually found guilty of manslaughter and sentenced to seven years' imprisonment. Significantly *The Times* of 3 May 1898, welcomed the verdict for the sake of 'the large class of female servants whose interests were involved, and who [were] often, through ignorance or poverty, as unable to protect themselves as was Jane Popejoy'. Although few suffered such ill-treatment as she had done, there is little doubt that the unsophisticated country child working in London was very much at the mercy of her employer.

Those girls who went into the kitchen began as scullerymaids, washing up stacks of dishes, cleaning saucepans and dish covers, 'preparing vegetables, and doing the kitchen scrubbing and other rough work. After a year or two of this, they became under kitchen maids . . .'[144] They were expected to do everything the cook told them, and had to treat all of the upper servants with the greatest respect. Even after World War I kitchen maids were expected to rise at about 5.30 a.m. and come downstairs to 'clean the flues, light the fire, blacklead the grate' and commence some of their other multifarious duties.[118] A few found the drudging work beyond their strength. Thus one of Amos Lelliot's daughters obtained employment in the kitchen of a large hotel on the Isle of Wight, but her health suffered from the heavy toil in the oppressive atmosphere of a basement kitchen. After a few months she returned home 'sadly pale and wasted and with her life almost despaired of'. Only after many weeks of rest and careful feeding up on milk and butter from Amos' solitary cow did she at last recover. Other victims, like Annie Langdown's cousin in Dorset, were less fortunate; they died of consumption.

Nor was it only that the hours were long and the work arduous. The accommodation provided was often inferior – many employers finding it convenient to subscribe to such views as that of Mrs J.E. Panton, in her *From Kitchen to Garret*: 'I should like myself to give each maid a really pretty room, but . . . I really believe servants are only happy if their rooms are allowed in some measure to resemble the homes of their youth, and to be merely places where they lie down to sleep as heavily as they can . . . A cupboard of some kind should be provided where they can hang up their dresses. But if this is impossible, a few hooks must supplement the chest of drawers, washing-stand, bedchair, and toilet-table with glass, which is all that is required in the room of a maid-servant. The sheets should be changed once in three weeks, also the pillowcases . . .'[116]

Free time was closely restricted. 'Like the children of the family, they had no evenings out, unless they had somewhere definite to go and obtained special leave.'[144] As late as 1899, the most generous holiday given by employers was reported to be: 'A fortnight in summer, one day monthly, half day every Sunday, evening out weekly.' But many fell far below this, especially in earlier years. Thus when the young Sarah Phipps (born 1869 at Broadwell in Gloucestershire) went into service at Loxley Hall near Stratford-upon-Avon, she only remembered going out 'once except to Church' during the few months she was employed there; and that 'once was to walk down to the main road to change a sovereign for the butler'. For most of the girls, in fact, their annual summer or autumn holiday of two weeks was their sole break with the daily grind. For those precious fourteen days they were able to return to the family home to meet their friends and relatives again. Very often at this time the younger children would be kept away from school in order to share in the excitement of the home-coming and reunion. At Brailes School in Warwickshire, for example, a regular log book entry in mid-October of every year during the 1870s was, 'Not so many children – sisters home for Holidays'. Or, 'Numbers much lower . . . sisters and brothers at home from service.'

Most of these young servants showed great generosity towards the more juvenile members of the family. At Juniper Hill it was said 'that some of them stripped themselves to help those at home . . .' Nor did their interest end with the holiday for, 'Many of them . . . would send half or even more of their wages home . . . [and] the mothers were so poor, so barely able to feed their families and keep out of debt, that it was only human of them to take what their children sent and sometimes even pressed upon them.'[144]

Of course, by no means all of the girls who left home for domestic service went to the kitchens. Some preferred housework and would be instructed in the arts of third or fourth housemaid by the 'upper servants [who] were their real mistresses, and . . . treated beginners as a sergeant treated recruits, drilling them well in their duties by dint of much scolding.'[144] Certainly these duties were extremely arduous: Mrs Beeton, for example, suggested that the housemaid should open the 'shutters of all the lower rooms in the house', take up the hearthrugs of the rooms 'which she is going to "do" before breakfast', sweep the breakfast room, remove the ashes and blacklead the grates – all before the family came down in the morning![30] Later there would be endless fetching and carrying to be done – coal to be carried up and down the steep stairs, and dusting, cleaning, and polishing to be completed. 'Architects put the coal store as far as possible from the kitchen in order to induce economy in the use of fuel.'[72]

One girl who became an under-housemaid in a large establishment in Scotland remembered that she was expected to scrub the main hall before breakfast, and then had to take the head housemaid a cup of tea in bed. Afterwards she was required to carry hot water in brass cans to her employers for their morning wash. The work was heavy, but she was allowed two hours off in the afternoon, after lunch, to go to her room. She then continued work until 9.30 p.m. when she was told to go to bed by the head housemaid. In addition, she had one half day a week off, plus every second Sunday half-day, but had to be back in the house by 9.30 p.m. on each occasion.

In many Victorian households, too, the servants were expected to attend regular morning or evening prayers, conducted by their employer, and on Sunday they were normally required to attend church. For this, as on all other occasions when they went out, maids must be 'neatly and plainly dressed'. Some even had to face inspection from their employer before they could venture forth. Nor did the matter end there, for not only had they to conduct themselves with propriety on the journey to church but when inside must observe the customary arrangements in regard to seating. At Langley Burrell in Wiltshire, for example, the two large houses in the village each had six maids who 'had to go to church on Sunday mornings, and sit in their proper order, from kitchen maid up to ladies' maid, or housekeeper – all wearing bonnets'. This was a typical situation.

Some girls became nursemaids. At its lowest level this could merely mean child minding for a neighbour or for members of a girl's own family – the sort of situation described by the mistress at Cublington School in Buckinghamshire during June, 1877: 'Agnes Beckill made twelve attendances in nine weeks – am told she is nursemaid to Mrs White in this village. Emily Biggs made nine attendances in nine weeks, helping her mother at home.' About three weeks later, Agnes was noted as having left permanently as she had 'gone out nursing'. Again, of the seventeen or so girls who left school at Brailes in Warwickshire during the period 1863–69 and for whom a specific reason for leaving was given, no less than five were to become nursemaids, as opposed to nine who went into general domestic service. School log books elsewhere reflected that general pattern, and it was no doubt this sort of situation which led Florence Nightingale to the discovery that at the time of the 1851 Census of Population 'nearly one-half of all the nurses, in domestic service, [were] between five and twenty years of age'.[54] Indeed, 508 were aged five to nine inclusive.

Of course, a number of girls earned a little money while still at school by looking after youngsters out of class hours. For instance, Sarah Sedgwick, the daughter of a gardener on a large north country estate, was paid around 4s a week for taking out children belonging to the big house. Then, when she was about fourteen, it was time to obtain a permanent situation, and so she moved to the nursery of a country house near Doncaster. There were two very young children to look after and as well as Sarah there was a head nurse, an under nurse and a maid to wait on the nursery. Sarah, as the most junior, had some of the least attractive chores to perform. As she recalled: 'I had to light the nursery fires at 6 o'clock, and

DOMESTIC SERVICE AND RURAL CRAFTS

I had my fire guard to clean . . . At 7.30 I had to call the head nurse with a cup of tea, and at 8 o'clock the children had their breakfast.' By ten the latter had to be out in their perambulators, and their walk would last for just over two hours. Luncheon was at one and was followed by a further outdoor excursion with the perambulators. After a 4 o'clock tea, the children were dressed up and taken downstairs to their parents in the drawing-room. Then came the return upstairs: 'there were their baths to get ready, all the water had to be carried. Then bed. I was supposed to be in bed myself at 9.30 but that was something which could not always happen to the minute, for with the washing, ironing and running in of ribbons I couldn't get done in time. We in the nursery lived very much on our own, in our separate world governed by the head nurse . . .

'The nursery staff were not expected to attend morning prayers, but we did go turn and turn about to church on Sundays. For this the staff and the two nurses wore black bonnets; in that first place I was considered too young for a bonnet, so I wore a little black hat. For Sundays and best I had a grey alpaca dress, in the nursery I wore cotton. All the uniform was paid for by the lady of the house . . .'[138]

Boys were usually employed in the larger establishments only – perhaps to help the gardener or as hall boys, or page boys or footmen: the hall boys were required to carry coals over the house, clean boots, and perform other miscellaneous functions. The range of duties required was made clear in the advertisements for boy servants, such as: 'Wanted – A strong respectable Lad, about eighteen to look after pony and trap, garden, clean knives and boots, and make himself generally useful. Wages 10s a week to live out.' Or, 'Wanted – A small, good-looking, and intelligent Boy, age from fourteen to sixteen. Strong, some knowledge of stable work and gardening, and to make himself generally useful.' Both of these advertisements appeared in the *Hampshire Chronicle* during August 1890, but there were many others of a similar type in all parts of the country during the Victorian period. Yet domestic service was never the draw for young male workers that it was for the females, and their numbers remained small.

During the first months and even years at work domestic servants had to endure much hard work and strict discipline. Most accepted the situation if not gladly at least with a certain philosophic resignation, seeing perhaps in the strict hierarchy of the large mansion an opportunity for their own advancement in the years to come. In addition, 'in the ordered, ceremonious life of the servants' hall, where distinctions of rank, from butler down to kitchen-maid, were meticulously observed . . . [a girl] would gain some idea of good behaviour.'[121] Food was normally plentiful, even if monetary payments were low and hours long. By 1899 it was estimated that, outside London, a female servant employed in general work and aged under sixteen years would receive an average annual money wage of £6 10s; at sixteen it would perhaps amount to £7 14s. For nurses employed in domestic service outside London and in the under-sixteen age group, the average wage was £6 8s per annum; for kitchen maids £5 18s and for housemaids, £8. But if these returns were pitifully small, equally there can be no doubt of the importance of young workers on the domestic scene.[23] It was they who filled the lowest ranks in the nation's army of servants, and who were expected to perform the least interesting tasks – and often the most laborious as well.

Although agriculture and domestic service continued to employ a large proportion of country children up to the end of the nineteenth century, a further, if less significant, outlet for boys lay in one of the traditional rural crafts. Sometimes this might take the form of apprenticeship in one of the large-scale workshops which were already growing up in the country districts – such as the quiet Anna Valley in Hampshire. Here 'it was the ambition of every boy . . . to work at Taskers', the local agricultural implement makers. For those who achieved their ambition, a formal indenture 'admitted them to the mysteries within the foundry gates' when they had reached the age of thirteen. Like all other apprenticeship indentures, its language was archaic but impressive, binding the youngster to serve for five years, during which term he was to serve his masters faithfully, 'their secrets keep, their lawful commands everywhere gladly do'. Care was likewise taken of the apprentice's morals: 'He shall not commit fornication, nor contract Matrimony within the said term. He shall not play at Cards or Dice Tables or any other unlawful games . . . He shall neither buy nor sell. He shall not haunt Taverns or Playhouses nor absent himself from his said Masters' service day or night unlawfully . . .' In the 1870s a further proviso was included: 'The said apprentice shall regularly attend a place of public Protestant worship twice on each Sunday during his apprenticeship.'[125] Yet irksome though these detailed restrictions may have appeared, they were a normal part of most indentures and were obviously accepted in that spirit by young workers at Taskers. (See Document J.) 'Few . . . transgressed and few left the works to become journeymen when sources of similar employment were so far afield. Instead, when they were "out of their time" most young men followed directly in the footsteps of their fathers in foundry, forge or erecting shop.' During the first year of their apprenticeship at the firm they were paid 3s a week, but this sum was gradually increased during the course of their training: and by the age of twenty-one a male employee could expect to earn about £1 a week. Work commenced at 6 a.m. and continued until 5 p.m., or later if overtime were required. There were two breaks during the day – one for breakfast, from 8 a.m. to 8.30 a.m., and the other, for luncheon, from 12.30 p.m. to 1.30 p.m.[125]

However, even at the end of the Victorian era employment opportunities in this type of establishment were limited, at least in the *rural* areas. More usual for the boy seeking apprenticeship to a country craft was a position in a small village

Helping father with deliveries for his florist's and gardening business, c. 1900. (The author)

workshop, where he would work alongside his master and perhaps one or two journeymen. And it was to the major crafts of smithing, wheelwrighting, shoemaking, carpentry and the like that these boys were normally apprenticed, although the actual numbers involved were always small (especially when compared to agricultural labour). For example, in Norfolk at the time of the 1871 Census of Population there were over 5,000 lads aged five to fourteen inclusive employed as farm labourers, farm servants or shepherds; but the blacksmiths in the same age range numbered a mere 67; saddlers 12; carpenters and joiners 64; and wheelwrights 9. A similar picture emerged in respect of Somerset, with 80 blacksmiths aged five to fourteen inclusive, 14 wheelwrights and 21 saddlers – compared to over 3,500 farm workers of the same age. In other counties much the same situation prevailed. And given that most boys would begin their apprenticeship at about the age of thirteen or fourteen, the figures indicate the small number of those engaged in learning the first stages of their trade at the time of the Census.

Furthermore, crafts of this kind tended to run in families, with a boy 'working in the shop where his father and his father's father had worked before him'.[75] Only a few boys came into a trade from outside – like Gaius Carley, a Sussex blacksmith who was born in 1888 the son of a farm bailiff, or the Tysoe blacksmith known to Joseph Ashby, who had been 'taken as a ploughboy' to learn his trade. Indeed, the premiums required in most cases for apprenticeship excluded the children of poorer families anyway, unless they could obtain help from a local charity or, still more rarely, from the Poor Law Guardians. The actual sums paid as premiums varied a good deal. Thus an indenture signed in 1841 by James Bennett of Walton-on-Thames in Surrey, a smith and farrier, and Frederick Woodruff, of the same place, the son of 'George Woodruff . . . Gamekeeper' required the father to pay the sum of fifteen pounds in order that his son might learn 'the Art of a Smith and Farrier'. In return for this Bennett agreed to accept Frederick for a five-year apprenticeship – under conditions similar to those listed by the Taskers – plus 'sufficient Meat Drink Lodging during the said Term'. The apprentice was also paid the sum of 6d per week for the first year, 1s per week for the second, 2s per week for the third, and so on until in the fifth year he received 4s per week. The father, for his part, was to find Frederick in 'all other Necessaries during the said Term'. However, at Southam in Warwickshire during the 1870s, the family of Timothy Blea, apprentice, had paid only an £8 premium when he was taken to learn the craft of wheelwright from a local craftsman named Urban Holt. Yet the premium paid by the family of James Woolgrove of Deddington, Oxfordshire to Moses Castle, a carpenter and wheelwright of Westcote Barton, in the same county, amounted, in 1860, to the substantial figure of £20. Obviously, sums of money like these were quite outside the scope of most agricultural labourers to pay for their children; and even the weekly wage of the apprentices was far too small to support them. For example, Gaius Carley, who did not live in with his master, only obtained 5s a week for the first year, and 8s for the second, when at the age of fourteen he began to learn the trade of blacksmith and farrier. He had been earning '6s a week . . . for bird scaring, muck spreading, stone picking and hop pole shaving' at the age of twelve on a local farm, before he made the change.[67] The benefits which would accrue to the craftsmen were, therefore, essentially long-term ones. (See Document J for conditions of other apprenticeships.)

Nevertheless, in certain parishes the existence of a charitable fund might open up the way to an apprenticeship for a boy whose family could not otherwise afford it. One parish where this regularly took place was Quainton in Buckinghamshire, and among the examples which could be quoted of the scheme in operation is that of William Jakeman 'a poor boy of the parish of Quainton' who was apprenticed to a carpenter for five years in 1900. Jakeman was aged sixteen at the time and, as was customary with this charity at the end of the nineteenth century, a generous premium of £40 was proposed – £20 being paid at once and the second £20 at the end of three years. In return the Master provided

An apprenticeship indenture of 1896 for Mark Padbury of Upper Tysoe, Warwickshire; he was apprenticed to William Gilks, a blacksmith, at Idlicote in the same county. (The author)

'sufficient meat, drink, washing, lodging and apparel, and all other things' or in lieu thereof the sum of 7s per week for the first year, 8s per week for the second, and so on. This was a similar wage to that paid to Gaius Carley in Sussex.

Badly-off boys who lacked the advantages of local apprenticeship charities might have a slight chance of obtaining an apprenticeship through the Poor Law Guardians – at least up to the middle of the nineteenth century. This was the continuation of a policy which dated back to the sixteenth century but which was then falling into disuse. Nevertheless, it was reported in 1843 that in the Hollingbourne Union of Kent, for example, a few labouring children were still being apprenticed – with premiums varying from £10 to £25 – to such trades as that of tailor or shoemaker; but significantly, it was also observed that the apprentices had 'commonly been cripples'. And, in the Holderness area of Yorkshire, a local witness, Christopher Sykes of Roos, recorded that in his part of the country 'parish apprentices [were] not common, excepting when a boy [was] not strong enough, and [would] not be able to gain a livelihood by out-door labour; then they [were] generally put to shoemakers and tailors.' Here the customary premium ranged between £5 and £10. In East Anglia rare cases of pauper apprenticeship were likewise mentioned, but most observers agreed that following the reorganization of the administration of Poor Law relief under the 1834 Poor Law Amendment Act the policy had largely been abandoned.[1] In its earlier days, too, it had been much abused, with children frequently 'apprenticed' to masters who treated them cruelly and gave them little or no real training.

But by 1850 most of these problems had been overcome and by whatever means a boy secured his apprenticeship, once the formalities had been completed he was ready to embark upon his new career. For those seeking to become blacksmiths and farriers, this normally meant a learning period of at least five years, at the end of which a practical test would have to be passed. Then it was customary for the young worker to go for two years as an 'improver' to another smith, 'a stage corresponding to journeyman in other crafts or trades. After this term he returned to his original master, as a master of the trade, qualified to set up as a smith in his own right.'[82]

The work of smithing was both heavy and tiring for the inexperienced. As Gaius Carley remembered, he had 'to get in the forge at six in the morning . . . My job was to keep the forge tidy, learn the size of iron nuts and bolts, stocks and dyes and different tools. Drill holes with the old machine . . . It was hard work swinging the heavy sledge hammer. One of the first tools I noticed and was taught to use. Soon I had to take the shoes off and finish the hoof and clench up . . . I began to get handy and began to master my fire and nail on a shoe and do several jobs at the fire.'[67] The blacksmith needed not only determination and diligence but also great physical strength, if he were to follow his calling successfully and this, too, had to be developed in the apprentice. At Brandeston in Suffolk it was apparently the custom after a few months to test a boy by requiring him 'to bend down, put both forearms under the anvil and lift it off the floor of the smithy. If at first he was unable to do this, he kept trying during the course of his apprenticeship till he had successfully completed the test. This . . . was a device to emphasize to the lad that he needed not only skill and intelligence but main strength to follow the craft of smithing.'[82]

Yet for boys who completed their training successfully there was the knowledge that their work played a vital role in the smooth running of the agricultural community – in repairing implements, shoeing horses and doing many other jobs, such as making 'a well-tempered hoe' or a sickle or scythe, perhaps produced with a particular worker's need in mind.[84] In addition, the smithy itself was usually one of the village social centres so a new apprentice was soon drawn well into the swim of local affairs. At Tysoe it was a normal thing for any man who had 'an idle moment to pass [to step] into the smithy to chat . . .

DOMESTIC SERVICE AND RURAL CRAFTS

Even the youngsters hurrying home from school [stopped] for a moment to watch the sparks flying from his hammer . . . and when the weather [was] inclement, and more especially when there [was] a long incessant downpour of rain, he [had] a company larger than the congregation of many a country parson at his Sunday morning services . . . Labourers with old overcoats or sacks thrown across their shoulders [turned] in to enquire of the smith whether the glass [was] 'up' or 'down' . . . The whole day long men and boys [were] coming to the shop with repairs to be effected . . . From mending the patten ring of Farmer Grimes's wife to soldering a kettle from the vicarage, mending the pedals of the schoolmaster's bicycle, fitting on the shaft of a navvy's shovel, or beating out a ploughshare, "orders" [were] poured upon the blacksmith.'[34]

A craftsman closely associated with the blacksmith in village life was the wheelwright, and here, too, the apprentice had problems to meet and overcome. As George Sturt recollected of his own early years in the family wheelwright's business at Farnham in Surrey, towards the end of the nineteenth century, the 'young apprentice's first task was to learn to use the tools of his trade', a job more easily said than done. Sturt recalled his own clumsy efforts to plane the surface of a felloe, i.e. one of the wooden sections on the rim of a wheel. 'The first step was to get a plane surface to work to – an apprentice's job – the beginning of all things in the wheelwright's craft. It is no exaggeration to say I hated it. Probably the plane was ill-sharpened and ill-set, and anything would have gone wrong; but resentment took hold of me against that innocent curve of the surface of the felloe under my plane . . . The felloe lay on one side, jabbed hard against the spiked bench-iron and with its rounded top surface towards me. It looked tractable enough. Yet when I tried to plane it, too often it jumped up over the bench iron, or proved cross-grained and would not let the plane "shoot" comfortably and smoothly from end to end.'[140] Indeed, according to Sturt it was a year or two before an apprentice was even 'equal to making and painting a wheelbarrow' – let alone moving on to the true purpose of his craft, making farm-waggons, carts, water barrels, barley rollers, etc.[140] Nor could the learner expect to emerge unscathed, for it was a saying in the trade 'that nobody could learn to make a wheel without chopping his knee half-a-dozen times'.

Many wheelwrights felt confident that once qualified they were masters not only of their own craft but also of that of the carpenter and joiner. At the same time they vehemently denied that a 'carpenter could . . . do wheelwright's work', because he lacked the appropriate apprenticeship experience. Nevertheless in many communities carpenters *were* employed on repairing and building waggons – among a multitude of other tasks. For an old Buckinghamshire village carpenter remembered, during his youth in late Victorian England there had been: 'No field for miles around, but had its gate that sooner or later would need repair; no farmer who did

147

not need his new cow-cribs, sheep-troughs, or ladders. No house, from the vicarage to the labourer's cottage, but had at some time or other a defect in its woodwork for which the services of our men would be required.'[126]

This particular carpenter had commenced his apprenticeship in the family business at Haddenham, Buckinghamshire, in the mid-1880s, when he was almost fourteen. Gradually he learnt the rudiments of the craft from the skilled men with whom he worked. He discovered 'how to saw upright and square, with the time-honoured threat of "hanging a plumb-bob from my nose" when I erred. They taught me the peculiar art of sharpening a saw, the irregular teeth of which were once described as "sow and pigs". With infinite patience they showed me how to plane wood straight, square and "out of wind"; how to drive a nail home without splitting or leaving the indent of the hammer on the face of the wood; the purpose and use of the various tools, the art of sharpening the rounds, hollows, and moulding planes, and the importance of keeping the left hand out of the danger zone when using a chisel, away from any slip that might occur. My neglect of this precaution resulted in a bad cut and a stiff finger joint . . .'

Other crafts, too, had their own special traditions and skills – crafts such as shoemaking, tailoring, baking, and even brickmaking. George Edwards, who was born in Norfolk in 1850, remembered helping to make bricks alongside his father in a local brickfield when aged barely seven: 'I was just man enough to wheel away eight bricks at a time'. In his village, brickmaking was a summer occupation, which was alternated with agricultural labouring, and there was, of course, no formal apprenticeship.[80] But the work was extremely heavy and proved beyond the strength of many of the children engaged upon it. (See Document I.)

Nevertheless even for those who did serve their 'time' in a trade in the approved fashion, by the end of the Victorian period certain of the old customs were already being undermined. The advances of technology were beginning to make some skills obsolete – the village tailor and shoemaker, for example, succumbed to the competition of mass-produced, machine-made clothing and boots; then, too, it was becoming less common for the apprentice to 'live in' with his master as a member of the family. An examination of the Census Returns shows that as late as 1861 the practice was still widely adopted. Thus, to take random examples, in the small south Oxfordshire village of Mapledurham at that date both the blacksmith and the wheelwright had an apprentice living with them. In each case the youth had been born in the nearby parish of Goring. And in the west of the county, at Spelsbury, the miller, John Martin, had a sixteen-year-old apprentice living in, while the shoemaker at Kingham likewise had a fifteen-year-old apprentice from Charlbury with him. These are but a few of the hundreds of similar instances that could be quoted from up and down the country. But by the 1890s the situation was changing; more and more apprentices were receiving a higher money wage in lieu of their keep, as both masters and lads sought to free themselves from the duties and responsibilities which residence by an apprentice in his employer's house inevitably entailed.

But some still stuck to the old ways, as Flora Thompson was to witness when at the age of fourteen she went to work in a village post office, near Buckingham, during the 1890s. Her employer (a woman) combined the job of postmistress with that of proprietorship of a business for shoeing and general smithing, which she had inherited. Here 'the foreman and three young unmarried smiths lived in the house, and each of these had his own place at table . . . [They] sat three abreast at the bottom end of the table . . . All meals excepting tea were taken in this order.' As befitted youngsters engaged in heavy work, the food provided for them was substantial and plentiful – 'boiled beef and dumplings, or a thick cut off a gammon, or a joint of beef. When they came in to go to bed on a cold night, they could be offered hot spiced beer, but not elderberry wine . . . Their huge meals and their beds in a row in the large attic were part of their wages . . .' Mrs Thompson significantly pointed out: 'The young men who still lived in did so from choice; they said they got better food than in lodgings, better beds, and had not to walk to their work at 6 o'clock in the morning.' While they ate their meals, they would 'talk of the horses they had been shoeing' and other matters connected with the trade.[144] But if they were content with their way of life, others were not and in the years that lay ahead they were to have few successors.

NOTES ON ADDITIONAL SOURCES USED

Reminiscences of Mrs Gertrude M.L. Anderson of Abingdon.

Reminiscences of Miss C. Pearce of Chippenham on life in Langley Burrell in the late nineteenth century.

Reminiscences of Mrs L. Bookham of Headington, Oxford, on life in a large mansion in Scotland.

Information on Sarah Phipps has been obtained from her daughter, Mrs Wallis, in a letter to the author dated 18 January 1970.

Information on Amos Lelliot and his family was obtained from the *Portsmouth Evening News* – 10 January 1969.

Pamela Horn, 'Female Domestic Servants in Victorian Oxfordshire' in *Top Oxon.*, No. 19, 1973/74.

Apprenticeship indentures have been consulted as follows: concerning Frederick Woodruff of Walton-on-Thames, Surrey, at the Museum of English Rural Life, Reading, D.63/1; concerning James Woolgrove of Deddington, Oxfordshire, at the Oxfordshire County Record Office, Misc. Gr. II; concerning William Jakeman of Quainton, Buckinghamshire, at the Buckinghamshire County Record Office, A.R. 47/66. Information on Timothy Blea obtained from Southam Petty Sessions Minute Book, QS. 116/10/1/4 at Warwickshire County Record Office – entry for 6 August 1877, dissolving the apprenticeship agreement at the request of Blea.

CHAPTER EIGHT

Church and Chapel

Oh ye, whom God has blest with wealth
  Have pity on the poor,
And snatch us from the sin and vice
  That lies around our door,
And let us by your aid be train'd,
  To walk in virtue's road,
To speak the truth, to live in peace,
  And learn the fear of God
Then shall we be content to dwell
  Where God has fix'd our lot;
Assur'd we all share in His love,
  For He forgets us not.

(Extracts from The Infants' Petition, which is included in *Wilderspin's Manual for the Religious and Moral Instruction of Young Children* (1845) and quoted by Rex C. Russell – *A History of Schools and Education in Lindsey, Lincolnshire, 1900–2* (Part 1, 1965), p. 7.

For most country children during Victoria's reign there were close links with organized religion – and especially with the Church of England. Indeed, prior to the 1870 Education Act, and to some degree thereafter too, it was the local vicar or rector who very often assumed responsibility for the establishment of a village school, and who helped to cover its running costs from his own income. In the eyes of both himself and his contemporaries 'the duty of educating the people had always been a religious one.'[122] Those clergymen who lacked the financial resources to carry out their duties in this direction often felt a deep sense of guilt and failure – as is perhaps exemplified by the incumbents of the two Oxfordshire villages of Blackbourton and Cottisford. In 1854, James Lipton, the vicar of the former, admitted pathetically to his bishop that his 'great want [was] a day school. I am shorn of my strength entirely for want of one. I could make use of the school for giving lectures at night and otherwise instructing my poor ignorant congregation.' At Cottisford, the rector similarly complained that only a 'most unsatisfactory' dame school existed but that nevertheless he could not 'see [his] way to raising funds for the building and maintenance of a school'. However, three years later the effort *had* been made in his case at least, and in September, 1857, the small, grey one-storied building was formally opened.

Sometimes, a clergyman would be able to obtain the financial help of a local landowner or certain of his well-to-do parishioners in order to discharge his educational obligations, but the response was an uneven one. For as HMI Blandford observed in respect of Lincolnshire in 1855: 'Great difficulty is experienced in raising adequate funds for the support of these schools, even under the most advantageous circumstances, and few persons are really aware what a heavy tax they are upon the parochial clergyman . . .'[129] The ungenerous attitude of Berkshire landowners was remarked upon by another HMI in 1858, when he reported that: 'Berkshire parishes are in general poor and thinly populated . . . and it does not appear that much interest is taken in the education of the poor by the wealthy lay proprietors, without whose aid the clergy, however great may be their exertions and sacrifices, cannot find the requisite resources for maintaining efficient schools . . .'[7]

Of course, not all children did attend Church of England schools. The British and Foreign School Society helped to set up establishments of a non-sectarian (but basically Nonconformist) character, while individual Nonconformists or Roman Catholics might take action on their own account. Thus in the Oxfordshire villages of Hook Norton and Launton, Dissenting schools were established as a result of local initiatives, and in the latter village the Congregational Day School dated back to 1845. It was held first in the Zion Chapel and then, from 1852, in a new purpose-built property. Even in 1878 its Supervisory Committee claimed that it had an average attendance of from 'thirty to forty children'. At Mapledurham, in the south of the county, the Roman Catholic squire financed his own school for the Roman Catholic children of the village from the 1850s to at least the 1870s.[100] These examples were mirrored in the experience of communities elsewhere.

However, one unfortunate side effect of this trend, where schools of different persuasions existed side by side within the same village, was the emergence of petty religious rivalries. At Loddiswell in Devonshire one such minor conflict arose between the National [Church] School and the British and Foreign School in the village. An entry in the National School log book for 1883 spoke of the British School master having 'enticed' children 'from this school to the British again', while in the following year, the British School log book complained of the vicar being 'engaged in a house-to-house visitation, and . . . trying to persuade the parents to send their children to the National School'.[133] Similarly at Crich in Derbyshire the master at the National School claimed in June, 1883, that when he and his wife were going home, about fifty of the pupils at the British School and their master 'shouted opprobrious epithets' at them; slightly earlier than this pupils at the National School had complained because children from the rival establishment had thrown stones and shouted 'names' at them. Not until the end of the decade were the two warring factions able to settle their differences.[103]

Rather more rarely, the conflicts might also be reported to the Education Department in London. Once such case arose in June, 1877, when the vicar of Bere Regis in Dorset wrote expressing concern that 'Inspection for Annual Grants [had] been promised to the Bere Regis British School, although the [Church] School accommodation provided by the Parish [was] amply sufficient to supply its educational requirements.' He obviously feared that the competition would weaken the Church School by attracting pupils away, and pointed out bitterly that: 'The Nonconformists in 1873 threw all the expense of fulfilling the requirements of the notice from the Education Department upon the managers of the Church Schools, by excepting their School from inspection. The Managers of Bere Regis Church of England Schools think that a great injustice had been done to them . . .' On this occasion the vicar's argument was accepted and the offer of inspection already made to the British School was withdrawn – to the fury of the Bere Regis British School Managers, who wrote an unavailing protest to the Education Department on 6 November 1877.

Fortunately, religious rivalries did not normally go quite as far as they appear to have done in these three cases, but there is no doubt that relations between Church and Chapel were often very strained.

In addition, after the passage of the 1870 Education Act non-denominational 'board' schools were set up in some villages, where the voluntary (i.e. religious) schools either did not exist or could not cater for all the children in the area. As we saw in Chapter 4, most clergymen were utterly opposed to the establishment of a school board in their parish and they exerted all their energies to prevent any church schools from falling into such hands. At the third annual meeting of the Lincoln Diocesan Conference in 1875, the Bishop of Lincoln expressed the fervent hope that members of his audience would 'do all they could to try to maintain the voluntary and denominational system of education . . . If they had a godless unchristian education they would have a godless unchristian people. If the system of School Board teaching was spread widely he would tremble for our civil and political institutions throughout the country.' His remarks were greeted with applause.[129] And as late as 1880 the Church was displaying its firm opposition in Derbyshire, when the Archidiaconal Conference meeting at Derby, in that year laid down as its policy 'never to allow a church school to pass out of the control of the Church so long as there is the power, at whatever cost of labour and anxiety, of maintaining it'.[103]

An examination of the situation towards the end of the nineteenth century leads one to the view that in the *country* districts at any rate clergymen were largely successful in their efforts. In 1895 it was estimated that 61.6 per cent of all elementary schools in England and Wales were Church of England ones – as opposed to 24.2 per cent connected with school boards and 6.2 per cent with the British and Foreign School Society. But in an agricultural county like Lincolnshire, Church Schools comprised no less than 71.7 per cent, and Board Schools 19.2 per cent of the total. Of course, some of these latter were established in the market towns of the county rather than the villages, anyway.[129]

Given the general links between education and organized religion, it is now necessary to examine the effect this had on the life of the individual country child.

First of all, despite the fact that the Church of England clergy took so active a role in the promotion of education, they sometimes had rather mixed views on the actual scope of the subject matter which should be taught. In 1858 it was noted that certain of them deemed 'the mechanical art of reading and writing, the text of the Church catechism and Mrs Trimmer, to be the aim of all education for the labouring classes, and conceive[d] that the development of the intellect which God gave to man for culture would tend to revolutionize society and unfit the poor man for his station in life.'[122] A year earlier than this, the then Bishop of Oxford, Samuel Wilberforce, had spoken about 'this outcry against taking children away from school to the land'. He had bluntly declared that, 'they did not want everyone to be learned men or to make everyone unfit for the plough, or else the rest of us would have nothing to eat.'[113] Although this was an extreme statement of one clerical viewpoint it was not entirely untypical. Nor had it completely disappeared by the end of the century – despite the effects of government education legislation in broadening the curriculum and, under the 1870 Education Act, in providing that 'no child was to be compelled to attend religious instruction' in any elementary school, church or otherwise, which was in receipt of a government financial grant.[64] Indeed, to the anger of many clergymen, school boards were even allowed to decide whether their school should give religious instruction or not. If it was provided, then 'no religious catechism or religious formulary . . . distinctive of any particular denomination was to be taught.'[64] And in order to facilitate the child's withdrawal from religious instruction, when desired, it was further laid down that this was to be given either at the beginning or at the end of a school session.

Nevertheless, only a minority of the more determined Nonconformist families took advantage of the latter provision. Roger Sellman notes that: 'Even in the most strongly nonconformist areas of North Devon, hardly ever was a child marked in

Boys at a Bible stall at St Giles's Fair, Oxford, c. 1880. They were doubtless more concerned to find out what was going on than to improve their religious knowledge. (Oxfordshire County Council, Department of Leisure and Arts)

the Admission Register as withdrawn from religious instruction in a church school, in villages where no British school was accessible'. He attributes this to 'parental ignorance' or 'unwillingness to stand in isolation against the local powers'.[133] More usual was the compromise adopted by the Purser family at Ilmington in Warwickshire. As young John Purser remembered, both of his parents were devout Methodists and 'Dad never went to work before he reached down the Old Book to read a few verses, and then they would pray together . . . I was not so attracted; I liked the chapel and its services. There was the village Bible Class, too, conducted by the Rector's eldest daughter . . . It was she who encouraged me, as well as others, to do a little Christian work, strengthening the influence of my parents. I distributed Christian tracts in some of the village homes on Sunday afternoon . . . as well as sometimes carrying with me the Wesleyan missionary box. Some of us were attending both Church and Chapel services.'[119]

Where religious instruction *was* given in the school, however, it tended to place great emphasis on the need for the labourer's child to 'know his place in society', and 'not to have ideas above his station'. Bible reading and the learning of the catechism were regarded as essential, and the vicar himself, or his wife or curate would normally visit the church day school each week to supervise these activities. As Joseph Ashby was to recall in connection with the school at Tysoe in Warwickshire, in the catechism the clergy 'laid much stress' on 'the Duty towards my Neighbour . . . Boys and girls must never "pick and steal", nor lie, nor have any envy of folk luckier than themselves; they must learn to labour truly to get their own living and order themselves lowly and reverently to their betters . . . the word "betters" was especially firmly underlined and annotated. It meant the Vicar himself and the man who paid your father's wage.'[63]

Similarly at Cottisford in Oxfordshire during the 1880s, Flora Thompson recalled the rector's Scripture lesson as consisting of 'Bible reading . . . of reciting from memory the names of the kings of Israel and repeating the Church Catechism. After that, he would deliver a little lecture on morals and behaviour . . . God had placed them just where they were in the social order and . . . to envy others or to try to change their own lot in life was a sin of which he hoped they would never be guilty. From his lips the children heard nothing of that God who is Truth and Beauty and Love; but they learned from him and repeated to him long passages from the Authorized Version, thus laying up treasure for themselves; so the lessons, in spite of much aridity, were valuable.'[144]

Sometimes the incumbent would extend his instruction beyond strictly religious matters, so that at Mapledurham School in Oxfordshire during the later 1880s the vicar gave dictation practice and geography lessons as well as teaching Scripture. And at Leckford Board School in Hampshire, the vicar, who was also the Correspondent for the Managers, 'tested the children in their Standard work' just before the annual visit of Her Majesty's Inspector, in November, 1876. Similarly, the clergyman's wife would attend at many village schools to give periodic guidance and even instruction on needlework or knitting to the girls. Apart from the importance of these subjects in the annual Government examination at the school, they were also regarded as essential accomplishments for children who were probably destined for domestic service on leaving school and who would later marry and have a home and family of their own to look after. At Mixbury School, Oxfordshire, during the 1870s the incumbent's wife regularly gave needlework instruction – as at the end of October and the beginning of November, 1875, when the master noted that she had visited the school each afternoon and had 'remained the whole time giving a sewing lesson'. But this was rather an intensification of her normal policy and usually she visited once a week only. At Wadenhoe Church School in Northamptonshire, similarly, the clergy

A YOUNG POSITIVIST.

Parson. "WHAT'S A MIRACLE?"——*Boy.* "DUNNO."——*Parson.* "WELL, IF THE SUN WERE TO SHINE IN THE MIDDLE OF THE NIGHT, WHAT SHOULD YOU SAY IT WAS?"——*Boy.* "THE MOON."——*Parson.* "BUT IF YOU WERE *TOLD* IT WAS THE SUN, WHAT SHOULD YOU SAY IT WAS?"——*Boy* "A LIE."——*Parson.* "*I* DON'T TELL LIES. SUPPOSE *I* TOLD YOU IT WAS THE SUN; WHAT WOULD YOU SAY *THEN?*" ——*Boy.* "THAT YER WASN'T SOBER!"

Village clergymen regularly visited the school to question children on their religious knowledge – or lack of it. (*Punch,* 1871)

156

took an interest in the school needlework – but here there might have been an ulterior motive in so far as it was the custom to sell the garments produced and the proceeds were used to help support the school. This was, incidentally, a not unusual way of raising extra funds, as the school log books clearly demonstrate. At Cublington, Buckinghamshire, an entry for 27 February 1877, recorded: 'The needlework and knitting sold; result very favourable.' And at Long Compton, Warwickshire, there was a rather sad entry on 30 July, 1898: 'Owing to the common use nowadays of flannelette, the sewing mistress has not found so ready a sale for unbleached and calico made garments as in previous years.'[120]

Nevertheless, despite the various examples of intervention in the teaching of other subjects, most clergymen confined their instruction to religious matters, and many took their duties very seriously – even if the results were not always what they would have desired. For instance, on 8 March 1872, the Revd Francis Kilvert, curate of Clyro, Radnorshire, ruefully confided in his diary that during the Scripture lesson at the local school that morning he had asked one of the girls, 'What happened on Palm Sunday?' and she had replied, ' "Jesus Christ went up to heaven on an ass." This was the promising result of a long struggle to teach her something about the Festivals of the Church.'[117] Other diary entries show that it was no isolated incident. In many cases children were set the task of learning hymns or prayers off by heart – often without understanding the meaning of what they were reciting. Mr G.A.N. Lowndes in *The Silent Social Revolution* (1969 edn., p. 9) records that his mother, who went to school in the 1880s, used to discuss 'with a bosom friend whether the words of the hymn they had been learning by repetition, ran "Pity me a simple T" or "Pity mice and plicity". Mice were obviously to be pitied because they got caught in traps and "plicity" was believed to be some unlucky type of lizard.' It was a confusion shared by many of their fellow pupils.

But apart from the necessity of satisfying the clergy – and teachers – on religious questions, children in church schools also had to face the prospect of an annual examination by Diocesan Inspectors, the first of whom were appointed in 1839 (the year which likewise saw the introduction of Government school inspectors). The Diocesan Inspectors were clergymen of the Established Church and at their examination a detailed knowledge of the Old and New Testament, the Catechism and the Prayer Book was expected, as well as hymn singing. In practice, the desired standard of achievement was not always forthcoming – as an investigation of their reports shows. Thus at Asthall School in Oxfordshire, the Diocesan Inspector noted in June, 1885, that although the 'catechism was fairly repeated . . . not much was known of its meaning . . . Standard I children were mostly very shy, some few answered pretty fairly questions on the early part of Genesis, but did not show much knowledge of the outlines of our Lord's Life. In the Upper Division, Standard II children did not answer much. Standards III and IV showed a fair knowledge of Genesis and Exodus and of the details of our Lord's Life, but they often answered at random. Repetition had been carefully prepared . . .'

In the middle of the century many of the Diocesan Inspectors seem optimistically to have expected still higher attainments and also to have examined in secular as well as religious subjects – albeit with the main emphasis on the latter. In the Woodstock Deanery of the Oxford diocese in 1854, for instance, the children were required to have 'acquaintance with the minute details of Scripture history. Old and New . . .' As a result, when the Inspector visited the village of Wootton he examined the pupils in 'Genesis and Exodus and the Gospel of St Luke – and [they] exhibited a thorough acquaintance with the text and history – also with the structure of the Church Catechism. The eldest class wrote a short history of some one of the Patriarchs with correctness and some cleverness.' Nevertheless, it is perhaps scarcely surprising that after this ordeal, by the end of the examination most of the girls were said to be 'beginning to flag'. At nearby Glympton it was approvingly observed that the small school was 'still remarkable for its quiet devotional character. The older children . . . continue to be well taught in Scripture Knowledge, Catechism, &c . . . Their quiet demeanour, general cleanliness, and Devoutness of manner is [sic], doubtless, owing to their continual intercourse with their superiors.'

Yet in spite of their efforts to maintain standards of discipline, religious instruction, etc., the Diocesan Inspectors were never regarded with the fear and dislike which were accorded to Her Majesty's Inspectors for much of the Victorian period. Indeed, as the century drew to a close the Scripture examination tended to lose most of the strictness and formality which characterized its government counterpart. In Derbyshire, for example, parents and friends were allowed to be present while the examination was in progress at some schools, and in a number of cases, too, the inspector would reward the pupils with a holiday because he 'wanted to make his visit as pleasant for the children as possible'.[103]

On the whole the reports issued also tended to be more complimentary than those produced by the HMIs – as a comparison of the two in school log books quickly demonstrates. Thus at the small school at Mapledurham in south Oxfordshire, the Diocesan Inspector spoke of the 'good progress' made by the scholars; 'much pains have, evidently, been bestowed on the Religious Instruction. The children showed good knowledge of their work and especially of the Old Testament subjects . . . The older children wrote some good accounts of the Old Testament characters.' On the other hand, the HMI found that although 'the discipline in School is satisfactory . . . I regret to say the condition of the attainments is not such as to justify me in recommending a Merit Grant . . .

Spelling is weak in all Standards, except the fifth . . . In Arithmetic . . . taking the School as a whole, only two sums out of every five set were correctly worked.'

This view of the relative kindness of diocesan inspectors is confirmed by Flora Thompson's memories of their annual visits to Cottisford. 'The examination consisted of Scripture questions, put to a class as a whole and answered by any one who was able to shoot up a hand to show they had the requisite knowledge; of portions of the Church Catechism, repeated from memory in order round the class; and of a written paper on some set Biblical subject. There was little nervous tension on that day, for "Scripture Inspector" beamed upon and encouraged the children, even to the extent of prompting those who were not word-perfect.'[144]

In addition to the regular instruction on religious matters given in school, children who attended church schools were usually expected to go to divine service on Sundays – and sometimes during the week as well. In certain places the entire school would march to church on at least one day per week, and in rare cases, still more frequently. For example, during part of the year 1870 children from Mixbury School in Oxfordshire were required to arrive at school as early as 8.15 a.m. every day in order that they might attend a church service before lessons began. At Tysoe, during Joseph Ashby's school days, part of each Wednesday morning was set aside for the same purpose, while at Asthall School, Oxfordshire, in the 1880s, Friday was the appointed day. Elsewhere – Long Compton and Wasperton in Warwickshire, and Wadenhoe in Northamptonshire are but three of hundreds of examples which could be quoted – attendance was confined to particular saints' days or important festivals of the church. Sometimes also the children took part in other church services – as at Long Compton on 26 April 1866, when an entry in the school log book recorded that the 'Children went to church because of a marriage in the village'. At Finmere in Oxfordshire in the middle of the century 'six white calico frocks' were kept specially at the school 'to be worn when wanted by as many of the school-girls at the funerals of infants. The girls were . . . required after a funeral to return straight to school.'[35] Again, on a rather different note, the Revd Francis Kilvert described in his diary the 'customary beautiful Easter Eve Idyll' at Clyro in 1870, with 'people arriving from all parts with flowers to dress the graves. Children were coming from the town and from neighbouring villages with baskets of flowers and knives to cut holes in the turf.'[117]

Nevertheless, whatever the practice in regard to week-day church attendance, at all of the schools Sunday church service had a special place in the lives of the pupils. Prior to the passage of the 1870 Education Act, it was not uncommon for the rules of church schools to include Sunday church attendance as one of their requirements. For example, at both Nuneham Courtenay and Launton in

Oxfordshire, the incumbent insisted upon the attendance of week-day scholars 'over seven years of age' at church on Sundays, and those who failed to attend without good reason were to be excluded from the church day school. In 1866 at least one Launton child was actually sent home from the day school because she had missed Sunday church attendance for eight weeks. At Bloxham in the same county, the school rules issued in January, 1855, similarly provided that: 'All children of churchmen that attend the week-day schools must also attend the Sunday schools, which commence at half-past 9 in the morning, and at 2 in the afternoon, when punctuality of attendance will be insisted upon equally as on weekdays.'[99] And at Kirton in Lincolnshire rules also produced about 1855 laid down that: 'All the Scholars are to attend both services in the parish church on Sunday, parents who prefer taking charge of their own children to church, are to state the same in writing on their admission. All others are to assemble at the school on Sundays at half-past 9 o'clock, a.m., and 2 o'clock, p.m.'[129] Countless other schools adopted a similar policy. Yet if the restrictions appear petty and authoritarian – as indeed they were in many cases – the reason for their inclusion can perhaps be appreciated by a consideration of what happened when they were not imposed. At the Oxfordshire parish of Tackley it was reported that the Wesleyan Sunday School had 'trebled its numbers when day scholars were not obliged to attend church Sunday school'. Few clerics were prepared to risk that situation arising in their own parishes if they could avoid it.

Yet despite all this careful emphasis on church attendance and on strict religious observance, before the enforcement of full-time school attendance from the 1880s onwards a number of children remained astonishingly ignorant on Biblical and doctrinal matters. In the Castleward area of Northumberland – a county with a fairly high reputation for educational achievement – a twelve-year-old boy interviewed at the end of the 1860s confessed that he did not know 'the name of Jesus Christ, Noah, Eve . . .' Again, in the Northamptonshire village of Cottingham at around the same time, the incumbent admitted that 'out of a confirmation class of 16 boys, one did not know the Lord's prayer, and five could not say two consecutive articles of the Apostle's Creed'. At Cranford in the same county, a boy of sixteen even told the obviously shocked rector *'that he had never heard of Jesus Christ!'*[2]

Furthermore, not all of the youngsters who regularly attended church and Sunday school derived a great deal of benefit from it. There were always a few who had to be reprimanded on Monday mornings by their teachers or the vicar for 'behaving badly in church' on Sunday or for playing marbles or playing 'irreverently' in the street on that day. And there were wilder spirits who were prepared to go still further. At Langley Burrell in Wiltshire in the early part of Victoria's reign it was apparently customary for the older boys and men to play 'football and hockey and other games . . . all over the common. The Revd Samuel Ashe, then Rector of Langley Burrell, used to go round quietly under the trees and bide his time till the football came near him when he would catch up the ball and pierce the bladder with a pin. But some of the young fellows would be even with the parson for they would bring a spare bladder, blow it, and soon have the football flying again.'[117] Such behaviour was regarded as disgraceful by most of the 'respectable' members of society, for in that age of strict Sabbatarianism the 'model' country child was expected to spend the brief hours away from Sunday school or church services in sedately reading an 'improving' book or perhaps, like Mrs Hilda Eriksen of Cropredy, in working at 'a special "Scripture puzzle"', which was 'kept in "the parlour" to do on Sundays'. A quiet walk round the village with father and mother, or a visit to relatives, was also permitted, but any form of play earned deep censure as unsuitable for the solemnity of the Sabbath.

For most children, then, Sunday was a day set aside for attendance at church or chapel, and for the young and active it was inevitably a rigid and daunting timetable – although one to be obediently followed, because rebellion was out of the question. Very often, as at South Marston in Wiltshire, the 'little boys and girls [would] march in all together, the boys cap in hand, cloutering along with heavy boots . . . The girls walk quietly round to the transept, leading little Jacky or Tommy by the hand, who turns his head over his shoulder and looks behind him all the way with wide open eyes, astonished to see so many people together.'[150]

Yet boredom and restlessness were unavoidable, especially on bright summer days, when the sunshine came into the otherwise dim church, sparkling through the small paned windows or entering via the open door. As Flora Thompson recalled at Cottisford: 'The afternoon service, with not a prayer left out or a creed spared, seemed to the children everlasting. The school-children, under the stern eye of the Manor House, dared not so much as wriggle; they sat in their stiff, stuffy, best clothes, their stomachs lined with heavy Sunday dinner, in a kind of waking doze . . . Only on the rare occasions when a bat fluttered down from the roof, or a butterfly drifted in at a window, or the Rector's little fox terrier looked in at the door and sidled up the nave, was the tedium lightened.'

A regular theme for the sermon at Cottisford Church – as at so many churches elsewhere – was the 'duty' of regular church attendance. But, as Mrs Thompson points out, the rector would hammer away at that for forty-five minutes, never seeming to realize that he was preaching to the absent, that all those present were regular attenders, and that the stray sheep of his flock were snoring upon their beds a mile and a half away. Another favourite subject was 'the supreme rightness of the social order as it then existed.'[144] Indeed, as Mrs Eriksen remembered, 'the sermon was a thing to be endured.'

SUNDAY SCHOOLING.

Teacher. "WHAT DOES ONE MEAN BY 'HEAPING COALS OF FIRE ON SOMEONE'S HEAD,' NOW, HARRY HAWKINS?"
Harry Hawkins. "GIVIN' IT 'IM 'OT, TEACHER!"

An idealized Sunday school class. (*Punch*, 1885)

For some youngsters the lengthy service would perhaps be enlivened by membership of the church choir – although this also carried with it the duty of weekly choir practices. Nevertheless, membership of the choir was regarded as an honour in some parishes; at Mapledurham, for example, only those children were permitted to sing in it whose 'scholastic achievements warranted it'. Elsewhere, and more logically, singing ability and a general 'good character' would be the relevant requirement. Other children found outlets for their boredom in whispering and giggling among themselves – offences which brought retribution on Monday morning. One such young transgressor, Thomas Hall, who attended Farnborough Church, Warwickshire, in the earlier part of the nineteenth century, later described his childish diversions: 'Old John Allen, the clerk used to occupy a desk by the side of the pulpit, he was a faithful old man but subject to the weakness and frailty of human nature, and sometimes on the

Sunday afternoon he would indulge in a short sleep during divine worship. John did not wish to omit any part of his duty and so when he awoke from his slumbers he sometimes said a-a-amen at a very improper part of the service and greatly to the amusement of the juvenile part of the congregation.

'In the chancel on the left-hand side sat the ladies and gentlemen from the Hall; on the right-hand side sat the servants and we school children occupied the steps leading to the communion table. We children always watched the arrival of the occupants of these pews with great interest and when the gentlemen and ladies had taken their seats the butler and footman also took theirs. These latter always turned towards the east and shielded their faces from the opposite side with their hats under pretence of performing their devotions but in reality to make ugly faces which caused the schoolboys to laugh. If we were detected in this we were punished on the following Monday morning at school although the fault was not ours.'

Sunday schools – those other Sabbath-day refuges of the children – were not very much more inspiring to the average youngster than divine service. Most of the time was taken up in Scripture reading and in study of the catechism – the sort of thing which was covered in the religious instruction at the day school. Sometimes the incumbent or his wife, or members of his family, would assist at the church Sunday school, but often voluntary help was relied upon – and this was, in any case, customary in the Nonconformist Sunday schools. Very often the teacher would be academically ill-equipped for his task, having only personal sincerity and integrity to recommend him. This was not always sufficient, as the Vicar of Deddington in Oxfordshire frankly admitted, when he wrote in 1854: 'The Sunday schools do not retain the young people, except now and then as teachers. The education in the daily school has been so good, that the first class of Boys know more than the old Sunday school Teachers; and are, as monitors, much better catechists than those who come on Sundays to instruct them.' Occasionally formal manuals were used to help in the instruction – such as J.M. Chanter's *Help to an Exposition of the Catechism of the English Church for the Use of her Younger Members*, or H. Hopwood's *Progressive Exercises on the Church Catechism*, but in general equipment was poor or non-existent. Nevertheless, encouragement to attendance was given by the provision of Sunday school prizes for those who had the best record in this respect, while each year there would be the Sunday school treat to look forward to. Furthermore, however boring the subject matter might be, any child who too obviously displayed a lack of interest or who became too high spirited and noisy ran the risk of receiving a sharp tap from the long cane which was kept by the teachers for just such occasions.

It seems, also, that the revivalist character of certain of the Dissenting Sunday schools served to keep the children more alert and attentive. William Edwards,

163

who was born into a Nonconformist family in the Lotting Fen area of Huntingdonshire in 1870, regularly attended the local Wesleyan Sunday school and later remembered: 'I used to be frit to death at the old men who run the chapel when I were a child . . . [They] were associated in my mind with the tales they used to tell us littl' uns at Sunday school about hell-fire and the bottomless pit, and the Angel of Death coming to fetch good children to heaven and the Devil coming to fetch bad children to hell, and so on. I used to sweat all over wondering which one on 'em 'ould come to fetch me, for I used to come out o' Sunday school convinced I coul'n't live till the next Sunday . . . Most o' the services were took by "local" preachers, though it depends what you mean by "local". They were lay preachers from the other villages round about, but some on 'em come from as far away as eight or nine mile . . . One man I knowed walked eight mile or so each way nearly every Sunday to take a service somewhere. The congregation used to take it in turns to have the preacher to tea, and a great occasion it were for the family. The child'en 'ould all be schooled for days aforehand about minding their manners, and then they'd all sit round the table scrubbed and washed and not daring to speak while the stranger was there.'[112]

Mr Edwards also explained why his family – like a number of other labouring people – attended chapel in preference to church: '. . . it seemed as if we 'ad more aright there than we 'ad in church, what was run by the big farmers and the rich folk. I used to like to hear the parsons at the church talk, with their eddicated voices and their long words, but they were a queer lot, all the same, and thought theirselves a lot better than the folk they were supposed to serve in the Lord's name. Whenever we met old Parson Harper or his wife, we had to stop until they'd gone by, and touch our caps and bow our heads, and the girls 'ould 'ev to curtsey.' Some youngsters felt still greater bitterness – like Joseph Arch, the Warwickshire-born agricultural trade union leader. In his autobiography Arch described, perhaps with a measure of sectarian bias, how in the parish church 'the poor man and his wife were shown pretty plainly where they came among their fellow-creatures and fellow-worshippers . . . In the parish church the poor were apportioned their lowly place . . . I never took the Communion [there] in my life. When I was seven years old I saw something which prevented me once for all . . . First, up walked the squire to the communion rails; the farmers went up next; then up went the tradesmen, the shopkeepers, the wheelwright, and the blacksmith; and then, the very last of all, went the poor agricultural labourers in their smock frocks. They walked up by themselves; nobody else knelt with them; it was as if they were unclean . . .'[27] Arch became a Primitive Methodist local preacher while still in his twenties.[98]

Yet if a few labouring families shared the feelings of Edwards and Arch towards the paternalistic but authoritarian village society of their youth, most accepted clerical interference in the running of village affairs with resignation. A number were no doubt grateful for the interest taken, for the patronage had its material compensations. Certain of the clergy, for example, provided clothing or uniforms for children attending their school; at Mixbury in Oxfordshire, Mrs Palmer, the wife of the rector, regularly bought the girls pinafores, dresses and bonnets, while in the early 1850s the incumbent of Mapledurham, in the same county, displayed a like generosity. He supplied a uniform of 'green tunics with black buttons and corduroy trousers, and peaked caps' for the boys, and 'green frocks and white straw poke bonnets trimmed with green ribbons tied in a bow under the chin' for the girls.[110]

Again, in times of illness, many clergymen provided special foods or even medicines. One such was Augustus Hare, incumbent of Alton-Barnes in Wiltshire in the early 1830s. In addition, Hare kept 'a shop, in which he sold at two-thirds of the cost price all kinds of clothing and materials . . . The shop was held in the rectory-barn once every week, when Mrs Hare attended and measured out the flannels, fustian, &c.' His gesture was greatly appreciated by the poorer parishioners. Similarly, at West Malvern in Worcestershire during the 1880s and 1890s, the curate's wife and some of the better-off ladies each took responsibility for a certain district of the parish; broths were provided for the needy families and the sick, and 'clothes which were worth passing on were passed on'. At one time, too, the local doctor and district nurse came every morning to consult with the curate 'as to who needed medical attention'. And at Wootton Courtenay in Exmoor the rector, alarmed at the shortage of milk for labouring children, kept a few cows so that he could provide free milk for them. This sort of practical help was apparent in the experience of other village communities in Victorian England.

A number of churchmen likewise expressed concern at the poor condition of cottage accommodation, and sought to arouse landowners and farmers to a sense of their responsibilities in this direction. One such was Archdeacon Lane Freer of Hereford, who bluntly told the Herefordshire Agricultural Society in October, 1856: 'It is in vain that we build schools, it is in vain that the clergyman preaches morality, and reverence to God and duty to parents; it is in vain that the schoolmaster teaches order, sobriety, and decency, if the moment the unfortunate scholars are released from school, they [return] to the abject misery and disgraceful wretchedness of a home, compared to which a well-ordered pigstye is a palace, and in which not one of you would place your horse for shelter on a winter's night . . .'[43] This was a theme to which he returned on more than one occasion.

Clerical patronage might also take a different form from a mere straightforward concern with the material conditions of the life of the poor. To the brighter child, the incumbent could on occasion give personal tuition, if his interest were aroused. Thus in the small Lincolnshire village of Welbourn, where during the 1860s and 1870s the school was said to be 'virtually owned' by the rector, the future Field–Marshal Sir William Robertson received assistance in this way. Robertson's father, the village tailor and postmaster, had little money, but the rector, 'although a stickler for social conventions . . . liked to encourage a promising boy. He soon picked out Will, and had him up to the rectory for extra lessons with his daughters, then learning French from a *Mademoiselle*.' After leaving school the young Robertson worked for a few months as garden boy at the rectory 'and so managed to continue his education'.[69] Four years later, in 1877, he joined the Army.

Of course, not all of the gifts bestowed by the clergy were of such a substantial or worthwhile character as those already quoted. Many incumbents were themselves too badly off to afford such ambitious schemes as, for example, the provision of a school uniform for large numbers of children. Nevertheless, to the children of labourers even small presents were acceptable. At the little Oxfordshire parish of Shutford during the 1860s, the curate gave an orange to 'each child who attended [school] twice on . . . Valentine's Day', while at Long Compton, Warwickshire, a log book entry for 3 February 1875, noted that the vicar had given the children 'a half holiday and also . . . two oranges to each of the little ones'.[120] But among the most exciting of these small celebrations were those which occurred around Christmas time. Very often they would include the singing of carols and recitations, which the clergymen and his wife, and perhaps some of their friends, would attend. Then the children were given sweets and oranges, or possibly, towards the end of the century there would be the special thrill of Christmas crackers and a magic lantern entertainment to follow. The impression made by these events was often a lasting one. Thus a former pupil at Blaxhall School in Suffolk could remember after more than seventy years that at Christmas 'the Rector made a Christmas tree at the school. The children sang carols . . . afterwards it was the Rector's delight to scatter nuts about the school and watch the children scramble for them.'[81]

Sunday school prizes and 'treats' were further ways in which the local clergy could give pleasure to village children. Although the prizes were usually of a rather boring character, chiefly consisting of 'improving' books or tracts, at least they were *something* in homes where books of any kind were rare. Certainly at Ilmington, John Purser was proud to recall more than half a century later that in 1890 he had received 'a large Family Bible' as a prize 'for being the best in religious knowledge'.[119]

But the 'treats' had a wider appeal. They might take the form of an outing by waggon or train, or, as at Tysoe, of a tea on the vicarage lawn. The young Joseph Ashby recalled with relish: 'There was cake at the tea – a wonderful change from bread and lard. Games on the slope of Old Lodge, the beloved familiar hill rising behind the Vicarage, finished the day for the young children.'[63] At Ilmington John Purser remembered the children being marched by the schoolmaster from the church school to the Rectory park. 'It was a beautiful place. There they would enjoy themselves, till called to sit in a circle for tea, a thing most of them had been looking forward to for days. Some boys would have no dinner, so that they could have a good "tuck in". It was good fare, such as they were not used to: fresh bread and butter, tea brought round in big jugs to fill their tin mugs, and two sorts of cake. The Rector, with his wife and four daughters, enjoyed the fun of serving, and seeing them eat. It was all done in perfect order; they said grace as they stood; and at the close, sang a retiring hymn, cheered their thanks, and left with a few nuts each in their mugs.'

Some of the 'treats' were rather more boisterous than this. In the Lotting Fen district of Huntingdonshire the young Kate Edwards remembered during the 1880s and 1890s that at the local Methodist Sunday school treat: 'We used to dress up in our best clothes and go off . . . about 3 o'clock in the afternoon carrying our mugs. Then we set down in a ring and the helpers brought tea round to us, and bread and butter and cake.

'After tea, there'd be the scrambling for nuts and sweets . . . the Sunday-school superintendent would pelt 'em about the field as far as he could all round him, we'd all scramble for 'em, and we kep' all what we could get . . . After the scrambling we'd play games. There were the round games like "Jinny sets a-weeping" and "Green Gravel" and "There stands a lady on the mountain . . ." Then there'd be round tag and long tag, and when the mothers began to come, they'd join in "There was a jolly miller" until it began to get dusk.'[112]

At Silverstone in Northamptonshire about the middle of the nineteenth century the church Sunday school treat was regarded as one of the major events of the year; at the same time it was also a chance to show rivalry with the Nonconformists (i.e. Meetingers) of the locality. As the Revd J.E. Linnell, who took part in the celebrations as a child, recalled: 'We had flags; [the Meetingers] regarded them as sinful vanities. We had a band; they considered it of Satan, satanic. Our march around the town was a triumph; theirs was the tamest affair imaginable. For more than fifty years the tea was held in the big Club barn of the "Compasses", while the sports took place in the adjoining paddock. Mine host, for many years an honoured church-warden of the parish, always saw to it that the barn was converted into a veritable bower . . . How the teetotallers of the present day would have regarded the arrangements I cannot imagine. All who wished well to the school sent home-made wine to the treat. This was carefully

A Sunday school outing on the Brecon–Newport canal near Gilwern, *c.* 1910 (National Museum of Wales (Welsh Folk Museum))

tasted on arrival by a select band of experienced teachers, who divided it into two classes, the less alcoholic to be drunk by the children, the strong to be set aside till later on in the evening. After the sports were ended . . . the Evening Hymn and the National Anthem were sung, cheers were given for the Royal Family, and then every boy and girl received a glass of wine and a piece of cake before departing to their homes.'[108]

Unfortunately, the element of sectarian rivalry displayed at Silverstone was often present in Sunday school celebrations elsewhere; only rarely was it possible for church and chapel to join together in a single celebration, as they did at Fulstow in Lincolnshire at the end of the 1860s, when about 300 'persons, young and old' went by waggon to Cleethorpes for their outing. 'The Fulstow band accompanied the expedition, and added greatly to the enjoyment of the day.'[129] But many Sunday schools organized outings on an *individual* basis, to the considerable excitement of their pupils. One child who remembered joining in regular expeditions from his small south Hampshire village to the nearby seaside resorts of Netley or Lee-on-Solent, recollected that 'everybody went in their best clothes. Their transport was a steam traction-engine, normally used for operating and pulling the threshing tackle, towing behind one or two trailers in which the folding wooden forms from the Sunday-school had been arranged for seating. Often the best clothes, after this trip, were punctured with small burn-holes, where tiny red-hot particles had blown back from the chimney of the engine. The speed would be about five miles an hour and the journey was one to be remembered . . . When the sea was reached, everybody paddled. Nobody bathed in those days. Tea, at Netley, was always taken in the Abbey grounds, followed by exciting chases around the ruins, while at Lee we ate in a kind of wooden hut, used, I think, as a café.' Yet if few children could boast such an impressive form of transport as a steam traction-engine and trailer, most who went on Sunday school outings would share in the other entertainments mentioned.

For Nonconformist children there was also the special anniversary celebration to look forward to, as well as the Sunday school treat. In some parishes, indeed, the two events were held on consecutive days. Kate Edwards remembered the Sunday school anniversary as 'the child'ens very own day . . . The Sunday school teachers had been teaching 'em special hymns for weeks, and between the hymns such children as dared and could learn their "piece" said recitations or sung little hymns in pairs or even an occasional solo . . . Among the girls, the secret o' what they were going to wear were kept as if their lives depended on it, and many a mother has dragged out to work for weeks in the field to be able to buy the new things for the anni.'[112] Most of the Sunday school anniversaries were of sufficient importance to be reported in the local press – as an examination of provincial newspapers soon reveals. Thus, to take one example, the *Norfolk News* of 29 May 1875, described the 'Sabbath school anniversary' held by Docking Primitive Methodists: 'In the afternoon and evening the children recited dialogues and other pieces, which they did in a very creditable manner . . . On Monday the children, teachers, and friends marched in procession through the village, after which 140 children and nine teachers and friends partook a nice tea, at the conclusion of which other pieces were recited. Mr Simmons gave each child an orange for every piece recited on Sunday or Monday.' Every year countless similar events were described from all parts of the country in the various local newspapers.

Finally, in a few communities the Sunday School movement became linked with the temperance cause – that persistent preoccupation of the Victorian social conscience. At Ilmington, for example, the Rector's eldest daughter started a temperance club for young people. To counter their beer-drinking habits, she hired a room and sold soft drink. But elsewhere the temperance cause would be more formally espoused by the establishment of branches of the Band of Hope. The term 'Band of Hope' had first been applied in 1847 by a Mrs Anne Carlile to groups of Leeds Sunday School children who were organized for temperance work. Mrs Carlile was the widow of an Irish Presbyterian Minister, and the movement enjoyed much early support from Nonconformists. Children who

Yeolmbridge Band of Hope, Cornwall, meeting at the end of the Victorian era. The Band of Hope was established to protect children against the 'demon drink'. (Museum of English Rural Life, Reading)

joined were encouraged to sing temperance songs and, if possible, to influence their parents on the evils of drink. In 1870, it was suggested by the leaders of the movement that meetings should begin with a temperance hymn and prayers, followed by music, readings, recitations, etc.[93] In addition, special outdoor meetings or picnics were to be organized for the young temperance supporters. In its early days the Band of Hope was primarily concerned with children living in the larger industrial centres, but gradually its influence spread and village branches were also established. For example, in the small South Oxfordshire village Mapledurham, an entry in the school log book for 25 November 1889, recorded that, 'A Band of Hope was opened today' by the vicar's daughter 'for the school children', while at nearby Whitchurch the school was closed regularly on one day each year during the 1890s, to permit the pupils to attend 'a

Temperance fête, at Purley . . . Many of the children [are] . . . members of the Band of Hope Union.' At the Wesleyan School at Childrey in Berkshire similarly an entry in the school log book for 15 July 1897, reads: 'School closed this afternoon. Band of Hope Temperance Fête . . .' In many other villages and market towns support was likewise demonstrated.

Yet not all of the efforts were a success. At Banbury, where a branch was formed in 1855, weekly meetings were held at the different Sunday schools in rotation; at the first meeting in the Unitarian Sunday School, 'thirty children signed the pledge; but the movement soon died out and had to be revived in 1861'.[94] Although some early converts remained loyal to their principles throughout life, few seem to have possessed the necessary crusading spirit to give the movement real impetus and the Band of Hope exerted but a limited influence within the temperance cause.

Nevertheless, through this, and through the other agencies which have been discussed, both church and chapel were able to exert a considerable pressure on the lives of country children during the Victorian period. If the impression made was not always as permanent as most clerics hoped, at least their teaching formed a background to day-to-day existence, and one to which some youngsters later looked back with nostalgia – 'how lucky are those families who were brought up to regard [church] as one of the most natural things in life – Sunday with church and quiet happiness at home'. Or perhaps (as with the young Richard Hillyer, in his autobiography, *Country Boy*) it was the chapel which 'brought independence, and a feeling that they had something of their own into lives that were stinted of every other freedom. It comforted them with warm and beautiful words like Beulah Land, Jerusalem the Golden and Redeeming Love.' Even for those who felt no such emotional attachment there were always the Sunday school treats and outings to look forward to – bright spots which ranked alongside other precious but all too few 'high days and holidays' in the juvenile calendar. (See Document K.)

NOTES ON ADDITIONAL SOURCES USED
Bishop Wilberforce's Visitation Returns for the Archdeaconry of Oxford in the year 1854 (Oxfordshire Record Society publication no. XXV, 1954).
For information on Bere Regis schools see Parish Records for Dorset at Public Record Office: Ed. 2.126.
Report of Diocesan Inspector of Schools – Deanery of Woodstock, 1854, at Oxfordshire Record Office, MS. Oxf. Dioc. Pp. e. 51; Report of Diocesan Inspector of Schools – Deanery of Reading, 1854, at Oxfordshire Record Office, MS. Oxf. dioc. Pp. e. 50 for examples of Diocesan reports on the schools.
Reminiscences of Thomas Hall of Farnborough. Thomas was born about 1817 and his reminiscences were written at the end of the nineteenth century. I am indebted to his

descendants, Miss Alice Hall and Miss Mildred A. Hall of Stratford–upon–Avon for this information.

P. Smith – 'Somerset and Dorset Labourers in 1872' (Unpublished article). I am indebted to Mr Smith, formerly of Oxford Polytechnic, for permission to quote from his article.

P.J. Bignell – 'Chapel Life of Yesterday' in *Hampshire County Magazine*, March, 1962.

Reminiscences of Mrs Gertrude M.L. Anderson of Abingdon in an interview with the author, winter, 1971.

Reminiscences of Mrs H. Eriksen, Cropredy, Oxfordshire, in correspondence with the author.

CHAPTER NINE

High Days and Holidays

Gentlemen and Ladies,
 We wish you happy May
We come to show our May garland,
 Because it is May-day.

(Verse of a May Day song from Souldern, in Oxfordshire, sung by children as they carried their garlands of flowers around the village, on 1 May. Quoted in J.C. Blomfield – *History of Souldern* (1893).)

Throughout the Victorian period most working-class country children had little time for recreation free from the cares of school, household chores and paid employment. Because of this, such opportunities for enjoyment as did come along were eagerly seized. As soon as the chance arose youngsters would hurry outside to amuse themselves with hoops, skipping ropes, tops and marbles, or perhaps merely run wild in the fields in search of flowers, birds' nests and the tracks of animals. As a Sussex farmer's daughter remembered of her own childhood: 'The appearance of a rare bird was a great excitement at the quiet farm. Once we watched for a whole morning a hoopoe investigating the ant hills around the tennis lawn but never once did it rear its noble crest. An eagle, unmistakable by its digitated wings, once flew over . . . Even the smooth hill turf was full of living interest. We used to lie on our stomachs to watch the many small creatures which were pursuing their busy lives among the grass roots.'[124]

At other times the games would be more formal – as at Juniper Hill in Oxfordshire and the Lotting Fen district of Huntingdonshire during the 1880s and 1890s, when the girls regularly organized dancing or rhyming games among themselves. On a summer evening, when their other chores were finished, they would gather on one of the green open spaces 'and bow and curtsey and sweep to and fro in their ankle-length frocks as they went through the game movements and sang the game rhymes as their mothers and grandmothers had done before them'. At Juniper Hill they had a large repertoire, 'including the well-known

173

games . . . such as "Oranges and Lemons", "London Bridge", and "Here We Go Round the Mulberry Bush"; but also including others which appear to have been peculiar to that part of the country. Some of these were played by forming a ring, others by taking sides, and all had distinctive rhymes, which were chanted rather than sung.'[144]

But the boys found such sedate pastimes dull and restrictive. They spent their time in tree climbing, fishing and 'fox-hunting', where one of the swiftest runners in the group would act as the fox, and would be chased by the rest. When eventually the 'fox' was captured, panting and hot, after an exciting cross-country run, he and the 'pack' would throw themselves down on the warm grass to rest. In their brief idleness some of the more restless souls would 'strip the bark of the young ash or sycamore, and make whistles or pop-guns from elder, or make cowslip-balls or plait rushes into whips . . .'[150]

Others, like the young Alfred Williams of South Marston in Wiltshire and Joseph Ashby of Tysoe, preferred impromptu games of cricket and football. Already by the 1860s cricket was coming into prominence at Tysoe; 'the fame of Surrey and Wiltshire county cricket had reached [the village], and the boys were making home-made bats and bowling along the smoother bits of road'. Elsewhere cricket teams were being formed at some of the schools and matches arranged with local rivals. At Long Compton in Warwickshire, for example, an entry in the school log book for 1 July 1868, recorded: 'Gave a half holiday in the afternoon, as the boys are going to play a cricket match with Whichford school boys.'[120] And at the Buckinghamshire village of Haddenham, later in the century, the young carpentry apprentice Walter Rose decided to add to his pocket money by making cricket bats in his spare time. He and another apprentice 'obtained some cleft red willow from the village hurdle-maker, and I entered into contract – the first of my life – to make a bat for the village junior cricket club for fourpence. Red willow, though suitable for the blade, is not strong enough for the handle . . . At the first time of using, my bat broke off short at the handle, and an indignant group of boys met me on the village green to get their money back.'[126] But for most youngsters a rough home-made bat or even a piece of wood had to serve their purpose. They could not afford more expensive refinements.

Stilts provided a further source of amusement; at Tysoe the boys would make their own and 'would act the beginning of half a dozen stories' while perched precariously upon them. At Langley Burrell in Wiltshire children were playing with stilts even in the 1890s, and one who took part in these games remembers them as a source of accidents for her youngest brother, who would fall off 'in the middle of a pond etc.' Many other small boys no doubt shared his misfortunes.

The late summer and autumn was, of course, the time for gathering nuts, blackberries, and mushrooms, while in winter skating and sliding on frozen streams or flooded meadows were favourite pastimes. The skates would usually be home made – rough and clumsy looking, but quite good enough to provide many hours of happy exercise. On the other hand, especially in the early and mid-Victorian period, some of the older lads would spend their time less satisfactorily, drinking in the public house, or playing bowls in the bowling alley.[27] It was they who often became the objects of the temperance movement's most determined efforts.

Yet, there were more respectable entertainments during the winter as well – such as the Penny Readings, which were warmly welcomed by both adults and children in those days when many were still barely literate. The Penny Readings at Clyro in Radnorshire in the 1870s were so popular that 'the room was . . . crammed, people almost standing on each other's heads'. On one occasion, those who could not get into the room, clung 'and cluster[ed] round the windows, like bees, standing on chairs, looking through the windows, and listening, their faces tier upon tier. Some of them tried to get through the windows when the windows were opened for more air.'[117] Similarly, if less enthusiastically, at Rollesby in Norfolk during February 1875, children as well as adults took part in a 'musical and reading entertainment' which was held in the evening. According to the local press, the Sunday school children sang 'Twinkle, Twinkle Little Star', and 'two juvenile scholars' recited 'The Spider and the Fly'. There were several other items of the same literary quality.

Very often the school room was used for this entertainment, and the pupils would spend part of their day in making everything ready for the evening's activities. At Ilmington, 'the school boys would be sent out to all who would lend chairs . . . as well as to take them back next day'. Most of the children naturally welcomed this as a break from lessons.[119]

At Juniper Hill it was also the custom for the children to play a part in the annual concert – their usual function being to sing 'mildly pretty spring and Nature songs from the *School Song Book*', to a somewhat critical audience of parents and friends. On the evening of the concert all of the inhabitants would turn out to listen appreciatively to the 'Squire and his Negro Minstrel Troupe', the comic songs of the curate, and other similar turns. The school children, too, were warmly applauded but criticisms of their efforts would certainly be made later on – even if they related 'more to how they looked than to their musical performance. Those who had scuffled or giggled, or even blushed, heard of it from their parents . . .'[144] The programmes adopted in most villages followed these predictable lines. Thus at East Hendred in Berkshire the school's concert held in December, 1897, in aid of its Prize Fund included such items as 'Maypole Dance', a 'communal song'; 'Cinderella', a sketch performed by four girls and a

All the fun of the fair at this feast day celebration, with William Taylor's Cinematograph show well to the fore, c. 1903–5. (Dr D. Buxton)

boy; and an 'action song' called 'The Children's Hospital', which was sung by four boys and four girls – no doubt with appropriate vigour.

Although such simple entertainment satisfied most audiences, rather more ambitious plans were put in hand in a few communities, and here one example must suffice. At the small market town of Witney, Oxfordshire, in December, 1897 the children attending the National School 'performed an operetta in the Corn Exchange entitled *Bold Robin and the Babes in the Wood*'. Though the local press praised their effort, declaring that 'the piece was well performed', few other pupils in rural schools would have cared to emulate them. Communal songs and a recitation or two usually proved the limit of their talents.

But if the youngsters enjoyed these home-spun amusements, their pleasure was still keener when the day-to-day routine was interrupted by more dramatic events, such as a local fair, circus, school treat or annual festival. As we saw in Chapter 8,

Sunday school treats and outings were events which were relished in this fashion, and the same was true of the other major celebrations. The attitude was summed up by one Victorian country child who declared: 'Living where we did and how we did, we used to make the most of anything a bit out o' the ordinary, and we looked for'ard from one special day to the next . . . I'm surprised to see how many high days and holidays there were during the year that we kept and we certainly made the most of any that children could take part in at all.'[112]

For youngsters of school age, there were first of all those events which were celebrated by a holiday from the school itself. Custom varied from one part of the country to another, but usually St Valentine's Day, Easter, May Day and Christmas were observed by a break of this kind. Nevertheless there were exceptions, and a few school log books contain disapproving comments on children taking the day off to go round with the May garland, for example, when no official holiday had been granted. But for the majority of children, for whom the old festivals *were* an official holiday, the approach of each was awaited with mounting excitement.

On the appointed day, boys and girls would often gather in groups before breakfast, dressed in their best clothes and would then walk or run round the village, singing the traditional songs and hoping to beg a few pennies from the better-off members of the community whom they visited. In Norfolk, it was customary for the children to rise very early on St Valentine's day in order to try to catch potential donors before sunrise. For 'if any child could say "Good-morrow Valentine", twice before he (or she) was spoken to, he was given a present, provided the sun had not yet risen; if it had, he could be refused on the ground that he was "sunburnt".'[97] To children who otherwise never had money to spend, pennies obtained in this way meant freedom to buy sweets and toys, or perhaps to provide a communal school tea, at which they could enjoy delicacies like cake or sweet biscuits, which they otherwise rarely tasted. It was for this reason that they anxiously displayed their money box whenever a suitable opportunity presented itself, and were not slow to express their disappointment if a donation was not forthcoming. Thus at Bodicote, Oxfordshire, the children set off early on St Valentine's day singing:

> *The rose is red, the violet's blue,*
> *Carnation's sweet and so be you,*
> *So plaze to give us a Valentine.*

But a variation of the second line after a churlish refusal was:

> *The devil's black and so be you.*[86]

177

Elsewhere the day was celebrated with other songs and other customs – although all were variations on the same theme. At Tuddenham St Mary in Suffolk during the 1880s, for instance, one girl remembered walking through the snow to sing at the rectory on 14 February: 'The Rector had a big bag of pennies, and he gave us a penny each out of his bag. One of the songs we sang was Good Morrow to your Valentine.'[85]

Yet however welcome the pence collected on Valentine's day might be, they were of small significance besides both the money and the pleasure which could be obtained from the celebration of May Day. For days before the great event children expended much time and effort in gathering the traditional flowers for the ceremonial garland which they would carry in their procession on 1 May or perhaps the 2nd, if 1 May fell on a Sunday. At Juniper Hill in north Oxfordshire, indeed, on the last Sunday in April some of the older boys walked as far as eight miles in order to gather bunches of primrose from a wood where they were known to flourish.[144] Very often teachers would also cooperate; at Ivinghoe in Buckinghamshire, the master of a private school in the village noted in his diary on 19 April 1864, that he had helped to make 'a frame for garland for girls' and elsewhere it was common for the school room to be used for the preparation of the garland. Desks, tables and floor would be strewn with the 'wallflowers, daffodils, cowslips, blue bells, violets, forget-me-nots' collected in readiness. The blooms would be fixed to the light circular wooden frame, and any necessary background greenery would be provided by sweetbriar, hawthorn, or other suitable bush. The whole was then crowned by a 'Top-knot', consisting of a 'bunch of crown imperial, yellow and brown', while set on a small ledge in the middle of many of the garlands would be a large May doll, known respectfully as 'the lady'. At Juniper Hill, 'A doll of some kind was considered essential. Even in those parishes where the garland had degenerated into a shabby nosegay carried aloft at the top of a stick, some dollish image was mixed in with the flowers.' Usually she was also covered with a white veil or frill and this was only raised, to reveal the full glory of the garland, to those who had already contributed their pence to the May Day procession.[144] At Edlesborough in Buckinghamshire and a few other villages the large doll would sometimes carry a smaller one in its lap, and this custom persisted into the last decade of the nineteenth century. As a contemporary noted, it was 'evidently intended to represent the Virgin and Child', even though the children themselves had no idea of the significance of the tradition they were following.[41]

However, the garland was not the children's only preoccupation. First of all, they had to choose a Queen of the May from among the older – and better-looking – girls. In the procession she would wear a crown of daisies or other spring flowers and a white veil; accompanying her would be the King,

Children at Iffley, Oxfordshire, c. 1905–6 with their May Day garlands. (The author)

selected from among the older boys and usually wearing a sash over one shoulder as a mark of distinction. In some May Day processions other boys, too, would wear sashes, as seems to have been the case at Iffley in Oxfordshire in the late nineteenth century – according to a contemporary photograph. But it all depended on the traditions – and resources – of the individual community.

The final touches were given to both garland and children when they assembled early in the morning of their great day. Usually the girls would be decked out in their lightest coloured dresses, while both they and the boys would wear 'bright ribbon knots and bows'. Wherever possible white veils and gloves would also be worn by the girls, but the poverty of many labouring families prevented these extra sartorial refinements and the Sunday-best hat would usually have to serve in place of a veil. By the end of the day most of the hats had slipped to rather a rakish angle – as can be seen on a delightful late nineteenth century photograph of children from Pitstone in Buckinghamshire. And here, in addition to the main garland, many of the children clutched small nosegays of their own – some of them fixed on to sticks so that their owners could hold them proudly aloft in the procession. But this was certainly not universal practice.

When the noisy and excited children had at last been gathered together in the cold early morning light, it was time for the procession to move off, headed by a

179

boy carrying a banner and, usually, a girl carrying the money box. Following them were the King and Queen with their attendants, and then came the rest of the children, walking two-by-two, under the admiring or critical gaze of parents, neighbours and friends. At Juniper Hill in Oxfordshire the hamlet children set off before 7 a.m., their first stop being at the Rectory, where they carefully struck up in timid and shrill chorus, a three-verse song beginning:

> *A bunch of may I have brought you*
> *And at your door it stands*
> *It is but a sprout, but it's well put about*
> *By the Lord Almighty's hands.*[144]

The door was then opened, a coin slipped into the waiting money-box and the garland duly admired before the procession wound its way to its next port of call – the Manor house. After that came the farm houses and cottages both of that small community and of the adjoining parishes. For children who otherwise rarely strayed outside the boundaries of their own village could be seen on May Day marching proudly along the country lanes and tracks, carrying their precious garland, on a prolonged series of visits. Boys and girls from the Brackley area, on the Northamptonshire/Oxfordshire border, frequently converged on that usually quiet market town for their May celebrations. As the *Oxford Chronicle* of 7 May 1870 recorded: 'On the 2nd the town was live with children carrying garlands, with a view to obtaining the customary "copper". Many schools from neighbouring villages also brought garlands, which they exposed at the doors of houses, singing appropriate songs.' With the money they collected the children might later celebrate with a special 'school tea', or else (as on St Valentine's day) the coins would be divided among them to spend as they wished. Quite considerable amounts might be obtained in this way, although the individual sums given naturally varied with the wealth and generosity of the households visited. Thus at Ivinghoe, Buckinghamshire, Mr Alfred Hart, the proprietor of a small private school in the village, noted in his diary for 1864 that he had given 3d to the 'garland girls'. But in another Buckinghamshire parish, near Haddenham, 'sixpence was given at the door of the manor house to every child that called on May Day. And one boy, who at a tender age had started work to lead the plough team, begged leave of absence and ran there and back rather than lose so cherished a gift.'[127]

At the north Oxfordshire National School of Cropredy and Bourton in 1863 the pupils collected the considerable sum of £3 9s. This they spent, as was their custom, on a tea.[130] At Steeple Aston School in the same county, the 1864 total was £2 10s 8½d; they, too, had their usual tea, but, in addition, each child received 2½d out of the surplus left when the tea had been paid for.

May Day celebrations at Iffley, Oxfordshire, c 1905–6. (The author)

At Haddenham, it was usual for the children to spend their spare pennies on sweets called *Suckballs*, which were on sale on May Day at certain of the cottages. Walter Rose (born 1871) remembered going to collect his own share of the delicacy: 'The compound from which those "Suckballs" were made was boiled and poured out on to sheets of newspaper, each sweet forming a disc the size and shape of a small round biscuit. When they had hardened, the whole paper of them was displayed in the lattice windows of the cottages. The children bought them (about six for a penny) still on their newspaper, the cottage wife cutting them off with scissors as she sold them.'[127]

Normally the May procession itself would continue for most of the day, and one or two of the older children would carry with them a basket in which the children's lunches of bread and cheese or lard would be carefully stowed, to be eaten picnic fashion at a suitable moment. But as the afternoon wore on some of the smaller boys and girls began to lose their earlier enthusiasm. Feet grew tired, especially when they were encased in shoes which were worn out or badly fitting, and it was perhaps with a secret sense of relief that some of them saw the procession at last draw near to home – and the prospect of a welcome tea. By their own firesides, too, youngsters could expect an interested family audience as they told of the great events of the day. For despite weariness and even the

181

squabbles which from time to time broke out among children grown crochety with their exertions, all considered the day a memorable one, whose passing was regretted. As one girl later recalled it was 'a day as near perfection as anything can be in human life . . . [but it] was over, for ever, as it seemed, for at ten years old a year seems as long as a century.'[144]

Although most May day celebrations followed this pattern, there were variations in a few areas. For instance, in the Anna Valley near Andover in Hampshire, the children of the employees of Messrs Taskers, the agricultural implement makers, celebrated their 'garland day', not on 1 May or thereabouts, but on the 13th of that month. This was known as Garland Day and in preparation for it boys and girls picked posies of wild flowers and made delicate yellow cowslip balls, with which they later ran from house to house singing: 'The thirteenth of May is Garland Day, please to see a fine garland, made early in the morning. The thirteenth of May is garland day, please to see a fine garland.'[125]

In the Huntingdonshire fen country another variant existed, since although the celebration was kept up at the beginning of May, in all other respects it differed from the junketings held elsewhere. Instead of the May Day procession, the custom in the Lotting Fen district was to set up tall posts, one on either side of the high way, with a clothes line running between them. Then an old rag doll, which acted as the May doll, was pegged to the middle of the line. When this had been arranged the children would take up little sawdust balls which had been prepared beforehand for them by their mothers and would 'pelt at the dolly to see if [they] could turn it over the line' – that being the object of the exercise. The lack of suitable bushes for a garland in the bare fenland countryside was the reason given for this particular departure.[112]

After May Day, the next great national festival in the child's year was, of course, Christmas – although 5 November (Bonfire Night) was celebrated by many in the appropriate fashion. But Christmas was special. Although most country families were too poor to give their children toys, unless the father was handy at making them himself, there would usually be a few oranges and perhaps nuts which had been carefully gathered earlier in the year against such an occasion. On Christmas Day the family would usually sit together round the cosy fireside, since even the menfolk normally had the day off. For the Christmas dinner there would perhaps be a piece of beef which had been given to the family by their father's employer, while the fire itself might be made up with coal derived from the same charitable source. Ivy, holly, and other evergreens festooned the plain walls of the living room, while in some districts 'the older kissing-bough [hung] from the ceiling . . . Iron hoops bent into the form of a crown [were] covered with greenery and decorated with apples and lighted candles. Usually a bunch of mistletoe [was] fixed to the underside, and in the north of England small presents [were] hung from it on long streamers of coloured ribbon.'[97] For the luckier ones there would be a bottle of home-made wine to sample and perhaps carols to be sung, as parents and children sat snugly in unaccustomed leisure; in the north of England 'every family that [could] possibly afford it' also had 'a Yule cheese and Yule cake provided'.[47]

But for boys and girls of school age there might be other treats as well. Some of the more daring anticipated the joys of Christmas by going out carol singing. Carrying lanterns 'made of swedes hollowed out, with a piece of candle fitted inside', they made their rounds from one house to another. However, not all parents approved of this form of begging – as they saw it – and Alfred Williams, the Wiltshire-born author and poet, remembered how as a child he and his sisters were soundly whipped when they disobeyed their mother's prohibition on carol singing.[70]

Christmas parties for school children were usually held after 25 December – where they were held at all. Sometimes, as at Saddlescombe in Sussex, during the 1860s, they might be organized by a large farmer for the children of his workers. On the appointed day those invited to the Saddlescombe party 'arrived shy and solemn, their faces shining with application of yellow soap, and their hair sleekly greased – probably with lard . . . Tea in the kitchen wore off some of the shyness of [the] guests and then came games in the school room, such as 'Hunt the slipper', when a little impromptu conversation between cobbler and customer was received as exquisite wit. To finish there was a Christmas tree and what a simple and inexpensive joy it was. A home-made garment for each, pinafore, hood or scarf, a bag of marbles, a penny Dutch doll gaily dressed, with a few bags of sweets, and coloured candles. 'One year the experiment was made to substitute a Father Christmas for the tree, but it was not a success, as the children mistook him 'for a bogey of the worst description and yelled with terror . . .' and so the following year the Christmas tree was restored. Soon after the presents had been distributed and excitedly examined, the fathers came with yellow horn lanterns to guide their offspring home, after what must have been a real highlight in their year.[124]

Elsewhere the local squire or a large landowner might provide a party, as the Duke of Marlborough did in January 1875, at the Oxfordshire parish of Hanborough; in this case the celebration was held in the school room, and 'a large Christmas tree . . . was the chief object of attraction. Some little toy &c., was provided for each child . . . When the Christmas tree had been lighted up . . . useful articles of children's clothing, &c., were distributed. Every mother, whose children attended both [Sunday and day] schools, received in addition a quarter of a pound of tea . . .' Or perhaps the better off members of the parish would join together to provide a suitable celebration – as at Shawford in Hampshire on

Boxing Day 1897. According to the *Hampshire Chronicle*, the entertainment consisted of tea 'to the children at 4 o'clock, Christmas tree at 5, and musical entertainment at 7.30. Certainly the picturesque fairy scene of the huge Christmas tree, standing some 15 ft high, laden with hundreds of sweet pretty things – fairy lights, oranges, crackers, sweet bags, toys, and lovely dolls – was a sight not readily forgotten. In the room right across [and] in and out were beautiful Japanese lanterns and hundreds of fairy lights . . .' In all, about two hundred children were catered for, and two of those who attended later wrote a letter to the *Hampshire Chronicle* expressing their appreciation of 'a very joyous day' and of the 'lovely things' provided as gifts; 'coats, jackets, boots, caps, knickers, stockings – and oh! I can't tell you how many different things . . . and then we all sang "God Save the Queen" and had bags of oranges, crackers, and sweets to carry home.' The letter was signed 'Harry and Jennie', and, if genuine, was perhaps written as the result of a little prompting by their teacher.

In some communities, like Whitchurch in Oxfordshire, the Christmas party was combined with the annual prize giving – even if (as with the Sunday school prizes discussed earlier) many of the books chosen for the purpose seemed rather unsuitable, given the age and level of attainment of the children involved. For instance, although the HMI had reported at Whitchurch in the early 1870s that the children's reading showed 'no sign of skill', while their 'intelligence [was] still imperfect', they were nevertheless given as prizes at around this time such books as White's *History of Selborne*, Defoe's *Robinson Crusoe*, and Joyce's *Scientific Dialogues*. But whatever the children's feelings may have been concerning their prizes, all could share in the pleasures of a substantial tea, a Christmas tree and usually a magic lantern display.

In a number of parishes traditional figures like the mummers still visited at Christmas time, although by the end of the nineteenth century their importance was sadly diminished. Nevertheless, as late as the 1880s, one country child could remember 'Molly dancers' calling at her fenland home at Christmas. One of them had a fiddle and another a dulcimer or a concertina, and they played the old familiar tunes while the rest of the group danced. The same child remembered that Plough Monday (the first Monday after Epiphany) was kept up by the children as well as the young men, whose traditional, somewhat boisterous, festival it was. The youngsters 'dressed up in anything [they] could find and blacked [their faces] with soot' as a disguise. Needless to say, this, too, was made an occasion for begging and singing songs, as the group of young 'plough boys' cried out for 'just one' penny, rattling their collecting boxes suggestively as they did so.[112]

But if these were the major festivals to which most country children looked forward, they were not the sum total of their celebrations. Varying from parish to parish, other dates were kept for events of considerable *local* significance like the Shrove Tuesday 'orange throwing' at Oving in Buckinghamshire or the rather rougher fun enjoyed by youngsters in Somerset, Devon and Dorset on that day even at the end of the Victorian period. Here it was the custom for the children to 'go about after dusk, and throw stones against people's doors, by what [was] considered by them an indefeasible right. They at the same time [sang] in chorus:

> *I be come a shrovin*
> *Vor a little pankiak;*
> *A bit o' bread o' your baikin,*
> *Or a little truckle cheese o' your maikin,*
> *If you'll gi' me a little I'll ax no more,*
> *If you don't gi' me nothin'*
> *I'll rottle your door'*[96]

In practice, they were not so much interested in gifts of bread and cheese as in those of sweets or small sums of money.

In some parts of the country, Good Friday or Palm Sunday would be marked by the eating of figs, while in the North of England during the 1840s and 1850s and perhaps later too, the traditional dish of 'Fig Sue' was prepared on Good Friday. 'The dish [was] a composition of figs, ale, white bread, sugar and nutmeg', and was 'alone partaken of for dinner on this day.'[47] In many villages Easter Monday was marked by the holding of sports and races, in which the children would also take part, while even harvest thanksgiving had a wide appeal in some quarters. As the master of Washford Pyne School in Devon noted with gentle irony, in 1888: 'This is the fifth [harvest] thanksgiving the children have left school to attend. Truly, we are a thankful people.'[133]

However, among this welter of local holidays there was usually one in every parish which was regarded as especially important by all of its inhabitants. This was the annual feast day, which might be marked by the Club Day celebrations of the village friendly society or by some other notable event, like a flower show or horticultural society display.

If it coincided with the anniversary of the village club, then members of the friendly society concerned would normally assemble dressed in their finery (including gloves, rosettes and sashes, where possible) and carrying before them appropriate banners. Alfred Williams remembered one such annual celebration during his childhood in South Marston, Wiltshire: 'It was quite the event of the year; Christmas and Easter were nothing to it . . . The anniversary was held on the second Tuesday in May . . . The procession was headed by three men bearing

Friendly Society meeting at Northiam, Sussex, in the early 1900s. This was held on the first Thursday in May and members paraded through the village, wearing white smocks and carrying staves, before attending a church service. They then visited a public house before games were organized on the village green. Such celebrations were among the highlights of the country child's year. (Mrs Elizabeth Rigby).

blue silk flags with tassels and fringes, a large one first, and two smaller ones, one on each side. The members wore . . . red and blue sashes and rosettes, and walked with blue staffs with gilt heads.'[150] At this stage in the proceedings the children were, of course, only onlookers, as the men and youths (for only rarely were females admitted) paraded the streets with bands playing before them. Usually the procession ended up at the church, where a special service was held, before the members repaired to their meeting place to do justice to the substantial dinner which awaited them. Meanwhile, the rest of the village were enjoying races, dancing and all the other diversions which characterized the 'feast day'. There were stalls selling gingerbreads and humbugs; hot potatoes and gingerade. Simple and crude toys were to be seen – wooden soldiers with scarlet tunics and white trousers. Jack-in-the-boxes, monkeys-on-sticks and many others – and here children could spend the pennies carefully hoarded in readiness for such an opportunity. At Cropredy in Oxfordshire at the annual fete 'all the schoolchildren were given 6d each to spend', but few parishes were fortunate enough to have benefactors willing to provide this. At many of the feasts there were also small simple roundabouts, which in the early days were pushed round by some of the village lads, in return for the chance of a free ride from time to time. Primitive roundabouts like these were owned by the Sanger family, in the early years of Victoria's reign, and according to 'Lord' George Sanger himself, the wooden horses fixed on them were nothing but 'enlarged examples of the rough penny toys that please the little ones . . . Their legs were simply stiff round sticks. Their bodies were lumps of deal rounded on one side. Their heads were roughly cut from half-inch deal boards, and inserted in a groove in the bodies, while the tails and manes were made of strips of rabbit-skin. They were gaudy animals, however, their coats of paint being white, plentifully dotted with red and blue spots . . .'[131]

In addition to the roundabouts there might be swingboats, Aunt Sallies and coconut shies, while sometimes, as at South Marston, the scope would be still more ambitious. Here there were 'shooting galleries . . . [and] generally a Punch and Judy show, with the "original dog Toby", and once a man brought a small menagerie with a "Rooshan" bear and a gorilla'. On the other hand, even this seemed insignificant compared to the Michaelmas Fair in the neighbouring parish of Highworth, during the later 1870s. As well as the traditional booths and shows there were 'exhibitions . . . of beasts and birds, waxwork figures, model machinery, glass-making, cotton-spinning, picture-galleries, and all sorts of things beside . . . A great Zulu and several negroes performed the war dance outside the [waxworks show], and a man blew loud blasts and fanfares with a trumpet, and invited the people to 'walk up and see the great Napoleon Bonnypart, the "Dook" of Wellington, and other celebrities, very lifelike and natteral . . .'[150]

But most country children had to be content with much less than this. Some small amusements and a tea of bread and butter, cake and lemonade, eaten in one of the marquees, were the usual limits of their aspirations. Yet there can be no doubt that they enjoyed themselves, for many made it their business to visit not only their own village's feast day but also that of as many of their neighbours as possible.

Furthermore, if the children were normally excluded, on grounds of age, from the activities of the friendly society which often provided the background to a village feast, occasional exceptions to this could occur in respect of the older boys. Sometimes quite young lads would be admitted to membership – as surviving records make clear. Thus in the Warwickshire village of Long Compton, the Assurance Society which was formed in 1869 with thirty-four members, included among these latter two twelve-year-old boys, who presumably took part in the annual parade when the 'Club day' was held on the 'last Tuesday of June'.[120] And towards the end of the century even some of the larger friendly societies, such as the Manchester Unity of Oddfellows and the Ancient Order of Foresters, began to establish junior branches, to cater for lads between the ages of fourteen and eighteen; the boys or their parents subscribed towards a small sickness benefit. However, this trend was deplored by at least one observer,

187

"STARTLING EFFECTS!"

Peep-Showman. "ON THE RIGHT YOU OBSERVE THE 'XPRESS TRAIN A-COMIN' ALONG, AN'
THE SIGNAL LIGHTS, THE GREEN AND THE RED. THE GREEN LIGHTS MEANS 'CAUTION,' AND
THE RED LIGHTS SI'NIFIES 'DANGER'" —

Small Boy (with his Eye to the Aperture). "BUT WHAT'S THE YALLER LIGHT, SIR?"

Peep-Showman (slow and impressive). "THERE AIN'T NO YALLER LIGHT—BUT THE GREEN
AND THE RED. THE GREEN LIGHTS MEANS 'CAUTION,' AND THE RED LIGHTS SI'NIF—"

Small Boy (persistently). "BUT WHA'S THE OTHER LIGHT, SIR?"

Peep-Showman (losing patience). "'TELL YER THERE AIN'T NO—" *(takes a look—in conster-
nation).*—"BLOWED IF THE DARNED OLD SHOW AIN'T A-FIRE!!"

The peep-show was of perennial interest to children at village feasts and festivals. (*Punch*, 1879)

Sir George Young, Bt, when he reported in 1874 to the Royal Commission on Friendly and Benefit Building Societies then in session. Sir George complained that: 'The society clearly does not appeal to a rationally formed judgment upon the comparative advantages which it offers, and does as clearly, in some cases, appeal to nothing but the childish desire of children to walk in a procession and wear ribbons . . . In so far as this appeal to the children has tended to nourish the taste for fine clothes and costly insignia it has done harm.'[9] His point concerning the appeal of the friendly societies to children's vanity was in fact unashamedly admitted by the spokesman of at least one Kentish society which enrolled young members; he declared that they 'got in' children of fourteen because of the 'flags and the music', presumably with the intention of retaining them for life.[9] It is perhaps also worth noting that after nearly eighty years Alfred Dodman of West Rudham, Norfolk, could remember belonging to a juvenile branch of the Oddfellows in his parish and proudly recalled that he had taken part regularly in their Whit Monday club feast. Bands played and amid all the general excitement, he and the other juveniles were allowed to attend the club dinner at the specially reduced price of 18d each!

Yet while the anniversary day of a local benefit society provided the focal point of many village feasts, it was by no means the only reason for such festivities. In some communities the local flower show performed a similar role, as in one north Oxfordshire parish described by Flora Thompson. In this village the flower show was 'the crowning event of the . . . year. It was always arranged to take place between haytime and harvest, so that the men of the village could be spared for a day from their fieldwork. The school children were given a holiday, and their mothers on that day did as little work as possible . . . From ten o'clock in the morning onward a stream of villagers and their friends . . . might [be] seen making its way over the greensward towards the big marquee flying the Union Jack and the smaller, but no less exciting, cluster of show booths, coconut shies, and gingerbread stalls by which it was surrounded. A brass band was engaged for the day, and the steam roundabout had an organ attached which was permitted to play by arrangement at such times as the bandsmen felt in need of refreshment . . .'[145]

Within the marquee parents and children could wander around enjoying the display of fruit and vegetables and sniffing appreciatively the moist sweet perfume which hung on the air. Some children, too, had a personal interest in these flower shows, for quite often a special section for wild flower displays would be included. At one horticultural show held at Tadmarton, Oxfordshire during September 1875, no less than five prizes were offered to the children of 'labourers and cottagers' for wild flower displays; and for those who did not win, there was always the consolation of taking part in the various entertainments offered – including 'dancing, cricket and other sports . . .'

Jennings' Fair on The Green, Devizes, c. 1900. One side-show, towards the back on the right, was William Taylor's Bioscope, which was sometimes used to show early moving pictures. Girls in costume performed on the front platform to attract an audience, who were then enticed inside – for a fee! (Dr D Buxton)

These well-loved festivals formed the nucleus of the high days and holidays to which youngsters looked forward from one year to the next. But equally attractive were the fairs and circuses which were often held in a nearby market town – although as regards the latter at least, not always as regularly as the other events mentioned. At the fairs there were all the thrills of the village feast writ large, and the youngster with a penny or two to spend felt rich indeed. At Ramsey Fair, held every July, one young visitor remembered that during the 1880s there were stalls 'where you could buy things to eat, like hot peas in a basin, or a dish o' whelks, or a packet o' brandy snap . . . There were the Fat Lady, all dressed up in spangles, a mountain o' flesh and blood, and a couple o' tiny dwarfs called Tom Thumb and his wife . . . In another booth there were the conjurors, and in another the performing fleas, that I remember being in chains. Then there were a boxing-booth, and a waxwork show, where when I were ever such a little girl I see the sad sight o' Queen Victoria and all her children round Prince Albert's death bed . . . Mother 'ould go with us for a ride on the "Sea-on-Land", as were nothing really but a boarded floor made to rock from end to end and from side to side. But we went in the "swing boats" by ourselves . . . The "flying-'osses" were another attraction, though they di'n't exactly fly, because they were only cranked round by a man by hand . . .'[112]

At many of the larger fairs there were also such superior attractions as a menagerie or, at the very end of the century, a moving picture or bioscope; at St Giles's Fair, Oxford in 1898, one such early bioscope showed Mr Gladstone's funeral procession to a packed audience, who had paid 3d each for the privilege.[61]

Nevertheless menageries and circuses were probably more likely to interest children than were the wonders of 'living pictures'. Some of these, notably Mander's Menagerie, whose 'great establishment' was valued at £50,000 in 1869, had a very large collection of animals and performed a useful educational function in days when few zoological gardens existed. When Mander's Menagerie was advertised as visiting Woodstock in Oxfordshire, during August 1872, the advance notice stated that a parade through the streets would first of all be held, with 'carriages drawn by elephants, camels, dromedaries, zebras, mules, &c. and accompanied by a Brass Band . . .' The excitement of the younger inhabitants of this normally quiet market town at witnessing such an event is easy to imagine.

At Banbury Michaelmas Fair a circus appeared 'almost every year' during the mid-Victorian period, and during the year 1858 there were even two of them – 'Sanger's Hippodrome came with its wild beasts and displays of horsemanship, together with Howe and Cushing's Great American Circus, which was possibly the most successful ever to visit Banbury. The band carriage was drawn into the town by forty cream coloured horses, and such was the popularity of the show that £470 was taken at the box office.'[147]

Yet apart from the fair's role as a provider of exciting merchandise and of entertainment, it had at least one other function, especially during the earlier part of the period. This was its position as a labour exchange, and although child workers were normally fixed in their first job by a local contact, a trickle at least came to the fairs (especially the statute or 'mop' fairs) to seek employment. Wide-eyed and timid they can be seen in the contemporary prints of such fairs, very often standing nervously by parents, as they waited to be hired. Even from Flora Thompson's little hamlet of Juniper Hill a few boys left 'to become farm servants in the north of England. To obtain such situations, they went to Banbury Fair and stood in the Market to be hired by an agent . . . They were usually well treated, especially in the matter of food; but were glad to return at the end of the year from what was, to them, a foreign country where, at first, they could barely understand the speech . . .'[144] However, by the end of the century this role of the fair had much diminished, except in the north of England, as advertisements in the local press or the work of employment registries took over the function. Already by the 1870s newspaper comments on the hiring activities of the fairs were regularly speaking of 'little' being done, as – to give one example – at Wallingford Fair in 1870. Many observers welcomed the trend, too, for as the *Illustrated London News* of 2 November 1872, pointed out, the practice of hiring at a fair exposed 'the young of both sexes to much danger of moral contamination, while standing idle together in the street of a market town or village, where the beershops were doing a brisk trade'; indeed, the journal critically compared the 'open assemblage of labourers for hire' to a slave-market. As might be expected, the agricultural trade union leaders were also opposed to the public hiring of the young, and in 1873 Joseph Arch, the National Union President, made clear his own 'repugnance' at the 'system which prevailed' at Statute Fairs, declaring that he had always kept his own children away from them.

But for most youngsters both fairs and circuses were purely of interest for the entertainment they provided, and the appearance of either in the neighbourhood would rapidly cause absenteeism at school. Sometimes, even at the end of the nineteenth century, schools bowed to the inevitable and granted a holiday for the duration of a fair; thus, at Grimsbury School near Banbury a full week's holiday was regularly given at the time of the annual Michaelmas fair, and at Headington Quarry School near Oxford the great St Giles's fair held in the city earned a similar remission.

Finally, there were always local events of a less predictable character to look forward to – the visit of a 'one-man band', or a dancing bear, or even the appearance of a motor-car in a village for the first time. At Asthall School in Oxfordshire an entry in the log book for 8 March 1898, shows that the children were let out of school 'to see a motor car that was passing through the village'. In other cases such as at Oving, Buckinghamshire, during January, 1868 a meet of hounds in the parish might lead to early dismissal, or perhaps the appearance of a troop of soldiers marching along the high road would provide the excuse. In any case, as we saw in Chapter Four, children were always prepared to play truant in order to share in any unusual activities which were on hand, if all else failed. At Wardington in Oxfordshire, the youngsters would look forward to the arrival of a German band which visited their parish each summer, 'perhaps ten to twelve strong, with shining brass instruments', ready to play their stirring tunes; but as one girl remembered, 'most memorable of all perhaps was the dancing bear, which we watched . . . with mixed feelings'. In the nearby market town of Banbury, another child recalled the excitement of the regular visits of 'a one-man band, one man having various instruments attached to different parts of him and somehow he managed to play them all at once. Drum sticks to his elbows, triangles, cymbals, bells on his ankles, pipe to blow and so on. Barrel organs or hurdy-gurdies made weekly rounds playing topical tunes often accompanied by

Performing bear at Topsham, c. 1900, this was a perennial source of interest to Victorian country children. (Topsham Museum Society)

dark pretty Italian women with bright-coloured head scarves and shining earrings. On or by the organ would be a cage with colourful love birds which we now know as budgerigars. If not birds there would be a small monkey wearing a little suit of scarlet and perhaps a feathered cap. He would hold a tin cup and chatter when a copper was put in.'[157]

In addition, special celebrations of great national significance – such as the ending of the Crimean War, or the Queen's Golden and Diamond Jubilees, in the summers of 1887 and 1897, respectively, would be marked by holidays and a tea for the children – plus, in the better-off communities, commemorative gifts as well. Jubilee mugs and medallions were widely distributed, while, as at Shipston-on-Stour, Warwickshire, in 1897, 'racing and rural sports' might also be held. Festivities here closed late in the evening, with the lighting of a bonfire and a display of fireworks.

By means of these 'extra' festivals, children could add to their basic school

ENGLISH COUNTRY LIFE.
A ZANY IN THE VILLAGE   TAUNT & CO.

One-man band performing at Kelmscott, Oxfordshire, c. 1900. Such events provided a welcome diversion for country children. (Oxfordshire County Council, Department of Leisure and Arts)

holiday period of about a week each at Christmas and Easter or Whit, plus four or five weeks' 'harvest' holiday in the summer. For example, during the period from September 1865 to September 1866, the pupils at Long Compton National School in Warwickshire earned an additional six and a half days' holiday in this fashion. An examination of other village log books shows that this was a fairly typical picture. Such breaks probably constituted the only true 'high days and holidays' in the child's year, since, as has been seen, during many of the formal 'holiday' periods, especially during spring and summer, children were employed at home or in the fields.

And despite the poverty and hardship which so often clouded their lives, country children were at least better off than their fellows in the great industrial towns when it came to the spending of their leisure hours. Instead of being confined to dirty noisy streets or confronted by the grimy bare walls surrounding many urban school playgrounds, they could enjoy the relative cleanliness and peace of their home surroundings. Even if they did have to work long hours at certain seasons of the year, they could at any rate savour to the full such diversions as came their way – be they fairs, menageries, or merely the sight of a party of soldiers marching along the high road.

NOTES ON ADDITIONAL SOURCES USED

Reminiscences of Miss C. Pearce of Chippenham concerning late Victorian Langley Burrell – in correspondence with the author, November 1971.

Diary of Mr Alfred Hart of Ivinghoe, Buckinghamshire, for the year 1864; in the possession of Mr J. Hawkins of Pitstone, Buckinghamshire.

Reminiscences of Alfred Dodman of West Rudham, obtained via Mrs R. Evans of Culham, Oxfordshire.

The photograph of Pitstone children during their May Day procession at the end of the Victorian period can be seen at Pitstone Local History Museum.

CHAPTER TEN

Sickness And Its Cures

'In those days the doctor was not called unless someone was really ill, for many of the women had as many as ten children, and knew a lot about sickness, and came in and helped each other . . .' 'The Country Doctor' in Noel Streatfeild (ed.) – *The Day Before Yesterday* (1956), pp. 251–2.

F or the children of the labouring classes, whether they lived in town or country, the very first months of life were the most hazardous. Although in rural areas the rate of infant mortality tended to be perhaps twenty-five per cent below that for the urbanized counties (see Table 3), nevertheless the average mortality of 138.8 per 1,000 male births which existed in the agricultural counties at the end of the century could not be considered satisfactory on any account – and even in those individual rural areas most favourable, it rarely fell below 100. In other words, at least one in every ten babies born in the country districts could be expected to die before it had reached the end of its first year. Furthermore, beyond those few especially vulnerable months, the position remained difficult. For example, in the year 1897 around one-quarter of total mortality for *all* age groups within such rural counties as Wiltshire, Westmorland, Herefordshire and Dorset comprised children below the age of five years. But at least this was better than the position in the urbanized counties, where over two-fifths and in some cases, nearly one-half of the very much higher level of deaths was accounted for by children in the under-five age group. In the year 1897, 46 per cent of total deaths in Cheshire came from this group, and in Lancashire, 44 per cent. (See Table 4.)

Yet if the country child had a slightly better chance of surviving to reach maturity than its urban counterpart, its position certainly did not warrant any complacency. Born in the close and confined atmosphere of a crowded country cottage, and frequently unable to secure proper food – with the shortage of fresh milk a particular problem – many infants fell an easy prey to disease. Thus in a letter to *The Times* of 30 August 1864. 'An Old Country Clergyman' claimed that in rural Wiltshire the farmers would not sell milk to the poor, preferring to feed 'all their skim milk to their pigs. I have heard mothers complain that they could not procure a drop for their pining infants, though pigs were fattening upon it.' He declared that he had 'ever found it the most acceptable charity to supply the poor with milk'. Nor had the position improved by the end of the century. At that date many young babies in the county were being brought up on nutritionally inferior tinned milk, because fresh was not available.[17] In other parts of the country similar examples could be quoted. (See Chapter One.) It is significant that according to official statistics, one of the most serious killers of young babies was 'atrophy', which was known to be caused by poor nutrition. It accounted for over one-quarter of all rural infant deaths in the 1870s and over one-fifth at the turn of the century. A second serious threat to survival for babies in both the mid-and late-Victorian period was convulsions, while a third was provided by stomach disorders – which could again be attributed directly to unsatisfactory feeding and to the unhygienic home environment. This was especially the case in cottages which lacked pantries and where food had to be kept in the living room, or in some cases, even in the bedroom. (See Table 5.)

Nor were these the only problems to be faced. One constant danger arose from the fact that many young babies had to share a bed with their parents because of lack of room, and a number of them paid the penalty by being 'overlaid', i.e. being accidentally suffocated by the parents while they slept.[57] Of course, where the family was already a large one, this accident might give rise to speculation among the rest of the community. Had it happened while the mother was drunk? Was another baby on the way? These and other similar questions were regularly posed by the less charitable whenever such a death occurred. Nevertheless, the problem was certainly not confined to country children, and in 1901 'national figures showed that no fewer than 1,550 infants had died in this way'.[123]

Another hazard to the well-being of *some* infants arose from an injudicious administration of opiates like Godfrey's cordial or laudanum, which was designed to lull a restless baby to sleep but which could, if administered too frequently and too freely, ultimately prove fatal. It has, indeed, been pointed out that: 'The British Medical Association reported in 1867 that Lincolnshire and Norfolk between them consumed more than half the opium imported into this country. There was not a labourer's house in the west [of Norfolk] without its penny stick or pill of opium, and not a child that did not have it in some form. Godfrey's cordial, a mixture of opium, treacle and infusion of sassafras, was the usual comfort administered to a squalling baby when its mother was too busy working in the fields to feed it.' Babies were commonly left in the care of a so-called 'nurse' while their mother was away, and it was she who administered the cordial. Occasionally she would give too strong a dose and then, 'frightened at its effects', would summon a doctor. He would arrive to find 'half-a-dozen

26

April 25	Mr Howlett visited the School.
28	More sickness amongst the children. Several away with sore throats. Four with Diphtheria.
May 1st	Whole holiday given
5	Another case of Diphtheria & several of sore throat. Average for week 63.6
12	Thirteen children away with bad throats
16	Mr Howlett visited the School
19	15 children away with bad throats
26	Many of the children ill. Average higher 75.6
June 2	Whole holiday given on Whit-Wednesday
9	Childrens health improved
15	Mr Howlett visited the School
23	The childrens health is much better Four away with Diphtheria
26	One of the above four died on Friday Evening
30	Average for week 78.1
July 3	All the children back at School
10	Children ill again, nine away.

Extracts from Sydenham National School log book, Oxfordshire, showing the incidence of epidemic and sickness among the pupils in the 1880s. Mr Howlett was the attendance officer. (Oxfordshire Record Office) babies, some snoring, some squinting, all pallid and eye-sunken, lying about the room, all poisoned'. It was not surprising that infant mortality was excessive. Indeed, Mr Henry W.T. Ellis, a surgeon of Crowle, in Lincolnshire, informed the *Royal Commission on the Employment of Children, Young Persons and Women in Agriculture*, in 1867, that in his district: '50 children under three months old died during 1865–6 . . . Twins and illegitimate children almost always die. I know a case here where a woman has had five or six children all of whom have died, having been given opium to keep them quiet.'

Fortunately, as the century moved towards its end and the opportunities for women's field labour in the eastern counties diminished, so this great reliance on Godfrey's cordial to quieten babies declined. Nevertheless, throughout the Victorian period laudanum was widely used to soothe the young child; indeed, it was the only painkiller normally available to both young and old, so that on these grounds, if no other, its popularity was assured. One girl who lived in a Warwickshire village in the early years of the present century, for example, remembers having laudanum to cure a toothache.

Furthermore, when a child did become ill, the poverty of labouring parents often prevented them from calling in the doctor because they feared the subsequent bills. Some learnt to overcome this by applying to the Poor Law for medical relief – but this for long carried with it the stigma of pauperism. Others tried to cope on a 'do it yourself' basis. Mothers discovered how to dose their children with simple remedies which they could prepare themselves, while in most villages and market towns a 'quack doctor' or herbalist was also on hand to give help. In Banbury, Oxfordshire, a Mr T.J. Norton plied his trade as a 'Botanic Electric Practitioner' during the 1880s, and a boy who lived in the town at that time remembered that: 'He was primarily a herbalist, selling such things as juniper berries, ginger and cough mixtures, but he also tried to cure people of various complaints by electric shock treatment.' Nevertheless cottagers usually preferred to rely upon the products of their own garden, for most would have a herb corner set aside for the purpose.

In a number of instances these homely simples consisted of a mixture of superstition and effective treatment. Thus for earache, the remedy would perhaps be to place a small heated shallot in the ear, and then wrap the head round with flannel – a measure which seems to have been successful. For mumps, goose oil and flannel would be used and for a cold on the chest a 'piece of brown paper cut out like a shield, on a piece of tape, and covered with hot tallow, would be worn until the cold and cough disappeared'. Elsewhere onion gruel was eaten to help cure sore throats and coughs, while mistletoe berries were regarded by some as a 'shure cure for the Hoping [whooping] Cough'.[102] Horehound mixed with honey was used to relieve sore throats and chest colds, while camomile tea was considered efficacious 'to ward off colds, to soothe the nerves, and as a general tonic'.[144] Celandines were said to be a valuable medicament for 'weak eyes', and 'elderflower in home-cured lard with boracic' provided a soothing ointment. Children were soon taught that 'for a cut that was bleeding fast there was nothing like a bunch of cobwebs; but if you were away in the fields the best thing was to rub the cut on a horse . . . presumably the scurf helped clotting.'[114] Many village people would also keep a few acorns in the house as a remedy for diarrhoea. The acorns were dried and grated, the powder thus resulting being taken when necessary.[150]

Then there were the measures adopted on the principle that 'prevention is better than cure'. Each weekend most children would be dosed with Epsom salts or castor oil, or even soap and water as part of the normal routine of cleansing them both inside and out. At times like these, protest availed the child nothing. In the spring time there were the regular doses of 'brimstone and treacle or nettle tea', administered to 'cool the blood'.[114]

Alongside these perhaps valid home cures, there were rather more dubious ones as well. In East Anglia a common remedy for whooping cough was to give the young patient a mouse to eat – usually fried. Even after about seventy years one who had endured the treatment remembered vividly the nausea with which he had faced it.[102] Nevertheless, it was a 'cure' which continued well into the present century, so that a doctor newly come to South Norfolk in the 1920s was 'completely at sea when informed that a small patient had continued to whoop with unabated vigour in spite of the fact that he had "had his mouse and all"'.[112] But there were other strange cures for whooping cough as well. At Bungay in Suffolk in the 1880s the children of St Edmund's Catholic School were apparently taken by their teacher to the gas-works when they had the disease. As an ex-pupil remembered: 'They used to go there of a morning and they'd sit around in the gas-works for about half-an-hour . . . It cured them: the fumes from the gas-works, I suppose.'[85] In Oxfordshire, the solution was to drive the patient 'round the sheep-folds before breakfast', as 'the smell of a sheep-fold' was thought to be a certain remedy.[114]

In some areas there was also an unashamed reliance on superstition or magical powers. For example, one old Norfolk lady's advice for nose bleeds was for the patient to 'get a skein of silk, and get nine Maids each to tie a knot in the skein, and then the sufferer must wear it round his neck . . .'[102] At Ringshall in Suffolk, a 'magical cure' for epilepsy in young babies was attempted by means of an ash-tree. 'An ash sapling was split down and the baby was passed through the cleft in the wood. The cleft was then tightly bound up, and the sapling as far as possible restored to its former state. If it lived the baby would then grow up in normal health; if it died the epilepsy would persist and nothing more could be done about it.'[82] In certain of the more remote districts a belief in witchcraft even

Mrs Betty Smith, district nurse at Colesbourne, Gloucestershire, 1908–10. Her area covered about fourteen villages and hamlets – hence the need for a bicycle. District nurses were recruited on a widening scale from the end of the 1880s. By their home visits they helped to improve the health of both mothers and children. They also raised standards of family hygiene. (Cotswold Countryside Collection, Northleach)

survived. Thus in 1853, a resident at Bridgwater in Somerset wrote: 'I was lately informed by a member of my congregation that two children living near his house were bewitched. I made enquiries into the matter, and found that witchcraft is by far less uncommon than I had imagined.'[74] Readers of Thomas Hardy's novel, *The Return of the Native*, will likewise remember that Susan Nunsuch, one of the villagers, believed that her child's sickness was due to witchcraft, and she sought by the same means to effect a cure.[158] Perhaps fortunately, such extreme examples as these were rare.

It was only when the various home remedies had failed that, in most cases, the doctor was called upon. To many country children he was an awe-inspiring figure and one whom they saw but rarely. Thus my mother (the daughter of a small farming family in north Warwickshire at the beginning of the twentieth century) only remembered visiting the doctor on two occasions during her childhood – once to have an especially troublesome tooth extracted and once to have treatment for blood-poisoning. About sixty years later she recalled that her fear of the doctor outweighed her fear of the blood-poisoning, but she was taken along by her elders to the surgery, and so had no choice in the matter. In this particular case, a linseed poultice was recommended, and fortunately for her, the treatment proved successful.

However, it was to cure such common childish ailments as whooping cough, and measles, as well as the more dangerous diphtheria and scarlet fever, that the doctor was most in demand. The mortality statistics indicate that whooping cough was an especially dangerous disease for girls in the Victorian period, and this is also substantiated by the evidence of a Wiltshire country doctor at the turn of the century, who regarded whooping cough as a killer of little girls. 'I never remember a boy dying of it.' Another disease recalled by this doctor as particularly dangerous was pneumonia, ' . . . it had a dreadful crisis, during which the patient very often died. During this crisis they would have a very high temperature, would be blue in colour with a hacking cough . . . If they lived their temperature would suddenly drop, and an hour or two later they would be sitting up in bed demanding a beef steak; but even then they needed careful watching, and stimulants had to be kept handy, to see they did not slip away . . .'[138]

Many of the childish ailments were passed from one child to another through the agency of the school. In the often ill-ventilated crowded classrooms poorly nourished youngsters quickly fell victim. Doctors noted, too, that among the earliest casualties in the epidemics were those who had to walk long distances to school and who frequently had to sit all day with wet feet during the winter months. One medical man observed, for example: 'I have repeatedly made notes of instances where, during the prevalence of diphtheria, children who have had to walk long distances through muddy lanes have suffered first and most severely.

Speaking generally, children in the chronic catarrhal condition, which is not uncommon with country children in the winter, are exceptionally susceptible to zymotic diseases, and this explains the undoubted fact that epidemics of scarlet fever and diphtheria spread as a rule, more frequently through school agency in the country than in town.'[45] His remark about the 'chronic catarrhal condition' of the children is also borne out by an examination of comments in school log books such as at Wadenhoe, Northamptonshire on 28 April 1899: 'Several children very poorly, work disturbed by the continual coughing'. Or at Odell School, Bedfordshire, on 24 February 1882: 'Had a bad week's work, so many having coughs making it almost impossible to teach'. Countless other teachers made the same sort of complaint each winter and spring.

However, the epidemics of serious diseases were obviously more alarming. Virtually all country schools experienced an outbreak of one kind or another every few years – and sometimes more frequently than that. A typical example is quoted below from the log book of Cholsey Board School in Berkshire in regard to an outbreak of scarlatina during 1877–8, but it must be emphasized that this random example was mirrored throughout the Victorian period in the experience of other schools and with other ailments.

1877

16 November – A few scholars absent with scarlatina. Warned all the scholars that if any of their brothers or sisters were taken with scarlatina *they* were not to come to school.

19 November – Three more cases of probable scarlatina. Warned Jesse Corderoy and his brother not to come to school for a fortnight as Rhoda, his sister, seems to be taken with it.

29 November – Still a few cases of scarlet fever . . . The sanitary inspector for this district came this morning and made enquiries about it and the precautions taken to prevent it spreading.

4 December – A few more cases of scarlatina.

20 December – Attendance still very low in consequence of illness. Walter Smallbones – scholar in the third class – died and was buried during Christmas week.

1878

1 February – C. Saunders, scholar in Infant School, having died of scarlatina the previous week, the rest of the family (including John, scholar in this school) went into Workhouse Hospital. One case of scarlatina in the village this week.

25 February – Scarlatina, which seemed completely gone, again made its appearance in Brewer family . . .

These entries make quite clear not only the damaging effect of the epidemic on school attendance, but also its prolonged nature – a characteristic which it shared with most similar outbreaks elsewhere. Indeed, Mr Alfred Hart, a private schoolmaster of Ivinghoe, Buckinghamshire, noted in his diary for 1864 that a smallpox epidemic in the spring of that year had altogether cost him £6 in lost school fees; for two or three weeks the school was closed altogether and for about eight or nine weeks, attendance was badly affected.

The lack of equipment for disinfecting either the school or the homes of victims added to this particular problem, as did the absence of proper medical treatment. Of course, where a family could not themselves afford to call in the doctor in these instances of severe illness, recourse must be had to the medical relief provided by the poor law authorities. In the case of the Saunders family of Cholsey quoted above, it will be seen that they were eventually sent to the local Workhouse Hospital, but more often treatment would be given at home in the form of outdoor relief – as an examination of surviving medical relief records demonstrates.

Unfortunately the standard of medical care provided by the poor law boards was not of a very high order. The salaries paid to medical officers were extremely low, and as one doctor pointed out in the early 1870s, there were many poor law unions 'where the medical officer [received only] 2½d or 3d a visit, for which he [had] to provide necessary medicines, keep of horse, turnpike fees, and general wear and tear'.[60] The result of this was that in many cases no medicines were provided at all, for it was only in 1864 that the poor law guardians were allowed to supply the sick with such 'expensive medicines' as cod liver oil and quinine, while even after that date most other medicaments were still the responsibility of the doctor. A very few poor law guardians went so far as to provide additional items like leeches or linseed meal. In these circumstances, therefore, medical officers who could not (or would not) afford proper treatment for their patients, fell back on a second line of defence. Under the Poor Law they could recommend to the guardians that additional food and stimulants be given to their patients. These extras were not classed as 'medicines' and were therefore paid for directly out of the poor rates and not the doctor's pocket. The result was, as a Kentish clergyman pointed out in 1854, that medical officers 'ordered wine and porter rather than provide a tonic medicine of their own', while at around the same time the senior physician of the Royal Infirmary, Bristol, noted that very often poor law doctors in the rural areas would prescribe entirely unsuitable medicine – to young and old alike – purely because it was cheap. One such man was said to have given, 'Epsom salts in peppermint water for gastric fever . . . he gave the patients nothing but Epsom salts'.[15] And despite the fact that from 1864 union workhouses were permitted to keep stocks of cod liver oil, quinine, etc. to supply to the sick free of charge, the situation remained unsatisfactory. In 1870 an official investigation showed that over one-third of pauper patients in eleven Poor Law unions in Bedfordshire, Cambridgeshire, Hertfordshire, Huntingdonshire and Northamptonshire were still receiving meat and stimulants at the recommendation of the district medical officer rather than more formal tonics. At the same time the inspector noted that: 'The kind of case in which these extras are most frequently recommended would be . . . a man with a wife and large family, a man in work receiving 11s a week, one of the children falls ill, he is unable to pay for the attendance of a Doctor, and consequently applies to the Relieving Officer for a medical order; it is granted and the Medical Officer recommends meat and wine. The man with 11s a week cannot possibly maintain his family and provide these necessaries, they are then ordered by the Guardians; when refused, which I certainly did hear on more than one occasion, it was always on the ground of the man being in receipt of sufficient wages to provide them, or that they were supplied from other sources – charitable.' Both this inspector and others found merit in the idea of establishing properly equipped dispensaries where an adequate stock of medicine could be kept by the poor law authorities, as an alternative to the existing system.[18]

But in the rural areas at least, these suggestions fell on stony ground, and as late as 1877 a minority of poor law unions were still not taking advantage of the powers they already possessed to supply cod liver oil or quinine to their pauper patients. Of nine Poor Law unions in Cambridgeshire, only *one* claimed to be providing such medical extras, while in Suffolk, the figure was eight out of seventeen unions – this latter level likewise being applicable to the North Riding of Yorkshire. In Wiltshire, too, a mere ten of the seventeen unions provided the 'extras'. Elsewhere the situation was more satisfactory.[19]

To the country child, these matters were of immediate importance, in so far as youngsters under nine years of age formed a sizeable proportion of the total sick aided by means of outdoor medical relief. Indeed, at the beginning of 1870 they comprised nearly 17 per cent of the total sick in receipt of poor law medicine, while in a few of the rural counties, such as Dorset, Gloucester and Rutland they formed almost 20 per cent.[16] Furthermore, despite all the efforts made, even in the 1890s records for some districts show that food was still more often ordered as an extra than cod liver oil or other medicaments which lay within the purview of the poor law authorities. For example, among the items provided in the Hungerford Union, Berkshire, during that decade for children under the age of sixteen, were eggs, milk and meat. However, in the 1870s, a few children in the union – aged as young as ten and fourteen – had been provided with half-a-pint of brandy per week or a pint of porter daily, when recovering from fever. Although no doubt a tribute to the contemporary faith in 'stimulants' half-a-pint of brandy

COTTAGE HOSPITAL AMBULANCE.

This ingenious ambulance was used to take sick children – and adults – to the Wrington Cottage Hospital. (From Horace Swete, *Handy Book of Cottage Hospitals*, 1870)

seems by twentieth century standards a very large quantity for a child of ten to consume in a week. Again, in the Brackley district of Northamptonshire, a four-year-old boy recovering from fever was supplied with meat and wine during June, 1871, while in August of the following year a six-year-old obtained meat and wine while recovering from an attack of measles. In Kingsclere Medical Relief area, Hampshire, a child as young as one year two months was provided with milk and brandy when suffering from an attack of diarrhoea, during December, 1875. Numerous other examples of the same type could also be quoted – both from these three districts and others.

Of course, an alternative to poor law relief – at least in some villages – existed in the form of charity. Although this, too, often took the form of food and stimulants rather than any other form of medical aid, it should not on that account be dismissed. For many country children were sadly in need of nourishing food and benefited from the 'extras' provided by Poor Law or charity, when recovering from illness. Sometimes the clergy of a parish would take the lead in the matter of charitable help. At Steeple Claydon, Buckinghamshire, the incumbent supported a benevolent society which provided meat, wine, porter and spirits for the sick, as well as cod liver oil and groceries. Again, at Finmere in Oxfordshire the rector provided cod liver oil and other simple medicaments from his own small dispensary in the middle of the nineteenth century, while early in Victoria's reign, at Combe Florey, near Taunton, the well-known cleric and wit, Sydney Smith, was very proud of the apothecary's shop which he had organized at the rectory.[115] It was filled with 'drugs and groceries for the benefit of everyone in the parish'. Some clergymen also favoured prevention rather than cure; at Finmere, the rector provided a brush and comb to the eldest boy and girl in each family. This measure, designed to prevent the occurrence of verminous heads, was reinforced by a further rule that 'no girl might wear long hair', while the head of each pupil had to be examined 'by a wise woman weekly'.[35] Another Oxfordshire cleric who advocated 'sensible precautions' was the incumbent of Yarnton, who issued a series of instructions to his parishioners during the cholera epidemic of 1853–4, not only warning them against eating raw fruit but also suggesting that all should wear 'flannel belly-bands and dry footwear'. He likewise warned against the dangers of dirt and infection and provided a supply of

Cottage hospital at Moreton-in-Marsh, first opened in 1873. Cottage hospitals were designed to cater for 'the respectable poor' and most had at least one child's cot to accommodate young patients. (Cotswold Countryside Collection, Northleach)

lime to every house in the parish for disinfectant purposes.[113] Many parishes could show similar provision by clergy or gentry. Indeed, in Oxfordshire during the 1870s, there are a number of instances of clergymen even 'qualifying and practising as doctors of medicine' in their own right.[113]

Another development along the same lines was the cottage hospital movement, which began at Cranleigh in Surrey during 1859 on the basis of subscriptions from well-wishers. 'A cottage was placed at the doctor's disposal, subscribers of sums, small and large equipped it as a hospital with six beds and one nurse in charge . . . All subscribers had equal privileges in nominating patients . . . Only cases which could not be treated at home were admitted, and all patients were expected to pay, if only 6d a week.'[137] The cottage hospitals were designed to cater for 'the respectable poor' – not the sort of people who usually relied on poor relief. It was estimated that on average the food required would cost 'rather more than $11\frac{1}{4}$d a day' per person, while the 'expense of drugs divided amongst the patients' would (somewhat ominously) probably 'amount to 1d and a fraction per day' each.[60] By 1870 about seventy cottage hospitals had been established in rural areas in most counties. The great majority would have at least 'one child's cot', plus a 'tray for toys, food, &c.'; then those 'little ones, who [were] well enough' could sit up 'in their cots in warm scarlet Garibaldis . . . playing with their toys in the sliding tray.'[60] Burford Cottage Hospital, Oxfordshire, was one which provided in this way for children and the log book at nearby Asthall School during the period autumn 1885 to spring 1886 mentions two pupils who were receiving treatment there.

A further alternative to poor relief – at least for the more prosperous rural families – was the assistance of a local friendly society to which the father of a family, and sometimes child workers, too, had previously contributed. In these cases a doctor would make a special contract with the friendly society to treat member patients as required. One example of this type of sick benefit scheme is provided by the Dorset Friendly Society, which in 1848 offered a contract to local practitioners for the treatment of its members on the basis of 2s 6d for each member; 2s for a wife; 1s for the first three children, and 9d for each additional child under the age of sixteen.[91] However, many friendly societies did not concern themselves with the whole family, but only provided help for the member himself. Such organizations as these latter were obviously of little help to the country *child*.

Given the limited medical treatment available to youngsters, therefore, almost any epidemic disease could present a serious threat to survival for the weaker or most ill–nourished children. In addition to the acute fevers which periodically descended upon most communities, there was, of course, the insidious threat of tuberculosis always present. As Walter Rose (born 1871) of Haddenham,

Buckinghamshire, remembered 'consumption' or 'decline' was 'the dismal ogre that haunted the lives of scores of young villagers with perpetual menace . . . [It was] a dread complaint that claimed its victims so relentlessly that the village at that time was never free from it. The symptoms were always the same; a delicate flush on an otherwise pale face, accompanied by a short, hacking cough; this continued for about three years, the sick one becoming weaker, until the end. There was no time of my early life when this experience was not daily before my eyes, the afflicted ones often being relatives or friends . . . [It] became a perpetual secret fear . . .'[127] Indeed, Rose himself even ate live snails because someone told him they prevented tuberculosis.

Although contacts made at school helped to spread these outbreaks, they were by no means the only source of infection – particularly in the case of fevers. The kind of environment in which disease flourished is made abundantly clear by the official reports prepared by government health inspectors in the later years of Victoria's reign. One example will perhaps suffice to show the conditions in which the greatest dangers were posed; each year many similar reports were prepared.

The extract relates to an investigation carried out in 1899 into the Biggleswade Rural District of Bedfordshire, which had a population of 21,864 in 1891. The cause of enquiry was the 'continued presence of diphtheria and enteric fever' (typhoid). According to the inspector's account: 'Diphtheria [had been] extensively prevalent in Sandy parish for many years past; in 1898 202 cases; great incidence in children of working class; probably spread by personal contact, especially in school; type of epidemic mild. Diphtheria also in Langford parish. During 1898, 42 cases with eight deaths. Personal contact mainly responsible, especially at schools, which were not closed. Type of disease moderately severe. Limited outbreak of enteric fever at Old Warden in autumn of 1898; 14 cases with four deaths; cause obscure, but first cases associated with consumption of contaminated water.

'Water supply throughout district generally from shallow wells, liable to be polluted. Sewerage and drainage defective; filth nuisances abundant. Public scavenging adopted for only one parish; in one other cesspools emptied by hand pumps and carts. No registration or regulation of dairies, cowsheds, &c. Byelaws as to slaughter-houses a dead letter. Practically no disinfection practised. Hospital accommodation insufficient.'[12]

Yet if diseases of the epidemic type accounted for the deaths of a number of country children, the majority fortunately escaped with such relatively minor ailments as coughs and colds or, in winter time, the pain of broken chilblains rubbed raw on stiff boots. Decayed teeth were another minor but unpleasant fact of life, for few youngsters were able to take more than rudimentary care of their

At the end of the Victorian era attempts were made to improve the health of children by giving relevant lessons in school. Here the mistress is showing her pupils how to clean their teeth. The legend on the board emphasizes the point: 'Spare the brush and spoil the teeth'. (The Mansell Collection).

teeth. The Medical Officer of Health for Worcestershire County Council complained in 1904, for example, that he thought 'the tooth brush [was] unknown in a labourer's house', and he did not think any satisfactory substitute was used. However, at Juniper Hill in Oxfordshire a 'clean, wet rag dipped in salt' was employed quite effectively for the purpose.[144] Defective eyesight likewise often went uncorrected and indeed undetected because of lack of medical attention, and if the random eye inspection at Grimsbury School, near Banbury, in 1898, is any guide it was a fairly large problem. Of 150 scholars examined, almost one-fifth were reported as having 'defective eyesight' of some kind. A further source of concern – and one with a strangely modern ring – was the growing use of cigarettes. The Worcestershire Medical Officer of Health in 1904 showed great concern at the 'juvenile smoking' which he considered was 'extremely common in the country districts'.[17] Yet it was not a new phenomenon.

Sickness and its Cures

Even in 1867/68 Mr W. Batley of Chichester, surgeon, had deplored the 'early age at which young lads begin to smoke, and the extent to which the practice is carried . . . Smoking lowers the nervous power of the body, prevents the proper assimilation of food, and thereby deteriorates the quality of the blood . . .'[2] A twentieth century critic could hardly be more forthright than that. Again, at Farnborough in Hampshire an entry in the school log book during 1872 indicated that the 'headmaster had occasion to cane several boys for smoking cigars'; but few youngsters could afford cigars even for experimental purposes, and cigarettes or pipes were the usual resort of boys engaged in surreptitious smoking.

So far most of the health problems considered have related to children of either pre-school or school age. However, for those who went out to work on the land or in one of the cottage industries at an early age, employment itself might prove damaging to their health. Although most medical men agreed that for the healthy child a moderate amount of work in the fields did not pose any particular danger, the story was different if they were weak and sickly. Those who were sent out with the horses when very young were thought to be particularly at risk. In Dorset, where lads went out to help with ploughing at the age of eight or nine during the 1860s, a local doctor claimed that this employment prevented 'proper muscular development, and very often [produced] . . . "tuberculous diseases" . . . The sameness and overhardness of toil mars the young yielding muscles . . . It is seen in their after life in a way . . . most clear; there is a want of physical energy – of what I may call labour pluck – a deadening of mind and body force . . . I see the effect of the early work in making the boys bow-legged.'[2] A colleague from Witney in Oxfordshire was of much the same opinion: 'I think that children are employed too young in heavy ploughed land; it tells on them in after life; when they get to be about 50 they go at the knees and are very much bent.'

Nor were the doubts confined to medical men alone. Some Church of England clergy entertained similar reservations, including the incumbent of Letcombe Basset in Berkshire, who noted in the late 1860s that there was 'scarcely one young man in the village reaching the height of 5 feet 6 inches. I entertain no doubt that, poor living also being taken into account, the physical frame is weakened and the growth stunted by the early period in life at which field labour is commenced.'[2] Certainly, one child worker – George Edwards of Norfolk – had no doubts on the subject. In later life he attributed 'his smallness of stature to being dragged into the fields when a boy of six years old; to overwork and bad living . . .'[134]

During the cold winter months bird scaring, especially, could be extremely uncomfortable and even harmful. One small child who was set to work in Norfolk in this fashion was later remembered by another lad to have been 'struck

211

by the cold; the Steward found him nearly dead, and picked him up and brought him into my mother. She treated him as best she knew, with hot blankets, and hot bottles, and hot sand, and they brought him round.'[102] Not all were as fortunate.

Likewise the domestic industries – notably lacemaking and glovemaking – often posed a threat to the well-being of the young workers. The sedentary nature of the work adversely affected the digestive system, while its confined character in small stuffy rooms, coupled with the poor nourishment of the children concerned, frequently provided a breeding ground for consumption. Again, in the winter-time the use of a 'dicky-pot' or earthenware pot containing hot ashes, for heating purposes led to the emission of fumes which stung the throat and caused the children to cough, while the practice of placing these containers on the ground by their feet caused chilblains and 'swelled ankles'.[3] On this account the pots were widely condemned by the medical profession. (See also Chapter 6.)

In most of the aspects discussed so far, the intervention of the *State* in helping to secure the health and well-being of the young was minimal – the poor law medical service, the Factory and Workshop Acts, and the Education legislation providing the sum total. However, there was one notable exception to this general passivity – namely the matter of small-pox vaccination. As early as 1841 'the first free specifically non-pauperizing medical service provided by the Legislature on a national scale', came into operation when all poor law guardians were empowered to vaccinate free of charge any children presented to them.[107] Thirteen years later, in 1853, the permissive approach was dropped – at least in theory – as a determined attempt was made to eradicate this dangerous and disfiguring disease. Under the new Act all children were *required* to be vaccinated within three months of their birth, but for various technical reasons – plus the opposition of parents suspicious of compulsion – the intention was not translated into reality until the early 1870s.

At this time the normal method of vaccination was that of 'arm to arm', and in country districts it presented a number of problems because of the scattered nature of the population. For example, the Medical Officer of the Privy Council, John Simon, pointed out in 1871 that in many rural areas public vaccination was only carried out once or twice a year, and when the vaccinator 'had one or two children well vaccinated', he would 'take one of them with him round in his carriage from house to house, and vaccinate the . . . children as he [went] about'.[24] In other places there were slight variations on this practice. In the Huntingdonshire fen country, it was usual for the doctor to vaccinate a child from another at his surgery. As one girl later recalled: 'When my brother had been vaccinated, the doctor at Ramsey sent for Mother to take the child to see him at a certain time on a certain day. He warn't very well 'cos his arm were paining him, and it were a pouring wet day, but Mother thought it were for his own good, so she carried him three mile and a half through the rain to the old doctor's. When she got there she found about a dozen other mothers with babies all waiting to be vaccinated from our baby.'[112]

Indeed, however worthy the intention of legislators may have been in trying to introduce free compulsory vaccination, by no means all parents subscribed to their views. The arm-to-arm method of vaccination was fraught with dangers of cross-infection and there were soon 'horror' stories published by the press of apparently healthy babies becoming fatally infected after being vaccinated. Although an anti-compulsory vaccination lobby developed in the early days it was only in the 1860s and 1870s that its real strength appeared. In 1866 an Anti-Compulsory Vaccination League was formally set up, and began to win support not only in the towns but in country districts as well. In July 1872, for example, the goods of four Banbury men were seized and 'conveyed to the Town Hall for sale', to pay the fines and costs they had incurred in prosecutions for not having their children vaccinated, while in late June, 1875, members of the Banbury and district branch of the League held a large demonstration 'on the occasion of the release from Northampton goal' of one of their members, who had undergone fourteen days' imprisonment for refusing to pay the fine and costs for not having his child vaccinated. 'After parading the town, the Vaccination Acts were publicly burned amid much enthusiasm.' Even in the remote Radnorshire parish of Clyro in March, 1871, no less than fifteen people were summoned at the local petty sessions for neglecting to have their children vaccinated.[117] And in Hampshire, as late as February 1897, an Andover tradesman was committed to Winchester Gaol 'under the Vaccination Acts for non-payment of costs. He has paid £40 12s 6d in sixty previous convictions, and refused to pay more', according to the account in the *Hampshire Chronicle*.

Yet if these parents' views appear over-alarmist, there was perhaps some justification for them. John Langley, who lived in Banbury from the 1880s onwards, remembered that he had 'a very nasty ear trouble' following his vaccination, while Dorothy Loveday, who was born at Wardington Manor House in 1883, recalled that her mother had sought an alternative to the arm-to-arm method. She had insisted instead on 'calf's lymph, even though it meant a worse arm, a more fractious baby and being called a cruel mother'.[109]

The resistance to vaccination grew in volume as the immediate danger of smallpox itself receded – ironically as a result of the now vilified vaccination campaign. In the end the growing public concern was recognized and during the 1890s a Royal Commission investigated the whole position, hearing evidence from both town and country women on the allegedly fatal effect of vaccination on their babies. Among other witnesses the Norwich secretary of the local branch of the Anti Vaccination League gave evidence, declaring that in 1890 his organization had investigated 'some twenty cases of injuries which happened in villages close round' his own city.[25]

It was in an attempt to meet these objections – coupled with an appreciation that poor quality vaccine *could* do harm – that in 1898 a new Vaccination Act was passed which went some way to eliminating the points at issue. In future, vaccinators were to offer 'glycerinated calf lymph' instead of the 'humanized lymph from arm-to-arm' as under the old method; and secondly, a conscience clause was introduced, whereby parents who did not wish to have their baby vaccinated could apply to the local magistrates. An examination of petty sessions records shows a steady flow of exemption certificates being granted in the course of the following years. However, it is a tribute to the effectiveness of the early vaccination movement that despite the fears and alarms of parents, in the rural counties in 1873–7, smallpox had been responsible for only 0.1 infant deaths per 1,000 births, while in 1898–1902 the number was so tiny that it could not be registered at all.[17] In the 1830s and 1840s the position had been very different – so that, for example, during the 1839 smallpox epidemic just over one-quarter of the 8,714 deaths recorded were accounted for by children under the age of one. And the annual rate of mortality from small-pox in that year for children up to and including the age of four, was 2.73 per 1,000 living – a rate far in excess of that for any of the other age groups quoted. Here at least progress had been made by the end of the Victorian era.

TABLE 3

REPORT OF THE REGISTRAR GENERAL FOR BIRTHS, DEATHS AND MARRIAGES FOR ENGLAND AND WALES FOR THE YEAR 1897 (From Parliamentary Papers, 1898, Vol. XVIII) p. xvi 'In the year 1897 . . . in registration counties the mortality of infants under one year of age in 1,000 births ranged from 101 in Hertfordshire and 109 in Buckinghamshire, Suffolk, Herefordshire, and Rutlandshire to 179 in Staffordshire and 187 both in Warwickshire and in Lancashire.' P. lxiv Deaths of children under one year to 1,000 births; averaging the ten year period 1887–96 and including the year 1897

	1887–96	1897
Urban counties		
Cheshire	150	161
Durham	161	156
Lancashire	173	187
Leicestershire	166	167

London	155	159
Staffordshire	165	179
West Riding of Yorkshire	162	165
Rural counties		
Wiltshire	102	113
Dorset	97	111
Oxfordshire	115	122
Herefordshire	112	109
Buckinghamshire	112	109
Westmorland	104	114
Sussex	112	117

TABLE 4

REPORT OF THE REGISTRAR GENERAL FOR BIRTHS, DEATHS AND MARRIAGES FOR ENGLAND AND WALES FOR THE YEAR 1897 (From Parliamentary Papers, 1898, Vol. XVIII)

DEATHS AT DIFFERENT AGES REGISTERED IN THE YEAR 1897

	Total deaths (all ages)	Total deaths under 5 years	Deaths under 5 years as a % of total deaths
Industrialized counties			
Cheshire	13,705	5,389	46
Durham	19,657	8,972	46
Lancashire	87,197	38,413	44
Leicestershire	7,016	2,938	42
London	79,613	32,228	42
Staffordshire	22,840	10,496	46
West Riding of Yorkshire	47,937	19,373	40
Rural counties			
Wiltshire	3,817	1,104	29
Dorset	2,913	802	28
Oxfordshire	2,937	820	28
Herefordshire	1,879	438	23
Buckinghamshire	2,352	688	29
Westmorland	948	240	25
Sussex	8,140	2,231	27

TABLE 5

(From *Inter-Departmental Committee on Physical Deterioration Report*, 1904, Parliamentary Papers, 1904, Vol. XXXII.)

p. 132   AVERAGE RATE OF INFANT MORTALITY UNDER ONE YEAR, PER 1,000 BIRTHS
AMONG MALE AND FEMALE INFANTS

(The urban counties – ten in number – had a population of 17.8 million in 1902; the rural counties – sixteen in number – included Buckinghamshire, Cambridgeshire, Cornwall, Herefordshire, Huntingdon, Lincolnshire, North Wales, Norfolk, Oxfordshire, Rutland, Shropshire, Somerset, South Wales (except Glamorgan), Suffolk, Westmorland and Wiltshire: they had a population total in 1902 of 4.28 million.)

| | Urban Counties | | | | Rural Counties | | | |
| | Males | | Females | | Males | | Females | |
	1873–1877	1898–1902	1873–1877	1898 1902	1873–1877	1898–1902	1873–1877	1898–1902
All causes	175.9	180.0	145.5	149.2	139.9	138.8	112.5	111.0
Selected causes only								
Smallpox	0.5	0.0	0.5	0.0	0.1	0.0	0.1	0.0
Diarrhoea, Dysentry, Cholera, Enteritis	22.1	36.6	18.8	32.5	11.1	18.5	9.3	14.8
Atrophy &c.	29.9	23.8	25.8	19.4	33.0	23.7	27.5	18.8
Meningitis, Convulsions	32.0	23.3	24.5	18.2	26.3	20.1	19.8	15.2
Premature birth	14.2	22.3	11.6	17.9	12.6	20.7	10.0	16.7

(NB: Deaths of infants from diarrhoea and atrophy were about twice as high among illegitimate infants as among legitimate ones.)

NOTES ON ADDITIONAL SOURCES USED
Reminiscences of my mother.
Diary of Mr Alfred Hart, private schoolmaster of Ivinghoe, Buckinghamshire, for the year 1864. I am indebted to Mr J. Hawkins of Pitstone for permission to use this.
Hungerford Union – District 3 Medical Relief Book, 1875–7, G/H/7/1 at Berkshire County Record Office.

Brackley District Medical Relief Book 1869–72, BK. 419, at Northamptonshire County Record Office.

Kingsclere Medical Relief Book 1872–6, PL.III–II/36 at Hampshire County Record Office.

Steeple Claydon Parochial Charities in 1872 Visitation Returns, Bucks. Archdeaconry, MS. Oxf. Dioc. Pp. c. 337 at Oxfordshire Record Office.

Petty Sessions Minute Books: Henley, MS. Dep. Deeds, Henley A XVI (11) at Oxfordshire Record Office; Wallingford at Berkshire County Record Office.

CHAPTER ELEVEN

'Crime and Punishment'

'As to the crimes most common amongst the class we have been considering, wood-stealing is the most common overt act of crime they commit; it is practised in some districts to an immense extent by women and young children. The boys at an early age but too often take to turnip-stealing and poaching.' Extract from a letter sent by the Hon. and Revd S. Godolphin Osborne, Rector of Bryanston-cum-Durweston, Dorset, to an Assistant Poor Law Commissioner, in connection with the *Report on the Employment of Women and Children in Agriculture* (Parliamentary Papers, 1843, Vol. XII, p. 75).

'The scourge of Juvenile delinquency affects very little the agricultural districts; it is chiefly confined to towns of large population.' Captain W.J. Williams – Inspector of Prisons for the Home District, in evidence to the *Select Committee on Criminal and Destitute Juveniles* (Parliamentary Papers, 1852, Vol. VII, Q.71).

There can be little doubt that among the various criminal offences with which Victorian country children were charged that of petty larceny predominated. Thus an examination of the Minute Book of the Henley Petty Sessions in Oxfordshire reveals that during the years 1862–76 inclusive, a period of fifteen years, there were forty-two offences involving children under the age of sixteen. Of these no less than twenty-nine concerned theft – as opposed to five cases of arson, two of assault, two of damage to property, two of breach of the contract of employment and one each for poaching and gambling (the latter relating to children playing 'tip cat' on the public highway). In all instances the goods stolen were of low value – 10s being the highest amount recorded – and many concerned such tiny items as the theft of walnuts valued at 6d; of apples worth 3d; of two eggs, valued as 2d; and 'one bundle of wood of the value of three pence'. There was even a case involving a pre-Christmas theft of ivy worth 1d, but in this instance the charge against the boy defendant was dismissed, although his adult male companion, a farm labourer, was sentenced to fourteen days' hard labour for the offence.

'CRIME AND PUNISHMENT'

An inspection of records relating to other rural areas confirms this prevalence of petty theft among young criminals. According to the Bicester Petty Sessions Minute Book, Oxfordshire, during the two years June 1855 to June 1857, five cases involving children were heard – four concerning theft and one a charge of obtaining food by false pretences. At Great Marlow Petty Sessions, Buckinghamshire, likewise, of three cases of juvenile crime heard during the period 1866–71, two were for theft and one a breach of the Turnpike legislation. In fact as Mary Carpenter, the Bristol social reformer who devoted much of her life to helping juvenile delinquents, wrote in 1853 'When [child] offenders are spoken of young thieves are usually intended; for an examination of the annals of crime will show that varied as are the offences of adults, those for which children are arraigned in a criminal court are almost invariably thefts more or less trivial . . .'[37] (See also Document M.)

Yet, as the examples quoted above perhaps indicate, the incidence of juvenile crime dealt with by the courts varied very much from one part of the country to another. In some areas the child was punished for minor offences by parents or perhaps the injured party himself, without being brought before the magistrates at all. But in other cases a more vengeful spirit seems to have ruled, and then punishments might be severe. At Henley Petty Sessions, during the 1860s and 1870s birchings were frequently ordered, while imprisonment was imposed for comparatively trivial infringements. In the case of the more serious crimes (such as arson) the defendant might be sent on to a higher court.

To modern eyes, however, those young offenders appear most unfortunate who were punished for stealing small items of food, such as turnip tops, bread and butter, eggs, etc. For in many cases the crime was no doubt prompted only by hunger. Thus on 13 March 1857, three boys were convicted at Bicester Petty Sessions with stealing '3 lbs weight of figs from the shop of Mr James Goble at Bicester – of the value of 2s'. They were each sentenced to one month's imprisonment with hard labour. On 21 July 1864, two boy labourers from the village of Northstoke, Oxfordshire, were convicted of stealing 'four pounds of Bacon and one four pound loaf of Bread of the value of three shillings and sixpence', and were sentenced by the Henley bench to twenty-one days' imprisonment with hard labour. And at Great Marlow Petty Sessions in Buckinghamshire two boys found guilty of stealing turnip tops valued at 1s were each given the alternative either of paying a fine, costs, and compensation, amounting to £1 9s 3d or else of facing one calendar month's imprisonment with hard labour. The sentence was imposed on 15 April 1871, and in the event only one of the boys was able to pay his fine. The other – as was hardly surprising for a farm labourer's son – could not raise such a substantial sum of money and so presumably was forced to serve a term of imprisonment.

In addition, the severity of sentences varied a good deal and by no means all offenders were punished by imprisonment alone. A whipping or a period of training in a Reformatory School might also have to be endured. In December 1869, a boy found guilty of stealing 17 lb of raisins at Weymouth in Dorset received 'three months' hard labour and five years' reformatory school'. Even more savagely, at Blandford petty sessions in the same county a ten-year-old labourer was sentenced to ten days' imprisonment with hard labour, followed by five years in a reformatory school, for taking 'three pennyworth of turnips from a heap in a field'.

Again, at Henley Petty Sessions, on 8 October 1863, a twelve-year-old labourer was sentenced to one day's imprisonment with hard labour 'and to be once privately whipped twelve strokes with a Birch Rod' for helping to steal twenty-eight apples. And before the same court about ten years later, two brothers (aged twelve and fifteen years) were each imprisoned for one calendar month, with hard labour, 'and then to be sent to a Reformatory School for four years' for stealing 'one bag containing Bread and Butter of the value of 6d.' Similarly, a ten-year-old boy from Benson, Oxfordshire, was sentenced by another bench of magistrates in January 1875, to ten days' hard labour in Oxford gaol, plus two years in a reformatory school, for stealing 56 lb of coal.

In fact, of the twenty-nine cases involving juvenile theft which were heard before Henley Petty Sessions in the period 1862–76, sixteen were punished by imprisonment, ranging from a day or so to three months – sometimes with hard labour. Five of these youngsters were also sentenced to a birching. Of the remaining thirteen, two were given the option of paying a fine, or in default 'seven days' hard labour'; four were punished by being birched only; four had their cases dismissed; and two were required 'to come up for judgment when called upon' and were given no immediate punishment. In addition, a ten-year-old boy, who had stolen a watch, was sent to an Industrial School for five years in May, 1874, and his father was required to contribute 1s 3d per week towards his maintenance. Industrial schools were first established in 1857 and, according to Mary Carpenter, were intended for: 'Those who have not yet fallen into actual crime but who are almost certain from their ignorance, destitution and the circumstances in which they are growing up, to do so if a helping hand be not extended to them.'[68] Finally, in three of the sixteen cases involving imprisonment, the young offenders were also sentenced to a period of training at a Reformatory School.

Reformatories were a fairly recent innovation, having received legislative sanction under the 1854 Act 'For the Better Care and Reformation of Youthful Offenders in Great Britain'. They were designed to assist young offenders below the age of sixteen by removing them 'from the scene of criminal life before they could become fully hardened.'[146] Unfortunately, the system had one very serious flaw. Before a youngster could be sent to a Reformatory School he or she must spend a minimum of about two weeks in prison, with all the undesirable impressions that this could make upon the young mind. Only when that time had expired could transfer to the Reformatory take place, for a period 'not less than two years and not exceeding five years'. Not until 1899 was this unsatisfactory position changed and imprisonment 'as a preliminary to going to a Reformatory School' abolished.

Within the Reformatories instruction in the three 'R's was given as well as a limited amount of industrial training designed to help with future employment. For the girls the main emphasis was on domestic service or laundry work. For the boys the training largely took the form of agricultural work (intended partly to fit the youngster for a new life in the colonies, should he choose to emigrate in later life[6]) and also instruction in such trades as tailoring, shoemaking, etc. The official annual reports on the schools give a flavour of this work. Thus in May 1883, boys at the North Lancashire Reformatory at Bleasdale, Garstang (with 125 inmates) were said to be employed as follows: 'The farm of 110 acres and the care of stock furnishes a large amount of useful labour. There are classes for tailoring and shoemaking, and a junior class for repairing and darning. The School takes a contract for road repairs and in the winter there is turf-cutting, wood-chopping, and stone-breaking . . .' At the Buxton Reformatory School for Boys near Norwich (with forty-one inmates) the training took a similar line: 'The farm of 40 acres gives plenty to do. The boys work occasionally on the neighbouring farms. There is a class for shoemaking, and the boys manufacture their own clothing and bake their own bread. There is a good garden.' The situation in most Reformatories conformed to this general pattern, although in some rather harsher conditions might apply. Indeed, in the more restrictive there were 'barred windows, locked doors and cropped hair', which converted them almost into prisons, while in a few 'industrial training' harmful to the children's health was embarked upon. In 1879 the managers of one Reformatory had to be formally requested 'to reduce the amount of labour applied to the brickfield'.

On the whole the number of country children felt to be in need of Reformatory School training was relatively small compared to the position in the more densely populated areas – as the table given below indicates. Thus in the year 1900, the three urbanized counties quoted provided about half of the children committed to Reformatory Schools, although at the time of the 1901 Census of Population they had only a little over a third of the total child population in the age group up to sixteen. Their share in the committals were clearly much larger than the size of their juvenile population should have warranted:

NUMBER OF CHILDREN COMMITTED TO REFORMATORY SCHOOLS IN
FOUR SELECTED YEARS FROM THREE URBANIZED AND THREE RURAL
COUNTIES

	1861	1883	1892	1900
National total	1,239	1,361	1,058	1,266
Urbanized counties				
Lancashire	222	329	194	287
Middlesex (including London)	231	152	121	208
Yorkshire	129	150	127	129
Rural counties				
Oxfordshire	8	6	3	3
Norfolk	12	13	9	12
Wiltshire	7	12	7	9

(From 27th, 40th and 45th Reports of Inspector of Reformatory and Industrial
Schools in England and Wales, Parliamentary Papers: 1884, Vol. XLIV; 1897,
Vol. XLI; and 1902, Vol. XLVIII.)

The young criminal: William Fleckney,
a sixteen-year-old Bedfordshire labourer,
was sentenced to five years' penal
servitude at Bedford Assizes in March
1868. The charge was that he 'did
feloniously kill and slay . . . George
Barrett at Luton' the previous January.
He had earlier been imprisoned for one
calendar month for theft. (Bedford Gaol
Records at Bedfordshire County Record
Office)

'CRIME AND PUNISHMENT'

Although some courts continued to send country children to both prison and reformatories for trifling offences, doubts on the wisdom of this course were steadily growing. Yet equally, even in the middle of the nineteenth century it was possible to find unenlightened critics who thought that conditions in a number of the gaols were *too comfortable* to act as a deterrent to juvenile offenders. The attempts at Reading Gaol, to reform criminals not by brutal treatment but 'through the influence of religion' soon found their critics. At Reading and other prisons which followed along the same lines the so-called 'separate system' of discipline was developed, with each prisoner confined in his own cell and having no contact with his fellow prisoners. Most of the young prisoners at Reading were said to be 'of the agricultural class',[6] and the recipe for conversion here was to set them 'large chunks of the Bible to learn by heart and repeat next day to a monitor'. In fact, the burden of learning and the solitude were regarded by some prisoners more as a deterrent than a reforming process and it was said 'that criminals had been driven from Berkshire to Buckinghamshire by the separate system at Reading Gaol.'[146] However, outside opponents of the policy were not convinced. One sourly pointed out that within the walls of Reading 'prisoners need not *work*, except for the purpose of recreation and healthful exercise'. There was no treadmill, and young and old alike were engaged on 'such light employments as pumping, oakum-picking and knitting . . . Ten hours out of the twenty-four are allowed for sleep, three for meals, two for bodily exercise or recreation, while the others are whiled away in mopish indolence and moody abstraction.' This critic self-righteously concluded that: 'A large proportion of recommittals is the inevitable result of such over-indulgence.'[40]

The dietary offered to prisoners was another subject of controversy. For most of the nineteenth century it was generally believed that convicts obtained better food than many free labourers, and the chaplain of Reading Gaol, who was a fanatical advocate of the 'separate system' reforms mentioned above, nevertheless commented on the 'excess' of diet offered in all prisons 'in which the Government Dietary [had] been adopted. It [was] incompatible with either punishment or improvement.' He also observed that: 'Many of our juvenile culprits have never feasted upon such luxurious abundance before they entered the prison . . . They become gross, and instead of giving proof of that moral activity which distinguishes other prisoners, they receive instruction with a sleepy indifference, and commonly disregard advice.'[42] Cautionary tales were told of young country boys who had committed offences purely for the purpose of receiving another prison sentence, since they had 'more good victuals' in gaol than they could get at home.

No doubt for the really destitute child, prison life was an improvement on the uncertainties of day-to-day existence outside on the streets. Nevertheless informed opinion was increasingly coming to question the validity of using prisons, no matter how organized, for minor juvenile offences. This was felt to be especially the case for those youngsters who had no previous criminal record. In 1847 a Select Committee of the House of Lords, examining the subject of juvenile offenders, had noted: 'That the contamination of a gaol, as gaols are usually managed, may often prove fatal, and must always be hurtful to boys committed for a first offence, and thus for a very trifling act they may become trained to the worst of crimes, is clear enough.'[38]

The same point was made in 1852 by Mr Sergeant Adams, an Assistant Judge of the Middlesex Quarter Sessions in his evidence to the Select Committee on Criminal and Destitute Juveniles. He declared that when, a few years earlier, he had visited Maidstone Gaol he had observed 'a group of children' confined together for fruit stealing: ' . . . there I recognized a vast number of my old acquaintances, who had been stealing from the markets at Deptford and other places. I saw a little urchin, about ten years of age, and I said, "Who is that boy?" "Oh," said the gaoler, "he has been committed by the county magistrates for stealing damsons." He had got over a garden wall and got a hatful of damsons, and had been sent to prison for a month. I said, "You put that boy, with your classification, with the most notorious young thieves in the neighbourhood of London. You will ruin that boy if you don't take him away." '

Twelve years later Mary Carpenter was likewise deploring the fact that 'young boys are still so frequently sent to gaol for trifling offences . . . For robbing gardens of apples, for breach of police regulations, young boys are constantly sentenced to imprisonment.'[38]

However, it was in 1875 that one of the more notorious cases involving imprisonment for petty theft came to light. Emily Davies, a thirteen-year-old Herefordshire girl, was sentenced to fourteen days' imprisonment and four years in a Reformatory School for stealing a peck of apples and a few plums. Her father was ordered to pay 2s a week towards her maintenance while she was away from home, and: 'The chairman of the magistrates solemnly told Emily and her father, that if they did not deal with such cases severely, it would be of no example to others.' But in this instance the severity of the sentence aroused the attention of journalists in London, Birmingham, Leeds, Manchester and Liverpool and editorials appeared condemning the action of the magistrates. Even *Punch* came to Emily's aid, while the Liberal MP for Leominster, Thomas Blake, raised the case with the Home Secretary. He pointed out that the value of the apples which Emily had stolen had only been a shilling, and appealed for aid 'in obtaining her discharge'. When he received no response to this request, Blake decided to organize a protest meeting at Ross, the girl's home town. On the appointed night, 11 November, a large crowd assembled in the old Market House and resolutions were passed demanding that the child be set free as 'the chief witness in the case, a little ten-year-old boy of dull intellect, himself an accomplice in the theft' had been allowed to give evidence on oath without understanding the 'solmen nature' of the proceedings. The protests at last bore fruit and on 1 December, Mr Blake was able to inform the local press that Emily had been released; at the same time the Home Secretary expressed his opinion 'that it was not desirable that young children on first conviction should be sent to a reformatory.'

There is little doubt that the publicity given to the case did good, even if, despite the Home Secretary's views, petty sessions records show that children *were* still being sent to prison or reformatory for trivial offences long after this date. But it is possible to detect a gradual mellowing of views on the part of magistrates. In 1881 they were formally asked to comment on 'the state of the law relating to the treatment and punishment of juvenile offenders', and although opinions varied in emphasis, a fairly common attitude was that taken by the Westmorland magistrates when they declared: 'It is desirable that the power of justices of the peace to imprison children and young persons should be used sparingly and with discretion, but imprisonment being in some cases the only suitable punishment, it would be very undesirable that the power should be entirely abolished . . . It is not, however, desirable that any boy or girl under 14 years of age should be sent to prison for a first or second offence, except as a necessary preliminary to sending to a Reformatory.' A number of respondents also agreed with the views of the Recorder of Tewkesbury, Gloucestershire: 'I have always been averse to sending them to prison, either on remand, or on summary conviction, or preparatory to being sent to a Reformatory or Industrial School, for, in my opinion, they never escape contamination . . . I would suggest that a correctional department should be attached to Reformatories to which bad boys should be sent for a longer or shorter period, at the discretion of the magistrates . . . I believe whipping, by a thoroughly responsible officer, to be very salutary as a punishment.'[11]

In the event, although a major change in the law to end the imprisonment of children was to be delayed until the Children Act of 1908, a growing reluctance to impose this punishment for petty crimes became apparent as the Victorian era drew to its close. Under the Probation of First Offenders Act of 1887, for example, courts were given power to discharge offenders in trifling cases or in circumstances where the youth, character and background of the person convicted justified it. The effects of this alteration in attitude can be seen in the records of the various Petty Sessions. At Henley during the period 1898–1900 boys charged with stealing pears and apples had only to face small fines of 1s, and even these were to be 'suspended during good behaviour', while all costs were

WHEREAS sundry persons, in violation of *His Majesty's Proclamation*, for the due observance of the *Lord's Day*, (and also of an Order issued by us to the same purport,) have practised *Playing at Ball* and other Games on the said Day, to the great annoyance of the Inhabitants;

Notice is hereby Given,

That if any person is hereafter found offending against the aforementioned *Proclamation of His Majesty*, they will be dealt with *according to Law*.

THOMAS SYMONDS, Minister.

RICHARD BOWERMAN, } Church-
SAMUAL DRUCE, } wardens.

JOSEPH FOSTER, } Constables.
WILLIAM BURCHELL, } Constables.

ENSHAM,
April 27, 1820.

J. AND T. BARTLETT, PRINTERS, OXFORD.

Prohibition on youngsters playing ball at Eynsham, Oxfordshire, in 1820. (The Bodleian Library, Oxford, John Johnson Collection: Sunday Observance 1) remitted. About thirty-five years earlier, two boys, aged eleven and twelve respectively, had been sentenced to 'one day's imprisonment with hard labour . . . and to be once privately whipped 12 strokes with a Birch rod' for jointly stealing twenty-eight apples. By the 1890s, indeed, leisure-time activities were the major source of conflict between the law and children in the Henley area. There were several instances of boys being charged with playing 'a certain Game called "Football"' on the public highway, during the year 1899, and fines ranging from 1s to 2s were imposed upon them. Again, in August of the same year, seven boys from the village of Caversham were accused of bathing in the River Thames 'without proper bathing dress or drawers contrary to the provisions of Bye-Law 80 of the Thames Bye-Laws 1898'. Three were fined 5s, plus costs of 1s 9d, and in default seven days' hard labour, while the others were fined 3d and costs of 1s 9d, or in default three days' imprisonment. They were 'allowed until Saturday next to pay'.

Of course many victims of these petty offences were always unwilling to press formal charges against children. They preferred to deal with the wrongdoers in their own way – if necessary by taking the law into their own hands. This was the reaction of Sydney Smith, when incumbent of Combe Florey in Somerset – although to modern eyes his methods were somewhat barbaric. Thus, 'a little girl who was caught biting one of his fallen peaches was made to spend all day on the lawn with a placard round her neck bearing the word "Thief" in large letters. A lad who was discovered looking covetously at the rector's fruit trees had his ears pinched with such vigour they tingled in old age at the remembrance of the episode.'[115] School log books provide other examples – as at Ivinghoe, Buckinghamshire, on 13 June 1879: 'Revd H.I. Rawlinson attended school on Monday afternoon and caned Edwin Dollimore for throwing stones over the vicarage wall into the garden'. Or at Leckford, Hampshire, on 25 April 1881: 'Rector on Friday obliged to warn some of the boys against chalking on the outer doors and railings'. Occasionally the policeman would also be asked to visit the school and speak to the assembled pupils about their misdemeanours – as at Elmdon in Warwickshire. Here an entry for the year 1898 recorded: 'Mr Grubb (the Policeman) visited school and spoke to the children about stone throw-ing'. For most youngsters this was enough to secure at least a temporary improvement in behaviour, for they had a deep-seated fear of the police and the law.

So far the main emphasis has been placed on cases of petty theft involving country children – since this was the most common form of juvenile crime. But poaching also provided a fertile source of law-breaking in many villages, even for youngsters. In the early 1860s the Chaplain of Bedford gaol considered that children who spent long hours in the fields bird-scaring, were particularly likely to become poachers: 'I think I am safe in saying that at least two-thirds of our poachers imbibe the taste for poaching from the temptations presented by that employment'.[51] And an examination of petty sessional records and the local press bears out the widespread nature of this particular offence.

Although young poachers probably embarked upon their career primarily to obtain food for the pot, a number quickly learned to enjoy the excitement and risks involved for their own sake. The sense of exhilaration was later recalled by one Victorian child poacher: 'I learned most of my woodcraft from the old mole-catcher. He was a little wizened, dried up man, and while supposed to be catching moles he wasn't above picking up a rabbit, or even partridge or pheasant eggs if the coast was clear . . . He taught me how to set a "snickle" in a rabbit run, and how to tickle trout as they floated under the bank in the beck. I was never lucky enough to "snickle" a rabbit, and the only time I caught a trout I fell into the beck with excitement. I took the trout home, expecting great praise for my prowess; all I got was an ash-plant across my sopping wet trousers, and I was sent to bed. I had committed a serious offence, though I was too young to know it, and "ashing a lad's behind" was the recognized form of punishment.'[105] Nevertheless, despite the unfavourable parental response, the boy was not deterred from continuing his 'hobby' in later years. Consequently, when he had enjoyed a ramble through the woods, he 'always brought home a couple of rabbits' for the pot. This casual offender – like most – was lucky enough to escape detection. But some lads who adopted a more businesslike and daring approach to poaching were less fortunate.

One such regular offender eventually became, at least in his own estimation 'The King of the Norfolk Poachers'. As he later recorded, his introduction to poaching came by chance one winter in the mid-1870s, when his father showed him where a hare had been eating greenstuff in the garden. The boy resolved to do something about it, and after discovering an old trap in the shed, he successfully set it to catch the hare. He received small thanks for his action. 'Father . . . caught me by the collar and gave me the soundest floggen a boy ever received.'

But the punishment served no purpose; a love of poaching had been implanted and soon the youngster was acquiring more traps and surreptitiously selling his ill-gotten gains to a local fish hawker. Even when he left school to work on the land he continued his poaching activities until one day the law caught up with him. 'It was this way. In the villige there was a large amount of Common land, of corse it was enclosed as there were plenty of rabbitts there, and I sone got to work snaren them. Some kind frend gave me away and wen I went one morning there was a Police man and a Keeper there waiten for me . . . In those days if a lad did a bit rong it was Prison for him . . . No doubt that the Maderstrates thought to

228

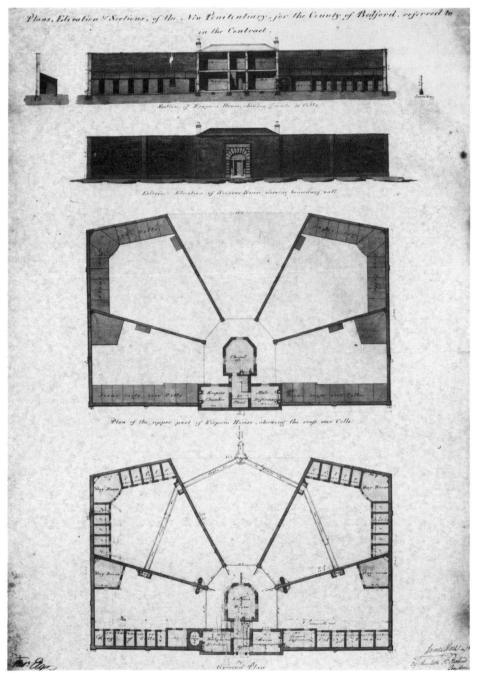

Bedford gaol where William Fleckney was confined after his arrest in January 1868. Its forbidding appearance must have intimidated even hardened criminals. (Bedfordshire County Record Office)

cure me with a lesson, specially as the Police had painted me so black to them.'[102]

He was sentenced to a month in gaol and departed for Norwich Castle by train 'handcuffed to a Police man'. 'Wen I got to Norwich I was led along through the streets the same way like a real dangerous fellow . . . at last we arrived at the Castle Entrance. . . I shall never forget what I felt when I first saw that gloomy Place, and I was just fit to cry, but held back my tears some how . . .'

Once inside he was made to take a bath before being dressed in a prison uniform 'covered all over with the broad Arrow and a number to wear on my Jacket'. Then he was escorted to his small, stone-flagged cell and was settled in for the night with bread and water for his first meal.

The impressions made upon this boy by this imprisonment – and the bitterness he felt – were no doubt reflected in the experience of many of the other Victorian boys and girls sent to prison for less serious offences than his. Certainly the visits of the chaplain were received in a spirit very different from what was intended:

'You had a Bible and prair Book and a himn book, and some times the Parson would come along and leave some littel track. He would some times come and se you, to tell you the enormity of your crime . . . I used to hate the sight of him.'[102]

Apart from the question of religion, however, there was the daily routine of prison life itself to contend with. The prisoners were expected to rise at six in the morning, dress, make up their bed and then scrub the floor and table. 'Breakfast at 7.30 to 8 o'clock then half an hour in Chappell . . . 9 o'clock we were marched off to the Weel room.' Working on the tread wheel was extremely tiring: 'It was like walking up steps and never getting any higher, but verry hard work and we was kept at if from nine till twelve.

'Then came diner, wich was one pint and a half of stirabout, composed of one pint of oatmeal, and half a pint of maze meal put in the oven and baked. We were put on the Weel again from 1 o'clock till four of the afternoon, then we were set to pick okum till eight, wen we went to bed . . .

The young prisoner's days continued to be spent in much the same fashion for the whole of his one month's sentence, although after the first fortnight the food at least was improved, so that he received a little cooked beef or bacon to supplement the earlier spartan diet.

In other gaols the circumstances were very similar, although by the end of Victoria's reign proposals were in hand to abolish the tread wheel for prisoners of all ages, and during the 1890s a more enlightened system of dealing with the younger prisoners was evolved, including the use of physical drill. The Governor of Warwick Prison spoke highly of these innovations, considering that 'the physical drill, habits of cleanliness and implicit obedience, with instruction both in religious and secular knowledge, cannot but bear fruit in a majority of these poor boys who are of an age apt to learn'. At Devizes Prison, where during the year ending 31 March 1902, there had been fifty-seven young offenders received, the governor noted that as well as physical training and educational instruction they had been 'employed at gardening, sawing wood, and mail-bag making'. So beneficial was the result claimed for this regimen that his chaplain even called for longer prison sentences for juveniles (of 'not less than six months') so that they could obtain the full advantage of the 'scholastic training, physical exercise and regular diet' which the prison provided. He considered that: 'The stigma which must attach to imprisonment is no greater, as it affects a boy's after-circum- stances, in the case of a longer or shorter period of imprisonment; and, therefore, where imprisonment is necessary, the sentence should be such as to allow the boy sufficient time to reap the full advantages the prison affords.'[20]

However, the days of the child in prison were now numbered, even if as late as 1901/2 there were still four offenders aged nine years, four aged ten, and eleven aged eleven years in the nation's prisons. But with the passage of the 1908 Children's Act this came to an end, for under section 102 of the Act no child under fourteen years was to be sentenced to imprisonment or penal servitude for any offence, or committed to prison in default of payment of a fine, damages, or costs.' Young persons, between the ages of fourteen and sixteen, were likewise protected, save only where the court certified them to be of such 'an unruly or depraved character' that they could not be accommodated elsewhere.

Children from both town and country benefited from this legislation but as the quotation from Captain Williams at the head of this chapter pointed out, the number of rural offenders was always limited compared to those from the urban areas. This is borne out by an examination of Table 6, which shows that in 1896 the ten rural counties of Berkshire, Cornwall, Cumberland, Dorset, Hereford, Norfolk, Oxford, Suffolk, Westmorland and Wiltshire together supplied only 97 boys committed to prison out of a national total of 1,395 for the year. The six industrialized areas of Lancashire, London, Northumberland, Staffordshire, Warwickshire and Yorkshire, on the other hand, provided 721 in that year, or nearly 52 per cent of the total, against the ten rural counties' share of 7 per cent. In 1900 the percentages were even more clear cut – with nearly 67 per cent of the total of boy prisoners committed in that year coming from the six industrialized counties and only 6 per cent from the ten rural ones. Yet at the time of the 1901 Census of Population these six industrialized counties contained only about 43 per cent of the total of children under the age of sixteen; as with the Reformatories mentioned earlier, the contribution of urban areas to the juvenile prison population was much larger than their share of the overall child population should have warranted.

The relatively low incidence of crime among country children was no doubt partly due to a lack of opportunity as compared to the temptations of shops, markets, etc. facing their urban counterparts, but it also seems likely that the hierarchical and paternalistic character of village society exerted a check. One writer in the middle of the nineteenth century pointed out that the 'proportions of crime' varied considerably, and the level for the 'Midland Agricultural Counties' was less than one-half that for the 'Northern Mining District'.[32] Nevertheless, particularly up to the end of the third quarter of the nineteenth century, those children who did break the law could be subjected – in certain rural areas at least – to harsh sentences out of proportion to the nature of the offence committed. But it is pleasing to report that by the end of the century an improvement had been secured in this respect – as in so many of the other aspects of the day-to-day experience of children discussed in earlier chapters. As compared with 1850, educational opportunities were wider, children were better clothed and fed, and the worst forms of exploitation of child labour had now been ended. In the new century a great deal of time and attention was devoted to carrying the advance in the status of children still further. But it was now an advance of prime benefit to the town-bred boy or girl, for by 1901 country children were but a minority in the nation's juvenile population. The countryman was no longer the typical Englishman.

TABLE 6

Annual Commitments of Juvenile Offenders to Prison from Sixteen Counties in England and Wales for three years ending 31 December 1900

(From 45th Report of Inspector of Reformatory Schools; Appendix. Parliamentary Papers, 1902, Vol. XLVIII.)

Counties	1896			1899			1900		
	Boys	Girls	Total	Boys	Girls	Total	Boys	Girls	Total
Rural									
Berkshire	25	–	25	10	1	11	22	1	23
Cornwall	1	–	1	3	1	4	–	–	–
Cumberland	2	1	3	9	–	9	6	–	6
Dorset	3	–	3	2	–	2	2	–	2
Hereford	6	–	6	3	–	3	5	–	5
Norfolk	24	1	25	11	1	12	4	1	5
Oxford	8	1	9	5	1	6	6	–	6
Suffolk	21	1	22	16	1	17	25	–	25
Westmorland	–	–	–	–	–	–	–	–	–

Wiltshire	7	–	7	6	–	6	8	1	9
Industrialized									
Lancashire	176	27	203	152	14	166	192	3	195
Northumberland	106	12	118	40	–	40	33	5	38
Stafford	56	–	56	14	2	16	19	4	23
Warwickshire	123	7	130	129	10	139	164	11	175
Yorkshire	152	6	158	124	9	133	92	3	95
London	108	8	116	354	4	358	363	1	364
National Total	1,395	103	1,498	1,286	72	1,358	1,295	58	1,353

TABLE 7

Number of prisoners under 16 years committed to prison during each of the years from 1887–8 to 1900–1. Up to 1892–3 the statistics included unconvicted prisoners, but after that year only convicted prisoners are included. The fall in numbers at the end of the period can partly be attributed to the Reformatory Schools Act, 1899, which no longer required that an offender ordered to be sent to a reformatory should, in addition, be sentenced to imprisonment.

Year	Under 12 years		12 years and under 16	
	Male	Female	Male	Female
1887–8	216	10	4,106	510
1888–9	222	17	4,243	583
1889–90	237	16	3,620	493
1890–1	180	14	3,276	402
1891–2	230	15	3,235	375
1892–3	198	14	3,486	338
1893	134	16	2,512	262
1894	82	2	1,942	226
1895	54	1	1,735	178
1896	59	1	1,336	102
1897	57	1	1,541	89
1898–9	42	1	1,586	93
1899–1900	18	1	1,193	60
1900–1	17	3	1,315	49

(The principal offences for which these children were sentenced, on a *national* basis, were said to be 'larceny, gambling, begging, sleeping out, &c.' See *Reports of the Commissioners of Prisons* for 1897, Parliamentary Papers, 1897, Vol. XL; for 1898, Parliamentary Papers, Vol. XLVII; for 1899–1900, Parliamentary Papers, 1899–1900, Vol. XLI; for 1901–2, Parliamentary Papers, 1902, Vol. XLVI.)

NOTES ON ADDITIONAL SOURCES USED

Petty Sessions Minute Books: Henley, 1862–81 at Oxfordshire Record Office, Ms. Dep. Deeds Henley A. XVI (10) and Henley, 1898–1903 at Oxfordshire Record Office, Ms. Dep. Deeds Henley A. XVI (11); Great Marlow Petty Sessions, PS/M/M/1 at Buckinghamshire County Record Office; Bicester, at Oxfordshire Record Office.

Dorset Magazine, No. 11, 1969, p. 29 for information on crime in Dorset in 1869. 'The Little Captive Maid' in *Hereford County Life*, June, 1971, p. 31 for details of the case of Emily Davies of Ross. Margaret May, 'Innocence and Experience: The Evolution of the Concept of Juvenile Deliquincy in the Mid-Nineteenth Century', in *Victorian Studies* September, 1973.

DOCUMENT A

COUNTRY COTTAGES

(i) *The Ideal:* Mr John W. Stevenson's *Cottage Homes,* as included in William Grey
– *Rural Architecture* (Edinburgh, 1852, pp. 24–5).
'. . . this author recommends to the adoption of builders of new cottages, as the
best and most economical style, work that is square on the plan. No house or
principal living-room, he says, should be less than 13 × 12, no bed-room less
than 11 × 9, kitchen 12 × 12, with 9 × 5½ for pantries or larders; lower rooms not
under 8 from floor to ceiling, and upper chambers 7½. [All measurements in feet.]
He requires closets for family purposes, or a wide stair-top landing for boxes,
chests, trunks, &c.; an outer detached room for coals, sticks, tools, &c., and
underneath a portion of the same roof, a privy, and connected therewith, large
sunk ash-pits. Following the injunctions of the Sanitary Reports, he urges the
discouragement of breeding or keeping swine, as detrimental to health and a
temptation to dishonesty; but recommends the keeping of fowls or bee-keeping.
Underneath the staircase, potatoes or vegetables, for winter use, may be stored.
All cottage erections should be privately approachable from both house and
kitchen. For reception of rain water, he recommends a tank, underneath a portion
of the kitchen floor, with a small sink-stone fixed over it; and to render the pantry
or larder cool, that apartment should be sunk a few steps in the earth. Eschewing,
therefore, ornamental workmanship . . . he lays it down as certain, that it is
not possible to erect and complete an improved cottage, with three sleeping
rooms, of sufficient size, and other conveniences, under £110, in any district of
England . . .'

(ii) *The Ideal in Practice:* Lord Wantage's Cottages at Ardington and Lockinge,
Berkshire, built in the 1860s – description from John L. Green, *English Country
Cottages* (London, 1899, pp. 56–7).
'The cottages are built of brick, with a slate or tile roof. There is a living room 15
ft square, 8 ft 6 in high, with a capacity of 1,912 cubic ft. The back kitchen has a
fireplace, a copper, and a sink; all washing and cleaning operations can be carried
on there, so that there is no steam about the house . . . There is a ventilated
pantry approached from the sitting-room, and a fuel store out of the back
kitchen. The floors are of brick or stone . . . The parents' bedroom is 15 ft by 12
ft; and 7 ft 9 in high, with a fireplace and ample window. There are two other
bedrooms about a hundred feet square, and 7 ft 9 in high, with ample window,
and a fireplace in one of them. Each bedroom has a distinct access so as to separate
the sexes. In addition to this there is generally an out-house, a good privy or an

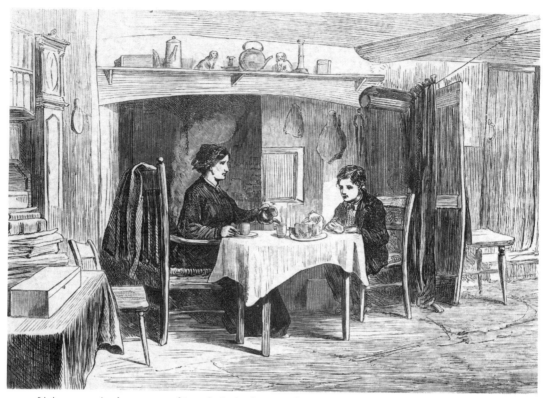

Living room in the cottage of Joseph Arch, the agricultural trade union leader, in 1872. Although Arch was a skilled worker, the furniture is plain and quite scanty. Mrs Arch presides at the tea table with her third son, Edward. (*Illustrated London News*, 13 April, 1872)

earth closet, and a water butt or a tank for each house; also an excellent garden of from fifteen to twenty poles in extent. In some places pigstyes [sic] are provided, and these "are of the greatest advantage to the labourer if removed to a sufficient distance from the house, and properly bricked and drained." The rent usually asked for these houses is 1s or 1s 6d a week . . .'

(iii) *The All-Too Frequent Reality*: From Frederick Clifford – *The Agricultural Lockout of 1874* (London, 1875), pp. 34–7. Mr Clifford was the special correspondent for *The Times* during the prolonged dispute in the spring and summer of 1874 between East Anglian farmers and those of their labourers who were members of agricultural trade unions.

Exning, Suffolk: 'In this parish there is no compensation for the absence of allotments in the extra size of the cottage-gardens . . . The crying evil of Exning, however, when I visited it, was the cottage accommodation. I do not speak on this point from mere outside views, but went into some of the labourers' dwellings. To the [better] class belonged a row of sixteen to twenty decent, respectable cottages, built by the squire, with two bedrooms overhead, a comfortable sitting-room downstairs, a nice bit of garden, and common offices in the rear, including ovens for bread-making. The rent was £4 16s . . . these are aristocratic mansions compared with some of the cottages in other parts of the village. I entered seven or eight of them. All had but one bedroom; all were occupied by labouring men with families. I am glad to say that all the children were young; but this description would not apply, I believe, to the tenants of other cottages of a like class. The ground-floor, without exception, was of brick. I think it is an over estimate to say that the sitting-room was 9 ft square. All the ceilings were low; I could not stand upright in one of the cottages. Then you went upstairs into a sleeping-room, with shelving, barn-like roof, lighted dimly by one small window; and in this one room, or rather loft, were thickly crowded miserable truckle-beds, in which father and mother, and in one case four small children, must lie and sleep. Another window, or any aperture for ventilation, would make the place more endurable . . . The rotten boards of one cottage swarmed with vermin – "Enough to run away with the children," the mother said . . . Upstairs and down-stairs, all was squalid and depressing. In one loft into which I put my head the children had been put to bed and already the air felt close and heavy . . . It was wonderful how in such dwellings, the women could look so clean and neat. Habitations like these are enough to crush nearly all sense of decency, or notion of tidiness and comfort among the women, while they must inevitably drive the husband to the public house . . . I asked whether many cottages in Exning had only one sleeping-room. My informant said, "Not less than half." Hovels like these must at times be nests of fever; and one cannot help asking why such small unhealthy dens should be allowed to stand for year after year in these villages? The sanitary machinery in rural districts must be sadly defective . . .'

DOCUMENT B

FAMILY DIET

From Maud F. Davies – *Life in an English Village* (London, 1909), pp. 192–5.
This book provided a survey of conditions in the Wiltshire village of Corsley
early in the twentieth century.

'. . . There is in Corsley no lack of competition for the custom of the labouring
classes. The housewife may purchase her groceries either from one of the village
shops or from the stores and shops in Frome and Warminster. Various butchers
and bakers drive round the parish with their carts, delivering goods to their
regular customers. Milk she can obtain from most of the numerous small farms.
Beer and ale are supplied by at least eight brewers from Frome and Warminster,
whose carmen deliver the casks at the houses. Coal and wood appear to be mainly
supplied by one local coal-haulier and timber merchant, and a competitor setting
up a few years ago failed to get any custom.

Most of the cottagers do the main part of their weekly shopping on Saturday at
Frome and Warminster, according to whether they live on the eastern or western
side of the parish. During the week they supplement their Saturday's purchases
from the nearest village shop, where credit is usually granted them if desired . . .

Milk is easily obtainable in all parts of the parish. Nearly all the farmers will sell
it to the poor in small quantities . . . The usual price of new milk is 3d per quart,
or 1½d per pint all the year round. In certain cases, in summer, or by special favour,
it is sold cheaper, at 1d per pint. In the winter it is sometimes scarce locally, and
the cottagers may then have difficulty in obtaining it, or may have to send farther
for it, and perhaps get short quantity for their money. This is, however, the
exception.

The greater number of households, irrespective of the number of persons, take
1d worth of new milk per day . . . A few families take separated or skim milk
instead of new, or to supplement it.

The produce of the garden furnishes a large proportion of the food of the
people. Potatoes, onions, greens, and other vegetables figure largely in the menu
of the poorest households, especially those with many children. Bacon is almost
universally eaten. Meat is eaten in all but the very poorest houses at least once or
twice a week, and it is an article of daily consumption in the majority of cottages.

At the midday dinner-hour in winter the wife or mother is very frequently
found preparing a stew with meat, potatoes, and vegetables, if well off, or if
poor, of potatoes and cabbage, or potatoes and onions alone. The well-to-do
sometimes have hot or cold roast meat, meat pies, chicken, where fowls are kept,
&c., by way of variety. They will also have a second course of tarts, pancakes, or

other sweets. If poor they will vary the stew of potatoes and vegetables by having bread with bacon, dripping, or pickles, children being sometimes fed on the latter. School-children who cannot return home to dinner take bread and butter, jam, or dripping. The mothers find that meat sent with the children is too often thrown away and wasted. On their return some mothers give the children hot vegetables or meat with their tea, or let them share in an early supper after a tea of bread and butter with jam or cake. Other mothers give nothing further but a plain tea, an inadequate diet for growing children who have a long walk in addition to their school work, and it must be remembered that little milk is taken per head in a large family.

The time and constitution of the meals taken subsequent to the mid-day dinner vary from one household to another. Most of the well-to-do have a good meal of bread and butter, and jam about 4.30, followed by supper later. In some poorer families one meal takes the place of tea and supper. At tea-time one sometimes finds prepared a meal of hot meat or stew, kippers and other fish, jam-tarts, &c., besides jam and cakes, and in one very poor family where the mother was out working the tea appeared to consist of bread and jam and the contents of innumerable jars and pots. There has been a great increase in the quantity of groceries consumed by cottagers within the last forty years, since the rise of wages. People dealing with a certain shop would, some thirty years ago, buy 1 oz of tea or of coffee to last a whole week, and 1 lb of sugar. Fifteen years later the same families would take $\frac{1}{4}$ lb of tea and 3 lb of sugar per week.

SPECIMEN FAMILY BUDGET No. 29

(Deficiency of Income, 10d)

Family: Labourer, wife, three children, also girl of eleven years for some meals. They reside in a three-bedroomed cottage with large garden ($\frac{3}{4}$ acre) for which they pay £6 per annum. Rent for water, 10s per annum.
The man belongs to a good club. Mrs T. pays 3d a week for each child into savings bank at Corsley School.
Mr T.'s wage is 15s. He keeps 5s out of which he pays his club, firewood (buying 40 faggots at a time for 10s), coal (half ton for 9s 8d), ale (5s per month), and all outdoor expenses, such as food for pigs and fowls. He pays for the clothing of the family out of the profits of garden, pig, &c.
Mrs T. receives 10s per week from her husband for the housekeeping, and she occasionally makes 6d for washing. During the fortnight the budget was kept she had a present of some liver from their butcher.

Mrs T. has been a cook and takes pride in her cooking and housekeeping. She cooks every day. Potatoes for breakfast, and meat, potatoes, and pudding for dinner. The children do not like milk puddings so she usually makes tarts, &c. They have cold food in the evening.

They take 1d worth of milk every day at 1½d per pint.

All the family are home for the midday dinner. The children do not take supper. The budget was kept very carefully by Mrs T. and is probably quite accurate.

30 December 1905 – STORE IN HOUSE:
Sugar, tea, ½ lb cheese, ¾ lb butter, 1½ lb bacon, a large loaf, five eggs, two bloaters, flour, currants, jam, pickles, store of potatoes.

DOCUMENTS

EXPENDITURE

Covering two weeks –30 December 1905 – 12 January 1906

	s	d
12 large loaves (2 have not been put down, but bread bill was 5s)	5	0
3 lb beef	1	9
1 lb butter	1	1½
1 lb mutton		8
Bloaters		3
7 lb sugar	1	2
1 lb lard		6
1 lb sultanas		4
Egg powder		2
¼ lb peel	1	0½
1 lb 14 oz cheese	1	1
Salt		1
¼ lb tea		4½
½ lb currants	1	0½
Tin mustard		1
Soap		3
Rabbit		6
Beef	1	3
Lamp oil		4
Flour		6
1 lb mutton		8
Fish		3
Lamp oil		4
Butter	1	1½
14 days' milk	1	2
Bacon	1	2½
½ lb tea		9
	£1 3	0

Debts incurred by the 'deficiency of income, 10d' noted in this budget – as in many of the other budgets quoted by Miss Davies – could only be met by 'extra' family earnings, for example at harvest time or by part-time employment of the mother and children. According to Miss Davies 65 of the 220 households in Corsley fell below the poverty line.

DOCUMENT C

AVERAGE QUANTITY OF THE PRINCIPAL KINDS OF FOOD CON-
SUMED BY AN AGRICULTURAL LABOURER'S FAMILY IN 1863 and
1903 RESPECTIVELY – PER WEEK

From: A. Wilson Fox – 'Agricultural Wages in England and Wales during the last
Half Century' in *Journal of the Royal Statistical Society*, Vol. LXVI, 1903, p. 295.

*1863 – Based on returns relating to 370 families in England, without distinction as to
number included in family*

Bacon, meat and bone	72¾ oz
Cheese	24 oz
Bread, flour, oatmeal, etc.	55¾ lb
Potatoes	27 lb
Tea	2¼ oz
Butter, dripping, lard, suet	25 oz
Sugar, treacle	2 lb
New milk, skimmed milk, butter milk	7.3 pints

*1903 – Based on 114 returns relating to families in England, consisting of man, wife, and
4 children*

Beef or mutton	53¾ oz
Pork	17¾ oz
Bacon	43¼ oz
Cheese	19¼ oz
Bread	19½ lb
Flour	14¾ lb
Oatmeal and rice	1¼ lb
Potatoes	25¾ lb
Tea	7½ oz
Coffee or cocoa	2½ oz
Butter	16¾ oz
Lard, margarine or dripping	17 oz
Sugar	4¼ lb
Syrup, treacle or jam	1½ lb
Milk, new	4½ pints
or Milk, skim	8¾ pints

(Wilson–Fox showed also that over three-quarters of the labourer's basic wage in
1903 was required to cover the average food bill.)

DOCUMENTS

DOCUMENT D

(i) HOME BACKGROUND OF A LOW-WAGE FAMILY IN GLOU-CESTERSHIRE IN THE LATE 1860s

Material collected by the Revd J. Fraser for the *First Report of the Royal Commission on the Employment of Children, Young Persons and Women in Agriculture*, Parliamentary Papers, 1867–8, Vol. XVII.

MARY PEART, of Kilcote, a hamlet in the parish of Newent [Gloucestershire]; husband aged forty-seven; works for Mr Hooper; earns 9s or 10s a week. Has five children at home, aged respectively 12, 10, 7, 4½ and 1¼ years; none of them earn anything, but she is trying to get the eldest (a girl) out to service. Requires 3½ pecks of flour a week for the consumption of the family; flour is now selling at 11s 6d a bushel. Has no vegetables, not so much as a potato left. Has had nothing but 'stark-naked bread', this month past; no butter, cheese, or bacon. Has had no cheese since harvest. Sometimes even the bread runs very short; has been two or three days without knowing where to turn for a bit. The rent of her cottage which contains two rooms on the ground floor, and two small bedchambers, with a garden about 30 perches, is £5, besides rates, which come to about 15s more. It is a good comfortable house; but the rent is too high for a labouring man to pay. Her husband is a steady man, and brings his money home.'

(Note by Mr Fraser: 'The Revd Morris Burland, who was present when I took this evidence, informed me that in his district, containing about 400 houses, there must be at least fifty families as badly off as this. I certainly hardly ever saw a district with more marks of poverty about it; many of the cottages ruinous, and unfit for human habitation; a low wage-rate, and a correspondingly low social and intellectual condition of the people; a great number of apparently truant children; a great aversion on the part of some of the worst-housed old people to take refuge in the workhouse, though they would be infinitely more comfortable there. The most wretched dens that I saw inhabited were such as had been erected by squatters on the waste; but there were others . . . not many degrees better in condition, for which rent . . . as high as £3 11s [per annum] is paid. – 28 January 1868.)

NB: A peck was equivalent to one-quarter of a bushel; a bushel of wheat equalled 60 lb – *Cassell's Concise English Dictionary*.

(ii) MORAL PROBLEMS ARISING FROM OVERCROWDED COTTAGES IN KENT, SURREY AND SUSSEX

From: Report by Mr Vaughan on the counties of Kent, Surrey and Sussex for the *Poor Law Commissioners on the Employment of Women and Children in Agriculture,* Parliamentary Papers, 1843, Vol. XII.

The undivided state of the larger families acting upon the scantiness of house-room and general poverty, or high rent, often crowds them together in their sleeping apartments, so as seriously to infringe on the decencies which guard female morals . . .

Mr Hart, a professional gentleman at Reigate, says –

'The great difficulty is to say at what age brothers and sisters do not sleep together in the same apartment, but generally until they leave home, be that at ever so late a period; many cottages have but one room, and the whole family sleep in one bed. I have often, when taking the examination of a sick man with a magistrate, an occasion which has more often taken me into a cottage than any other, observed upon this, and I consider its effects most demoralizing.'

In the neighbourhood of Cuckfield, in Sussex, it is said to be common for children of both sexes to use the same sleeping-room and bed, up to the age of twelve and even fourteen.

The Revd W. Sankie, the curate of Farnham, in Surrey, mentioned a case within his own knowledge where two sisters and a brother, all above fourteen, habitually slept together. In cases where the habits are less offensively alarming, it is still clear that the common sentiments of personal shame and personal respect may be so impaired as to leave no natural security but such as hardy principle or deep religious feeling may give. The admission of strangers, too, into the cottager's home produces an effect of a kind sometimes similar, occasionally the same . . . Where the letting of a room to a whole family is prohibited, as in some cases by the owner of the house, and a single lodger only is allowed, the danger strikes more directly at the chastity of the family.

Mr Rammell, a farmer on a large scale, living at Sturry, near Canterbury, says –

'Cottage-rent is very high. Cottages, with two rooms, are sometimes let for 1s 6d, without a garden; sometimes, though not commonly, for 2s; 2s 6d and 3s are paid for four-room cottages. It is common for persons in roomy cottages to let off a room to a stranger. The benefit of an airy abode is thus lost; and other evils follow, from the intimacy between a stranger and the grown-up daughters.'

DOCUMENTS

DOCUMENT E (i)

Extract from Chambers's Narrative Series of Standard Reading Books – published by W. & R. Chambers in 1862 (Standard IV). Some of the books in this series were in use at Mixbury School, Oxfordshire, in the mid-1870s, according to a log book entry.

ROBERT FENTON

'I wish I was big, and could help you, mother, that you need not work so hard,' said Robert Fenton.

'You can help me, my dear boy,' answered his mother.

Robert's mother was a widow, and had to work very hard to support her four children, of whom Robert was the eldest. He was ten years old, and had hitherto been able to go to school; but now, when his father was dead, his mother would perhaps wish him to give up school, that he might be able to earn a few pence daily. As Robert went to school that morning, he thought over his mother's words. How often, when his father had been alive, had Bob thought it tiresome to be obliged to go to school! He had looked at the bright poppies in the field, and had wished he might be allowed to linger there, to hear the birds sing, and watch the butterflies. He had wished to be like the clear little brook, that he might wander on and on, he knew not where; but now, when there was a chance of getting free from school, Robert felt sorry. 'What could mother mean when she said I could help her now?' thought he. 'Did she wish me to give up school to work in the field?' And as Robert went along thinking, he met Dick, a neighbour's son, who was going to pick potatoes in the field. 'I would not like to be like Dick,' thought he; 'he can neither read nor write, and keeps bad company. If I could get something to do after school – that mother could let me go to school one year longer, I would learn with all my might.' Poor Robert! it was early in life to begin with cares and troubles, but Bob was a fine manly fellow, who would not sit down with his hands before him, when he knew he ought to work. His teacher had said: 'If God puts you in a place where you must live by the work of your hands, you may be sure that is the very thing that is good for you.' And Bob knew that his teacher was right; he had found out already how pleasant it is to feel you are useful, when he had mended the wall of his mother's little garden, or helped her in the field; but it brought in no money, and Robert knew that his mother must pay the rent, and how should he manage to help her in that. At last a bright thought seemed to strike him. 'I know what I will do,' said he aloud, as he leaned against the low wall of a garden. 'Farmer Bennet is a good man. I will go and tell him all about my trouble, and if he can give me anything to do after school-hours, I am sure he will do so.'

'So I will, my little man,' said Farmer Bennet, who had heard the boy's words. He had been bending down to tie up a rosebush, and had listened to Robert's words. He now asked him to tell him his request, and promised to grant it if the schoolmaster gave a good report of him. Robert was not at all afraid that he would not, for he was one of the best boys in the school.

Farmer Bennet was as good as his word. He gave the little fellow only such work as he could do without overtasking his strength, and as Robert made good progress at school, he made him afterwards keep his books for him. Robert felt very proud and happy at this mark of confidence, and you may be sure he did his best to deserve Farmer Bennet's kindness. But the best of all was, that he could give his mother the help he had wished, even before he had become a man. He always kept the same rule for himself with which he began. When he knew that he ought to do a thing, he thought first about the way he could do it, and then set to work with all his heart; and as he never forgot to ask God's blessing for all he did, he was successful in almost everything he undertook.

(The extract ended with an instruction to 'write from dictation the last two sentences'.)

DOCUMENTS

DOCUMENT E (ii)

FROM ASTHALL SCHOOL LOG BOOK AT OXFORDSHIRE COUNTY RECORD OFFICE: T/SL.4(i)

Object Lessons for Infants for 1898

Animals
1. Paws and Claws of Animals and their Uses.
2. Tails   "   "   "   "   "
3. Tongues   "   "   "   "   "
4. Beaks   "   "   "   "   "
5. Feet   "   "   "   "   "

Plants
1. Herbs, Shrubs, Trees.
2. Apples and Pears.
3. Oranges and Lemons.
4. The Strawberry Plant.
5. Flowers of different Seasons.

Properties of Bodies
1. Sweet, Sour, and Bitter Tastes.
2. Hard, Soft, Rough, Smooth.
3. Brittle, Flexible, Tough.
4. Transparent and Opaque.
5. Adhesive Substances.

Form
1. Vertical, Horizontal, and Oblique Lines. (Position)
2. Straight, Bent, and Crooked Lines. (Shape)
3. The Square.
4. The Oblong.
5. The Circle.

Object Lessons for Standard I, II and III grouped for 1898

Animals
1. Feet, legs, and other means of Locomotion of Animals.
2. Teeth and Bills of Animals.

 3. Coverings of Animals.
 4. Homes of Animals.
 5. Animals which furnish food (when alive).
 6.   "   "   "   "   (when dead).
 7.   "   "   "   clothing.
 8. Insects.
 9. Bees.
10. The Spider and his Web.

Plants
 1. How plants grow.
 2. Parts of a Plant.
 3. Roots as Food.
 4. Stems as Food.
 5. Leaves as Food.
 6. Flowers and Seeds as Food.
 7. Plants giving us Clothing.
 8. Flowers of different Seasons.
 9. Parts of a Flower.
10. Uses of Wood.

Common Inorganic Substances and their Properties
 1. Adhesive Substances.
 2. Porous Substances.
 3. Brittle, Flexible and Tough Substances.
 4. Inflammable Substances.
 5. Solids, liquids, and gases.
 6. Gum and Glue.
 7. Chalk.
 8. Earthenware.
 9. Coal.
10. Water, Ice, Steam.

DOCUMENTS

DOCUMENT F

THE VAGARIES OF REVISED CODE FINANCE AND SPECIMEN REPORTS OF THE HMIs

(i)
By 1878 grants were available on the following terms:

	s	d
Grants based on average attendance		
For each child	4	0
plus If singing is taught	1	0
If organization is satisfactory	1	0
Grants on Individual Examination		
For each pass in Reading, Writing and Arithmetic,		
if 250 attendances have been made, 3s each	9	0
Grants for Class Subjects		
On average attendance of children over 7,		
if classes pass a creditable examination in		
one (or two) of grammar, history, geography,	2	0
plain needlework	for each subject	
Specific Subjects		
For every child in Standards IV–VI who		
passes in not more than two from the list. (On		
the whole, the specific subject list (including		
such subjects as mathematics and eventually		
even Latin) proved irrelevant to the modest	4	0
attainments of a country school)	for each subject	

(See Mary Sturt – *The Education of the People* (London, 1967), pp. 344–5.)

(ii) Specimen Reports by HM Inspector on Childrey Wesleyan School, Berkshire – Ref. C/EL.14, at Berkshire County Record Office. It will be seen that the conditions of the grants had changed yet again.

Report for 1888:
The discipline is good, and the scholars of the second and upper standards have made very fair progress in the obligatory subjects. The younger children appear

to have received insufficient attention. The Registers should be tested by the managers at least once a quarter at irregular intervals . . .

Average attendance – Boys 15.4; Girls 13.8 – 29.3 Total.

Fixed Grant – 4s 6d; Merit grant – 1s; Singing – 6d.

Percentage – 5s 7d;   *Total* – 11s 7d.

Needlework – 14s

No. presented and present (at examination) – 24;

Passes – Reading, 17; Writing, 16; Arithmetic, 15 – Total 48.

Grant – 29 at 11s 7d = £16 15s 11d; Needlework – 14s; *Total* – £17 9s 11d.

Report for 1890

The room is bitterly cold and draughty. The children in the first and second standards have passed a good examination, and the Infants have improved in their attainments, but the school can scarcely be considered to be in a satisfactory state as there is only one pass, easily obtained, in Writing, or in Arithmetic above the second standard. Needlework is scarcely satisfactory and more pains should be taken with this subject.

With reference to an entry in the Log Book dated the 11 August, to which HM Inspector requests attention, I am directed to state that if the school is opened the register must be marked, however small the attendance may be. If the children reach the school so wet, that sitting in school for the usual school hours is likely to be injurious to their health, the Managers may properly send them home at once and not open the school or give any instruction to them.

The school must be properly warmed.

Fixed Grant –	12s 6d
Discipline –	1s 0d
Singing –	6d
Total Grant –	£18 18s

(iii) Report for Austrey School in Warwickshire for 1890.

Discipline is very well maintained. The children read unusually well, in a natural voice and with good intonation. Handwriting also deserves praise; Spelling very fair, as is the mechanical Arithmetic. The first and second standards know their tables well, but the third and upwards should solve easy problems and do better in mental arithmetic. English fails, parsing being poor in the fourth standard. The school has been much improved by the addition of a class room, improvement of play-ground, etc. More pictures are needed. Considering that the children live near the school, the attendance should be much more regular than it is.

Master: Henry James Kesson, Trained Two Years; Certificated First Class. Emily Kesson, Sewing Mistress and General Assistant.

DOCUMENTS

DOCUMENT G

BIRD SCARERS

Extract from *Joseph Arch* by Revd F.S. Attenborough (Leamington, 1872). Mr Attenborough was a Leamington Congregational Minister and helped in the formation of the National Agricultural Labourers' Union in 1872, with Joseph Arch, a Warwickshire hedgecutter, as union president. In 1872 he also wrote the first (brief) biography of Arch and included in this a description of contemporary village life. The extract relates to this aspect of the booklet. (pp. 24–5)

In the country lanes we have met young gentlemen of tender years, whose general appearance and 'get up' have excited our attention. Carefully inspecting them we have found them to be odd bundles of disproportion. No proportion between their feet and boots; the former, small, weak, and tender – the latter, thick, studded with huge nails, caked with great clods, so heavy that we have wondered how the little chaps managed to drag them about, and so spacious that we have feared their little contents to be hopelessly lost. No proportion between their legs and breeches; the former, young and slight – the latter, various, venerable and straggling. No proportion between their frames and coats; the former, small and thin – so thin! – the latter, long, loose and roomy. Their boots may, perhaps, have some relation to modern times, but the coats are matters of antiquity, the history of them no man knoweth. Strange head gear, too, have these youths. Hats, caps, 'billies', and sundry battered relics, which may have been these, or anything else. Greatly varying, there are two features which these coverings frequently have in common, a hole at the top exposing the head, and a fragmentary brim in the front concealing the face. If you give these youths the chance they always speak; their utterance never varies; find them where you will, in a thin dreary voice they propose the question 'Plase, Master, can ye tell us wot toime it is?' And if you pass them seven times a day, they will seven times urge their enquiry. 'Who are these little men, these compounds of youth and age, these, whose forms are of to-day, but whose attire is of so remote a past, these on whose hands time hangs so heavily?' 'These, sir, are the noble army of British bird-scarers; the field police who guard the germinating seed and tender growths against the depredations of our winged creatures.' One would think that no creature having wings, or any other means of flight, would tarry in their presence for a moment, so grotesque and unnatural are they. The British farmer however has trained himself to gaze upon them without emotion: and, having overcome their first amaze, the birds seem somewhat drawn to investigate them, and can with difficulty be removed.

To a shrill battle cry, to rattles, to strange mechanical devices set in motion by means of strings, and, now and then, to gun and powder these youths resort in the prosecution of their war; with all these, however, they scarce restrain their foes, and in recompense for their utmost endeavours, they receive, it is said, fourpence per day.

DOCUMENTS

DOCUMENT H

CHILD WORKERS ON THE LAND

(i) *First Report of the Royal Commission on the Employment of Children, Young Persons and Women in Agriculture,* Parliamentary Papers, 1867–8, Vol. XVII.
(Evidence collected by the Revd J. Fraser, Assistant Commissioner)

ALBERT MERRITT, of Almondsbury (Thornbury Union) [in Gloucestershire], aged 10 the 21st of last June. Has been working for farmer Carter; earned 3s a week; drove plough; liked school better; found himself tired with his day's work; got so much walking. Would leave home at 5 or 5.30 a.m.; go to farm, help to clean out his stable and get the horses ready. Then got his breakfast, which he had brought with him, bread and cheese, and half a pint of cider, allowed by his master. Went with the horses on the land, at work till noon; then got a quarter of an hour for dinner, bread and cheese and cider. Kept on ploughing till three, then took the horses home, that would perhaps occupy half an hour. When they got home to farm, the ploughman went in to get his dinner in the house while he looked after the horses, fed them; helped to cut the chaff. Did not get home till 7 o'clock; had his supper, potatoes and bacon, with nothing to drink. Goes to bed at 8 o'clock.

(ii) *Second Report of the Royal Commission on the Employment of Children, Young Persons and Women in Agriculture,* Parliamentary Papers, 1868–9, Vol. XIII.
(Extract from the Report by Mr F.H. Norman on the counties of Surrey, Wiltshire, Herefordshire, Warwickshire and Worcestershire.)

The age at which children are first employed varies so much that it is impossible to state accurately what that age is . . . but few are employed under ten years of age. The result of the evidence upon this point may, I think be fairly stated to be the age at which boys commence to work regularly in farm labour is about eleven or twelve in Surrey and Herefordshire, about ten or eleven in Warwickshire and Worcestershire, and about nine or ten in Wiltshire. This is a very general statement, and is subject to many exceptions. These ages refer only to the times when continuous employment first commences. There are, however, many other operations to be done on a farm which occupy only a portion of the year, and for which boys younger than the ages given above are employed.

Girls are not generally employed under the age of fourteen or fifteen years. At that age they accompany their mothers and assist at whatever work their mothers may be engaged. In Wiltshire they work rather younger. I have met with a few instances of little girls being employed in the same light work of the farm as that in which the younger boys are engaged in, but these instances are quite exceptional.

253

Women and children making hay at Carmarthen, c. 1900. (Carmarthen Museum)

The great majority of farmers think that ten is the youngest age at which boys should ever be employed. It is thought that the work which boys under that age can do on a farm is of little or no value, and that they have ample opportunity of learning the business to which their lives are to be devoted if they begin at ten. Some few maintain that unless they commence at eight or nine they never become really useful; but quite as many farmers of the greatest experience think that the age of commencing to work might be advantageously postponed until eleven or twelve. I feel sure that an impartial perusal of the evidence I have collected will lead to the conclusion that ten is the very youngest age at which they are wanted in any of the counties I have visited, and that the inconvenience to which farmers would be exposed would not be serious if they were not employed until somewhat older than that.

The ordinary farm operations in which the youngest children are employed are bird-minding, planting potatoes and beans, minding cows, sheep, and pigs, picking and gathering potatoes, and collecting acorns; they are also occasionally sent out to weed, but as a general rule the weeding is done by men and women. The special occupations in which they are engaged are hop-picking, at which children of all ages are employed in every district in which hops are grown; apple-picking, i.e. collecting the apples and pears which have fallen from the trees. In the fruit gardens round Evesham and Pershore, in Worcestershire, children are extensively employed from the ages of seven and eight upwards. Their work consists in bird-minding and weeding, tying up radishes, onions, &c., and picking currants, and gooseberries, and vegetables. In fruit picking young children under ten years of age are of but little use, as they are likely to crush the fruit and thus render it unmarketable; but as a general rule there is work to be done by children in the gardens, of one sort or another, throughout the whole summer, and education in this neighbourhood suffers in consequence.

It is important to observe in which of the above kinds of labour the children are employed by the farmers, and in which they work independently of them. In the operations of planting beans and potatoes, and in gathering potatoes, the farmer cannot, strictly speaking, be said to be the employer of the children. In these operations the work is done by contract, and the man who takes the contract generally brings his own children to assist him, and in picking acorns children work on their own account, and sell the acorns they collect to the farmers . . .

Boys are generally hired by the week; the old practice of hiring by the year and boarding boys in farm houses is gradually dying out, although it is still practised to a considerable extent in Herefordshire and Wiltshire. The discontinuance of this practice is the necessary result of the improvement which has taken place in agriculture; the farmer who now occupies 500 acres of land is quite a different person from the farmer who formerly occupied 100, his feelings and his mode of life are different, and he will not tolerate the inconvenience caused by a troop of noisy farm boys living in his house. In consequence of this change the farm houses which are now being built are not generally provided with the accommodation necessary for boarding labourers, and however much the science of agriculture may have advanced while this change has been going on, the friends of labourers must, I think, regret the abandonment of a system which supplied farm lads with good food, and subjected them, in many cases, to wholesome control at a time when they particularly required it, and relieved the overcrowded cottages in the villages of some portion of their inhabitants.

Little boys, when employed at scaring birds, minding pigs, &c., receive from 1s 6d to 2s 6d a week; when they begin to drive plough they have from 2s to 3s a week, and their wages are gradually raised as their strength and efficiency increases.

Boys who are boarded in farm houses commence at about 30s a year, besides their food.

THE VICTORIAN COUNTRY CHILD

DOCUMENT I

STRAW PLAITING AND LACEMAKING

First Report of the Employment of Children, Young Persons and Women in Agriculture, Parliamentary Papers, 1867–8, Vol. XVII.

(i)
Evidence attached to Mr Culley's Report on Bedfordshire and Buckinghamshire; No. 98 – Copy of Memorandum by Revd Joseph Simpson, Tilsworth, dated 22 April 1868.

'The children begin straw plaiting at four years old; if they do not begin young they never make good plaiters. It is the general practice for parents to keep their children indoors all the day at straw plaiting. Children are at straw plaiting schools about seven hours in the day, and are generally employed at home about three or four hours besides, if they have not done the number of yards set by their parents. At some plait schools each child gives to book learning three or four minutes each day, or as much time as is taken up in reading five or six verses of the New Testament; but at most plait schools there is no reading whatever. The position of the body adopted by straw plaiters for convenience and expediting their work cannot be conducive to health. A bundle of straw is placed under the left armpit from which three or four straws are taken, and placed in the mouth to be moistened by the saliva; the fingers being all the time engaged in plaiting, the head is bent forward each time a new straw is required, which recurs constantly as the straws are only a few inches in length, thus a stooping habit is acquired from the constant bending of the head and cramped position of the left arm, to say nothing of the injury done by the constant habit of holding dyed straws in the mouth. The children often have sore lips, and they no doubt suffer from the abstraction of saliva sufficient to moisten many yards of plait per day. It was formerly the custom to moisten the straw with water, but the saliva is considered by the dealers to give it a better appearance, and hence the present filthy custom. Straw plait carried out in moderation is a great source of benefit to the district, inasmuch as it keeps away poverty, but as at present conducted in the case of children sadly needs restriction.

(ii)
Evidence No. 119.
'Mrs Hart, Thurleigh, used to have a lace school of fifteen and will have again in summer. Girls between eight and sixteen all pay 3d per week. School hours from 8 a.m. to 6 p.m., with one hour for dinner.

An attempt to revive the craft of lacemaking was made by Mrs Skinner of Periteau House Private Asylum, Winchelsea, in the early 1900s. Like similar charitable efforts elsewhere, it had little long-term success, and the domestic lace trade continued its inexorable decline. (Winchelsea Museum)

'They hadn't ought to begin while they're nine years old, but their parents can't afford to keep 'em and pay their schooling; I have a little one in her eight (i.e. seven years old). I can't send her to school, and she's been learning at her pillow for two years; my girl of thirteen works from 7 till 7, with an hour for dinner.'

'Mrs Hart has two girls of sixteen and thirteen, neither of whom can write, and were never at school, except Sunday school, after they were six years old.'

THE EMPLOYMENT OF CHILDREN IN BRICK AND TILE MAKING – 1870

(iii) From: George Smith – *The Cry of the Children from the Brick-Yards of England* (London, 1879 edn.) (pp. 5–7)

When I was a child of about seven years of age, I was employed by a relative to assist him in making bricks . . . At nine years of age, my employment consisted in continually carrying about forty pounds of clay upon my head, from the clay heap to the table on which the bricks were made. When there was no clay, I had to carry the same weight of bricks. This labour had to be performed, almost without intermission, for thirteen hours daily. Sometimes my labours were increased by my having to work all night at the kilns.

257

THE VICTORIAN COUNTRY CHILD

The result of the prolonged and severe labour to which I was subjected, combined with the cruel treatment experienced by me at the hands of the adult labourers, are shown in marks which are borne by me to this day . . .

A Sub-Inspector of Factories informed me the other day that he had visited several brick-yards in the Midlands, and found the children to be in precisely the condition described by me. The children were of various ages, from nine to twelve, but mostly nine to ten. They were of both sexes, and in a half-naked state. Their employment consisted in carrying the damp clay on their heads to the brickmakers, and carrying the made bricks to the 'floors' on which they are placed to dry. Their employment lasts thirteen hours daily, during which they traverse a distance of about twenty miles . . . Imagine a child of nine or ten, with features prematurely old, toiling from six in the morning until seven in the evening, and receiving nothing but curses and blows from the men, because he is not quick enough in his movements . . . Ignorance and immorality prevail to a fearful extent among the workmen and children so employed.

NB: Of course, some of the worst exploitation of child labour in the brick-yards occurred in the industrial areas, e.g. the Black Country, rather than in the rural. However, largely as a result of Smith's agitation, in 1871 a Brick-yard Act was passed prohibiting the employment of females under sixteen and of boys under ten. Restrictions were also imposed on the employment of young males; they were to work (between the ages of ten and thirteen) on the 'half-time' system already introduced for Factories and Workshops. The usual problems of enforcement of the legislation were encountered, but by the end of the 1870s Smith was satisfied that progress was being made.

DOCUMENTS

DOCUMENT J

APPRENTICESHIPS

(i) Preserved at Buckinghamshire County Record Office, A.R. 30/50. (Dated 1853)

This indenture Witnesseth That Robert Frederick Miller of the age of fifteen years son of Maria Miller Schoolmistress at the Eton Union Workhouse of his own free will and with the consent of his said mother testified by her executing these presents doth put himself Apprentice to Henry Graveney and James Graveney of Slough in the parish of Upton cum Chalvey in the County of Bucks Whitesmiths Locksmiths and Bell hangers Coparties to learn the Arts and with them after the Manner of an Apprentice to serve from the twentieth day of April now last past unto the full End and Term of Six Years from thence next following to be fully complete and ended. DURING which Term the said Apprentice his Masters faithfully shall serve their secrets keep their lawful commands every where gladly do he shall do no damage to his said Masters nor see to be done of others but to his Power shall tell or forthwith give warning to his said Masters of the same He shall not waste the Goods of his said Masters nor lend them unlawfully to any he shall not commit fornication nor contract Matrimony within the said Term shall not play at Cards or Dice Tables or any other unlawful Games whereby his said Masters may have any loss with their own goods or others during the said Term without Licence of his said Masters he shall neither buy nor sell he shall not haunt Taverns or Playhouses nor absent himself from his said Masters service day or night unlawfully. But in all things as a faithful Apprentice he shall behave himself towards his said Masters and all theirs during the said term AND the said Henry Graveney and James Graveney on consideration of the sum of ten pounds sterling to them in hand paid by the said Maria Miller on the execution hereof the receipt whereof is hereby acknowledged do hereby covenant and agree with the said Maria Miller that they the said Henry Graveney and James Graveney their said Apprentice in the arts of Whitesmith Locksmith and Bellhanger which they use by the best means that they can shall teach and Instruct or cause to be taught and instructed Finding unto the said Apprentice sufficient Meat Drink Medical assistance Working tools Lodging and all other Necessaries during the said term save and except Wearing apparel and the washing and mending thereof which are to be found and provided for the said Apprentice during the said Term by the said Maria Miller AND for the true performance of all and every the said Covenants and Agreements either of the said Parties severally bind themselves unto the other by these Presents IN WITNESS whereof the Parties above named to this Indenture have put their Hands and Seals the twenty-first day of December and in the seventeenth Year of the Reign of our Sovereign Lady Victoria by the Grace of God of the United Kingdom of Great Britain and Ireland QUEEN Defender of the Faith and in the Year of our Lord One Thousand Eight Hundred and fifty three.

Signed Sealed and delivered   SIGNED: Robert Frederick Miller

in the presence of Mr G. Chack   Maria Miller
Clerk to Mr Barrett,   Henry Graveney
Solicitor Eton.   James Graveney

NB: No provision was made in this indenture for a *money* wage to be paid.

(ii) Preserved at Oxfordshire County Record Office, Misc. Gr. II. (Dated 1858)

This Indenture Witnesseth That Thomas Edward Grimes of Milton in Parish of Adderbury in the County of Oxford by and with the consent of Charles Grimes of the same place, Weaver, his Father, testified by his execution of these presents doth put himself Apprentice to William Franklin of Adderbury West in the said Parish of Adderbury, Builder, Carpenter, Joiner and Wheelwright to learn his Art and with him after the Manner of an Apprentice to serve from the day of the date hereof until the full End and Term of six Years from thence next following to be fully complete and ended DURING which Term the said Apprentice his Master faithfully shall serve his secrets keep his lawful commands every where gladly do he shall do no damage to his said Master nor seek to be done of others but to his Power shall tell or forthwith give warning to his said Master of the same he shall not waste the Goods of his said Master nor lend them unlawfully to any he shall not commit fornication nor contract Matrimony within the said Term he shall not play at Cards or Dice Tables or any other unlawful Games whereby his said Master may have any loss with his own goods or others during the said Term without Licence of his said Master, he shall neither buy nor sell he shall not haunt Taverns or Playhouses nor absent himself from his said Master's service day or night unlawfully. But in all things as a faithful Apprentice he shall behave himself towards his said Master and all his during the said Term. AND the said William Franklin in consideration of the services of the said Thomas Edward Grimes covenants with the said Edward Grimes, the father, to pay the said Thomas Edward Grimes, his apprentice, three shillings per week during the fourth year, four shillings per week during the fifth year and five shillings per week during the sixth and last year of his said apprenticeship. And the said William Franklin also covenants with the said Charles Grimes his said Apprentice in the Art of a Builder, Carpenter, Joiner and Wheelwright which he useth by the best means that he can shall teach and Instruct or cause to be taught and instructed Finding unto the said Apprentice sufficient Tools and all other Necessaries for learning his trade during the said Term. And the said Charles Grimes hereby covenants to and with the said William Franklin that he will find and provide unto and for the said Apprentice during the said term sufficient Meat, Drink, Clothing, Washing, Mending, Medicine and medical attendance, in case of sickness or Accident and all other Necessaries during the said term. AND for the true performance of all and every the said Covenants and Agreements either of the said Parties bindeth himself unto the other by these Presents. IN WITNESS whereof the Parties above named to these Indentures interchangeably have put their Hands and Seals the seventeenth day of August and in the twenty second Year of the Reign of our Sovereign Lady Victoria by the Grace of God of the United Kingdom of Great Britain and Ireland QUEEN Defender of the Faith and in the year of our Lord One Thousand Eight Hundred and fifty eight.

Signed sealed and delivered by the above named parties in the presence of Henry Churchill, Solicitor, Deddington.	SIGNED: Thomas E. Grimes Charles Grimes William Franklin

NB: In this particular case – and unusually – no premium was required by the master. However, it remained the father's responsibility to feed, clothe, etc. his son and not until the fourth year of his apprenticeship did the boy obtain any remuneration.

DOCUMENT K
'HIGHDAYS AND HOLIDAYS'

(i) From *Oxford Times* – 17 July 1880.
DEDDINGTON SUNDAY SCHOOL CENTENARY

The Nonconformists of this town celebrated the centenary on Sunday and Monday last. On Sunday the scholars met at their respective schools, and were joined by the children from Clifton, Hempton and Great Barford. Being formed into a procession, they marched three abreast into the Market-place, where they stood in two blocks, eighteen in each line. After singing a hymn they were told off in threes, forming one large procession, and marched from the Square, through the Horse Fair, High-street, and the Grove, to an orchard kindly lent by Mr J. Clarke. Here a religious service was held, conducted by the Revs H. S. Payne, Independent; G. E. Butt, Primitive Methodist; and Mr K. Whetton, Wesleyan Reform. There were about 470 scholars, and there could not have been a less number of spectators and friends on the field. At the close of the service, the same order was observed in marching to the Market-place, through Hudson street, where, after singing another hymn, they dismissed. On Monday the festival took place, commencing with a cricket match, in the Castle grounds, between the Independent Sunday School Club and eleven from Hook Norton, which resulted in a win for Deddington. At two o'clock the three schools of the town again met in their respective places and, headed by some beautiful banners, marched through the Market-place, Hudson street, and High street to Hempton Way, where the waggons and vehicles were waiting to convey the party to Tornhill farm, which was again kindly placed at the disposal of the committee by F. Gulliver, Esq. Tea was served at four o'clock, after which some jolly games were indulged in, and heartily enjoyed until eight o'clock, when the rain caused a somewhat hurried gathering and reloading for home. Cheers were given . . . after which the whole party hurried to the town and, although the rain was drizzling, proceeded to the Market place and sung a hymn, after which they gave three hearty cheers and dispersed. There could not have been less than 800 on the grounds at Tornhill during the evening.

(ii) From *Hampshire Chronicle* – 1 February 1890
WEST MEON – SCHOOL TREAT

Through the kindess of Mr & Mrs Leroy Lewis, of Westbury Park, the children attending these schools, to the number of 160, received their usual treat on Tuesday last. The children assembled about four o'clock, and very soon afterwards they sat down to the plentiful spread which had been provided for them, and to this excellent repast it need scarcely be said ample justice was done. As soon as the feast was concluded the tables were removed as another entertainment which had been arranged was about to take place . . . The second part of the programme consisted of conjuring and ventriloquism by Mr Paul Howard from London. For about an hour and a half he kept his audience in a continual state of wonder and delight, which was manifested throughout by the vociferous applause which constantly greeted his efforts. At the conclusion of the entertainment the rector, the Rev R.M.G. Browne, called upon the children to express their thanks to Mr & Mrs Leroy Lewis for their great kindness by giving three cheers for them and their baby, which was heartily responded to. On leaving the children had smart bags containing oranges, apples, and nuts, presented to them by Mrs Leroy Lewis and her brother, Master G. Newcomen. The remark of the children on their way home was that "this was the best treat they ever remembered."

(iii) From *Hampshire Chronicle* – 3 July 1897
DIAMOND JUBILEE CELEBRATIONS – HEADLEY

The celebration of the long reign of the Queen was held on Saturday, the 19th ult. in the rectory field. Early in the morning Mr W. Gamblen, with his staff of workers, was busily engaged in erecting awnings, flags, etc., and the general arrangements of the field. The building of the bonfire also fell to this gentleman's charge, while Mr J.H. Viney, jun., builder, Ferndale, supplied a capital new bandstand in the Jubilee colours (red, white and blue), with decorations of flags and fairy lamps, and at the entrance gate near the church a well contrived triumphal arch was erected in the same colours. Unfortunately the inclemency of the weather prevented the illuminations being lit up. At the rectory flags were out, and at the top of the chestnut tree the Royal standard was hoisted. Many others in the vicinity displayed bunting. At four o'clock the National School children living in the parish, numbering over 500 . . . assembled, when the Haslemere Institute Brass Band played the National Anthem. At 4.30 tea was provided in the schoolrooms. Each child was presented with a Diamond Jubilee mug, the gift of Mr & Mrs A. Ingham Whitaker, of Grayshott Hall, Lady Wright, of Headley, giving each a Jubilee button with a design of the Queen, etc. The little ones were served with tea, cake and buns by a large staff of willing ladies and gentlemen . . . Tea over, three hearty cheers were given, on the motion of the Rector (Revd W.H. Laverty), to Mr & Mrs Whitaker and Lady Wright for their Jubilee gifts. Mr C.H. Beck proposed three cheers for the Rev W.H. Laverty, which received a ringing response . . . Besides the children about 100 old people and widows were each presented with pretty baskets lined with coloured tissue paper containing pastry, sweets, buns, orange, bottle of mineral water, and glass, supplied by Mr W. Rogers, who added a buttonhole of Jubilee colours. With the basket was given a quarter of a pound of tea. Each child had free swings and cocoa nut shies . . .

(iv) From *Kendal Mercury* – 13 November 1869; Westmorland.
KENDAL MARTINMAS FAIRS

The usual Martinmas fairs were held on Monday and Tuesday in this week. Fortunately the weather was in every respect most favourable. The early trains on Monday morning brought in large numbers of country lads and lasses; others arrived on foot, or in carts and 'shandries', and altogether there were more strangers in the town than there have been for some time past . . . As usual there were shows and shooting galleries, and vendors of 'poisonous' gingerbread and bad toffy [sic], nut hawkers and ballad singers; in fact that class of frequenters of fairs who pick up a living as they can, were present in large numbers, and that they made a good thing out of the buxom lads and lasses of Westmorland there is no doubt. 'Beware of pickpockets' was, at the instigation of Supt. Bird, posted in placards on the walls, much to the surprise of the country folks . . . The dancing rooms, as usual, were crowded, and the public houses drove a thriving trade; and it is to be hoped that those philanthropic purveyors of hot coffee, located in Market Hall, likewise received a fair amount of support. A man, in terms more forcible than polite, was literally screaming religion into the ears of some few bumpkins and bumkinesses, likewise stationed in the Market Hall; and another fair frequenter administered, of course by the aid of a battery, galvanic shocks at the 'small and reasonable charge of only one penny.' Other sights there were, but none of importance, and we think there was less drunkenness, and riotous behaviour than is usually seen at fairs.

DOCUMENTS

DOCUMENT L

DIARY OF A COUNTRY SCHOOLMASTER

Below are extracts from the diary of Mr Alfred Hart, who kept a small private school at Providence Place, Ivinghoe, Buckinghamshire. Most of the events mentioned in the diary relate to the parish of Ivinghoe (then a small market town) and the adjoining village of Pitstone. I am indebted to Mr J. Hawkins of Pitstone for permission to use the diary.

1864

August

Monday, 8th: Teaching. Very few scholars. J. Dell, the man reported to have had the small pox went to work this morn. W. Parsons came. Dug a few potatoes this eve.

Tuesday, 9th: Teaching. Rained a great part of the day after a long drought. Went up into the town this eve.

Wednesday, 10th: Teaching. Dug up all the potatoes in the right or high side of the garden. Fine day.

Thursday, 11th: Teaching. Got the potatoes in the house this eve, also pulled up peas and pea-sticks and watered some of the trees, kidney beans and plants. Pump got choked up, took the bucket out, &c.

Friday, 12th: Teaching. Swept school-room and yard this eve. Went at noon to Pitstone to fetch a name tin for Mr Hawkins, also brought one from Mr Tompkins's. Wrote Mr Hawkins's this eve. [NB: The 'name tin' was a name plate, probably to be fixed to the side of a waggon.]

Saturday, 13th: Went up town this morn. and afterwards went to Pitstone with W. Parsons to take Mr H.'s name. Wrote Mr Tompkins's when I came back; after dinner went to measure wheat cutting, outer piece 15 a[cres] Mr Tompkins.

Sunday, 14th: Recd. letter and P.O.O. for £3 0 0 from Niece Grew. Went to Church this afternoon. Wife went to see Mr Hedges. Also recd. letter from Mrs Meacher – Bromley.

August

Monday, 29th: Teaching. Cousin W. Soper & wife call'd to see us. Wife went with them to Mr G. Archer's. I went this afternoon to measure up Mr Tompkins's Harvest land, finish'd. Sent a letter to Mrs Bradbury.

Tuesday, 30th: Teaching. Br. John C[ollyer] also Ann Collyer came to see us. Went up town twice to paint Ann Hawkins's grave stone, also wrote an application to Directors of S.E. Railway for Cornelius Short, in the eve. went to

Mr Jolly's Cheddington to take the measuring accts. Rec'd note from J. Hiley (Birmingham). [NB: He was paid 8d. by Cornelius Short for writing the application.]

Wednesday, 31st: Teaching. Wet morning but cleared up towards the eve. Messrs. Peach and Kinns called to see us. Went up town this eve. painted stone the 3rd time.

September
1st, Thursday: Teaching. In the afternoon broke up for fortnight's holiday. Went in the eve. to measure some land for Mr Jno. Simmons, Seabrook.

2nd, Friday: Went up town this morn. thinking to write A. Hawkins's grave stone but found the sheep had been on it, so obliged to clean it & paint it over afresh, and put some hurdles round it. Settled with Mrs Norris. In the afternoon wrote a name for Js. Weatherhead (cart tin). In the eve. went to see the ruins of Mr Beesley's boiler house, the boiler having burst in the afternoon, and blowing over 2 horses and a cart, standing by the mill into the middle of the front yard, the tall chimney also blown down but most providentially no one hurt. Afterwards went to see Mr T. Green about his Will. [NB: He received 1s 8d for writing Weatherhead's cart tin.]

3rd, Saturday: Went to take Mr Simmons's Accts., then went to measure for Mr H. Williamson, North Field, Pitstone Green & the Leys. In the afternoon commenced writing A. Hawkins's grave stone. In the eve. went to Mr Tompkins's harvest supper. [NB He received 4s. for writing Ann Hawkins's grave stone.]

4th, Sunday: Went to Church this afternoon.

[NB: In an entry made on 18 September 1864, Mr Hart noted that he had 'earned £6 3s 5d during the holidays' for measuring work for local farmers etc. This was by no means uncommon; in Lincolnshire during the 1850s and 1860s the Lincoln Diocesan Education Board recognized that summer conferences were very difficult to arrange because 'School-masters cannot so easily attend during the Season of Harvest in consequence of the demands made upon their time for land-measuring.' This comment related to the year 1859, but similar ones were made both earlier and later. See Rex C. Russell – *A History of Schools and Education in Lindsey, Lincolnshire* 1800–1902, (Lindsey County Council Education Committee, 1966), p. 41. For poorly renumerated teachers these opportunities were valuable ways of earning a little extra money.]

November and December
30th, Wednesday: Teaching – and writing coffin plate for Mr Heley & writing up weekly accounts. Mrs Hawkins, Pitstone, confined of twins, girls, this week.

1st, Thursday: Went up town to take the coffin plate, also to take Mrs Norris some eggs.

2nd, Friday: Teaching: Swept school room and other jobs this eve. Mr Green and Mr H. Dimmock called and signed his Will [NB: For preparing the Will Mr Hart was paid 5s.]

3rd, Saturday: Up town this morn. to prepare for going up town to write Mr Paradine's cart name, finished by morn. – came home, swept yards &c., afterwards went up town.

4th, Sunday: Went to Church this afternoon. Old Mr Heley buried. Wife went this eve. to see Uncle Hedges. [NB: Mr Hart gave 1s to a special missionary collection at Church.]

The diary is of interest because it indicates the range of activities in which a schoolmaster could involve himself, in addition to teaching. Indeed, in Mr Hart's case teaching seems to have been relegated to the position of a regular, not very interesting, chore.

Alfred Hart was born on 7 March 1812, at Kirkby-on-Bain, Lincolnshire, and appears to have settled in Ivinghoe some time in the late 1840s. At the time of the 1851 Census of Population he had a mixed boarding school, with four girls and nine boys as resident pupils. However, within ten years it had been converted to a day school, for at the 1861 Census there was only one boy resident at the school. By 1864 he, too, had left. The pupils were local – mostly the children of tradesmen or farmers in the Ivinghoe area. See Census Returns for Ivinghoe at Public Record Office: 1851 – H.O.107. 1756; 1861 – R.G.9.1008; 1871 – R.G.10.1564.

The Post Office Directory for Buckinghamshire, etc. for the year 1864 gives the following occupations and places of residence for some of the people mentioned in the diary entries:

George Archer, farmer, Ivinghoe Aston.
Francis Beesley, baker and miller, Pitstone.
John Collyer, grocer, Pitstone. Thomas Green, wheelwright, Ivinghoe.
John Hawkins, farmer, Pitstone.
William and George Heley, plumbers and glaziers, Ivinghoe.
John Kinns, draper and tailor, Ivinghoe.
Eleanor Norris (Mrs), King's Head Inn.
William Paradine, shopkeeper, Ivinghoe.
John Simmons, farmer, Seabrook, near Ivinghoe.
William Tompkins, farmer and miller, Ivinghoe.
Humphrey Williamson, farmer, Pitstone.

DOCUMENT M

Extracts from Calendars of Prisoners at Oxfordshire Quarter Sessions – 1851–64 – Cases involving children up to and including the age of 15 (QSP 1/4 Oxfordshire County Record Office.)

Name	Age	Educational Ability	Occupation*	Charge	Sentence
Epiphany Quarter Sessions – 1851					
Daniel P.	14	Illiterate		Stealing at Handborough, one cotton handkerchief, value 6d.	6 calendar months' hard labour in the house of correction, and to be whipped once in the first and once in the fifth months.
Easter Quarter Sessions – 1851					
Rowland L.	15	Reads and writes imperfectly		With an older youth, stealing at Kelmscott, fifteen ounces of bacon, value 5d.	6 weeks' hard labour in the house of correction.
Trinity Quarter Sessions – 1851					
Mark G.	14	Illiterate		Charged, with 2 older males, with 'stealing from the person at Salford, 2 shillings, 1 sixpence, 4 pennies, and one half-penny.'	3 months' hard labour in the house of correction. (His older companions received the same sentence.)
John P.	14	Illiterate		With his father, 'stealing, at Bicester, 20 lb weight of wood, value 2d'.	14 days' hard labour in the house of correction and to be once whipped.

Epiphany Quarter Sessions – 1852

Name	Age	Literacy	Offence	Sentence
Luke B.	14	Illiterate	Stealing at Eynsham, with his older sister, one piece of wood, value 1s 6d.	Acquitted (The sister was imprisoned.)
George P.	15	Reads and writes imperfectly	Stealing, at Caversham, one tame rabbit, value 1s.	9 calender months' hard labour at house of correction and to be whipped at the end of the first six months.

Michaelmas Quarter Sessions – 1852

Name	Age	Literacy	Offence	Sentence
William C.	14	Illiterate	Receiving (with a 20-year-old man) £20 at Nettlebed, knowing it to have been stolen.	4 calendar months' hard labour in the house of correction and to be once whipped.
Edward G.	12	Reads and writes imperfectly	Stealing, at Nettlebed, £20.	3 days' hard labour in the house of correction and to be once whipped.

Epiphany Quarter Sessions – 1853

Name	Age	Literacy	Offence	Sentence
Mary N.	14	Illiterate	Obtaining, by false pretences, at Watlington, 2 pairs of boots.	21 days' hard labour in the house of correction.
Jane L.	14	Reads and writes imperfectly	Stealing at Southstoke, 2 half crowns, 4 shillings and sixpence.	3 weeks' hard labour in the house of correction.
James B.	14	Reads and writes imperfectly	Stealing (with a 16-year-old boy) at Watlington, 1 smock frock.	1 calendar month's hard labour in house of correction.

Trinity Quarter Sessions – 1853

Name	Age	Literacy	Offence	Sentence
Charles K.	15	Reads and writes imperfectly	Assault with intent to ravish, at Chadlington.	4 calendar months' hard labour in house of correction.

Michaelmas Quarter Sessions – 1853

Name	Age	Literacy	Occupation	Offence	Sentence
Sarah B.	14	Reads and writes imperfectly		Stealing a cotton dress at Souldern.	1 calendar month's hard labour in house of correction.
John S.	15	Reads and writes imperfectly		Stealing, with an older man, two beech spokes at Rotherfield Greys.	To be whipped and discharged.

Trinity Quarter Sessions –1861 (QSP. $\frac{4}{6}$)

Name	Age	Literacy	Occupation	Offence	Sentence
Arthur T.	13	Reads and writes imperfectly	Labourer	Stealing 1 revolver pistol at Enstone.	2 months' imprisonment with hard labour at house of correction and 4 years at Reformatory.
Thomas H.	12	Reads and writes imperfectly	Labourer	Stealing a gallon of peas at Rotherfield Greys.	2 calendar months' hard labour at house of correction.

Michaelmas Quarter Sessions – 1861

Name	Age	Literacy	Occupation	Offence	Sentence
George G.	14	Illiterate	Labourer	Breaking and entering a house at Newnham Murren and stealing 1 oz of tea, a ½lb of sugar, and other articles.	1 month's hard labour in house of correction and at the expiration thereof to be sent to the Philanthropic Farm School at Redhill, for 2 years.

Epiphany Quarter Sessions – 1862

Name	Age	Literacy	Occupation	Offence	Sentence
Robert F.	15	Reads and writes imperfectly	Labourer	Stealing 6 trusses of hay at Bampton.	21 days' hard labour in house of correction.
Michael H.T.	12	Reads and writes imperfectly	Labourer	Stealing a concertina at Deddington. Also a pipe and case at Deddington.	21 days' hard labour at house of correction for each offence, the second sentence to follow from the first, and to be once whipped with a birch rod – 20 stripes.

Lent Quarter Sessions – 1862

Thomas H.	12	Reads and writes imperfectly	Labourer	Stealing 3 weights at Henley-on-Thames (previous conviction).	1 calender month's hard labour at house of correction, and at the expiration to be detained in a Reformatory School for 3 years.

Trinity Quarter Sessions – 1862

Thomas J.	13	Reads and writes imperfectly	Labourer	Stealing one gold watch and chain at Bampton.	6 calendar months' hard labour in house of correction.

Lent Quarter Sessions – 1864

Thomas F.	15	Reads and writes imperfectly	Labourer	Stealing (with others) 62 lb of bacon.	1 calendar month's hard labour at house of correction.

Trinity Quarter Sessions – 1864

Stephen S.	11	Reads and writes imperfectly	Labourer	Unlawfully wounding Henry Banbury at Eye and Dunsden.	14 days' hard labour at house of correction.
Henry C.	10	Reads and writes imperfectly	Schoolboy	Stealing 2 purses containing money at Northleigh.	14 days' hard labour at house of correction.

*Occupations were not provided during the 1851–3 period.
NB. Houses of correction were used for the imprisonment of persons convicted of minor offences. However 'the distinction between gaols and houses of correction was abolished by the Prison Act, 1865.' – See Earl Jowitt – *The Dictionary of English Law* (London, 1959).
(The surname of the young offender has been omitted in each case so as to avoid giving embarrassment to any surviving relatives.)

271

DOCUMENT N

LABOURING LIFE IN COWDEN, KENT IN THE YEAR 1843

Extract from evidence provided by the Revd T. Harvey, Rector of Cowden, Kent to the Special Assistant Poor Law Commissioners on the *Employment of Women and Children in Agriculture*, Parliamentary Papers, 1843, Vol. XII.

Boys are employed profitably in wood-cutting, and their fathers prefer this to sending them to school; little value, indeed, seems to be placed on education, and the farmers give no encouragement to carrying it out: it . . . does not form part of a poor man's pleasures; after working all day he gets his supper and goes to bed; nevertheless, when books are lent which interest them, their children sometimes read such to their parents; but reading is not among the solaces of a labourer's life. Through this district great efforts have been made to promote education; many schools have been built by subscription, and endowed by landed proprietors and the clergy. The great obstacle is the difficulty in providing a yearly salary. Annual subscribers, where the small parishes are inhabited chiefly by tenantry, and boys enough to form a school of such numbers as to justify the high salary required by masters, can with difficulty be found.

I think that the children cannot be said to be badly clothed; they are warmly clad generally; the clothing-clubs have greatly added to their comforts; at the same time these clubs have shown what a small regular saving will effect; nevertheless it must be confessed that the labourers have been led to lean too much on such assistance, and do not so much feel the necessity of depending on themselves.

Another great and oppressive misfortune to the labourer's family is the difficulty of expending the earnings to advantage. Confined to the limits of his little circle, and perhaps only late on the Saturday evening receiving his wages, his dealings are solely with the village shop. In these shops articles for consumption are sold of but moderate quality at very high prices. There are numerous instances of large fortunes made in places where the farmers and labourers are the only customers – such fortunes as could only be accumulated by excessive profits and want of competition. It is a hard case to have earned 12s by the sweat of the brow, and to be able to procure not more than 9s would command in a town where competition exists.

The cause of the high price of village shops, I apprehend, arises from want of competition. A labourer (it is considered) is allowed credit for a small amount, and then obliged to deal under fear of having his debt called for, and thus of being left destitute for the time. It may be true that the shopkeeper, by deaths and other causes, loses money, but with such large profits the effect is slight; and, as he knows everybody, he has good tact, and generally avoids a bad creditor. Millers commonly pursue the same system. Blankets are double the price of a wholesale shop in London; shoes, too, are excessively high; the labourer in consequence finds himself ill off, and complains that he cannot live upon his wages, when in fact he cannot lay them out to advantage.

Bibliography

(A) Parliamentary Papers

1. Agriculture, Report of Special Assistant Poor Law Commissioners on the Employment of Women and Children in, Parliamentary Papers (P.P. 1843, Vol. XII.).
2. Agriculture, Royal Commission on the Employment of Children, Young Persons and Women in, P.P. 1867–8, Vol. XVII, and 1868–9, Vol. XIII.
3. Children's Employment Commission, Second Report, P.P. 1843, Vol. XIII.
4. Children's Employment Commission, First and Second Reports, P.P. 1863, Vol. XVIII and 1864, Vol. XXII.
5. Children's Employment Commission, Sixth Report, P.P. 1867, Vol. XVI.
6. Criminal and Destitute Juveniles, Select Committee, P.P. 1852, Vol. VII and 1852–3, Vol. XXII.
7. Education, Annual Minutes and Reports of the Committee of Council on
8. Factories and Workshops Commission, Report, P.P. 1876, Vol. XXIX.
9. Friendly and Benefit Societies, Royal Commission on, P.P. 1874, Vol. XXIII.
10. Honiton Lace Industry, Report, P.P. 1888, Vol. LXXX.
11. Juvenile Offenders, Report on the State of the Law Relating to, P.P. 1881, Vol. LIII.
12. Local Government Board, Annual Reports of (from 1871).
13. Labour, Royal Commission on (The Agricultural Labourer), P.P. 1893–4, Vol. XXV.
14. Medical Officer of the Privy Council, Sixth Report of, P.P. 1864, Vol. XXVIII.
15. Medical Relief, Select Committee on, P.P. 1854, Vol. XII.
16. Medical Relief (Return), P.P. 1870, Vol. LVIII.
17. Physical Deterioration, Report of Interdepartmental Committee on, P.P. 1904, Vol. XXXII.
18. Poor Law Board, Annual Reports of (to 1871).
19. Poor Relief (Expensive Medicines) Return, P.P. 1877, Vol. LXXI.
20. Prison Commissioners, Annual Reports of.
21. Reformatory and Industrial Schools, Annual Reports of Inspector of.
22. Registrar-General, Annual Reports of.
23. Servants, Report by Miss Collet on Money Wages of Indoor Domestic, P.P. 1899, Vol. XCII.
24. Vaccination Act of 1867, Select Committee Report, P.P. 1871, Vol. XIII.
25. Vaccination, Royal Commission on, P.P. 1896, Vol. XLVII.

(B) Newspapers and Journals
Dorset Magazine
Hampshire Chronicle

BIBLIOGRAPHY

Hampshire County Magazine
Hereford County Life
The Illustrated London News
Jackson's Oxford Journal
Kendal Mercury
Labourers' Union Chronicle
Leamington Chronicle
Leicester Chronicle and Leicester Mercury United
Midland Free Press
Norfolk News
Oxford Chronicle
Oxford Times
Portsmouth Evening News
The Queen
The Times
Warwick Advertiser

(C) Books and Articles published before 1900

26 Anonymous, *Life and Experiences of a Warwickshire Labourer* (1872).
27 Joseph Arch, *The Story of His Life Told by Himself* (1898).
28 Matthew Arnold, *Reports on Elementary Schools* 1852–82 (reprinted 1908).
29 Revd F.S. Attenborough, *Joseph Arch* (1872).
30 Mrs I. Beeton, *The Book of Household Management* (1863 edn.).
31 Mrs I. Beeton, *Cookery Book and Household Guide* (1898 edn.).
32 Thomas Beggs, *An Inquiry into the Extent and Causes of Juvenile Depravity* (1849).
33 J.A. Benson (Joseph Ashby of Tysoe), 'Gleaning' in *Land Magazine*, Vol. 3, 1899.
34 J.A. Benson (Joseph Ashby of Tysoe), 'A Rainy Day in a Blacksmith's Shop' in *Land Magazine*, Vol. 3, 1899.
35 J.C. Blomfield, *History of Finmere* (1887).
36 J.C. Blomfield, *History of Souldern* (1893).
37 Mary Carpenter, *Juvenile Delinquents* (1853).
38 Mary Carpenter, *Our Convicts* (1864).
39 Frederick Clifford, *The Agricultural Lockout of 1874* (1875).
40 S.P. Day, *Juvenile Crime, its Causes, Character and Cure* (1858).
41 P.H. Ditchfield, *Old English Customs Extant at the Present Time* (1896).
42 J. Field, *Prison Discipline* (1848).
43 Archdeacon Freer – Memoir of (privately printed, 1866).
44 F.W. Galton (ed.), *Workers on their Industries* (1895) (Chapter on 'The Agricultural Labourer').
45 J.L. Green, *English Country Cottages* (1899).
46 William Grey, *Rural Architecture* (1852).
47 James Hardy (ed.), *The Denham Tracts* (1895).
48 Augustus J.C. Hare, *Memorials of a Quiet Life* (1872).
49 F.G. Heath, *The English Peasantry* (1874).
50 Richard Jefferies, *Hodge and His Masters* (1880).
51 F. Digby Legard (ed.), *More About Farm Lads* (1865).
52 John C. Morton, *Cyclopaedia of Agriculture* (1855).

[53] John C. Morton, *Handbook on Farm Labour* (1861).

[54] Florence Nightingale, *Notes on Nursing* (1859).

[55] Mrs B. Palliser, *A History of Lace* (1865) (A revised edition was published in 1902).

[56] Bessie Rayner Parkes, *Essays on Woman's Work* (1865).

[57] *Sanitary Condition of Oxfordshire* (1874).

[58] Mary Simpson, *Scripture Lessons for the Unlearned* (1861).

[59] George Smith, *The Cry of the Children from the Brickyards of England* (1879 edn.).

[60] H. Swete, *Handybook of Cottage Hospitals* (1870).

(D) Books and Articles published from 1900

[61] Sally Alexander, *St Giles's Fair, 1830–1914* (1970).

[62] A.W. Ashby and M.K. Ashby, *Development of English Agriculture and Rural Life*, National Home-Reading Union Pamphlets, Science Series, No. 1, 1918.

[63] M.K. Ashby, *Joseph Ashby of Tysoe* (1961).

[64] H.C. Barnard, *History of English Education* (1966 edn.).

[65] E.N. Bennett, *Problems of Village Life* (1914).

[66] Richard Bourne and Brian MacArthur, *The Struggle for Education 1870–1970* (1970).

[67] Gaius Carley, Memoirs of (1963).

[68] J. Carlebach, *Caring for Children in Trouble* (1970).

[69] Victor Bonham-Carter, *Soldier True – The Life and Times of Field-Marshal Sir William Robertson* (1963).

[70] Leonard Clark, *Alfred Williams – His Life and Work* (1945).

[71] *Crime and Punishment*, Northants. County Record Office, Archive Teaching Unit (Folder One, 1971).

[72] Duncan Crow, *The Victorian Woman* (1971).

[73] Maud F. Davies, *Life in an English Village* (1909).

[74] Trevor Davies, *Four Centuries of Witch Beliefs* (1947).

[75] Freda Derrick, *A Trinity of Craftsmen* (1950).

[76] J.W. Docking, *Victorian Schools and Scholars*, Coventry and North Warwickshire History Pamphlets, No. 3 (1967).

[77] J.G. Dony, *A History of the Straw Hat Industry* (1942).

[78] E.L. Edmonds, *The School Inspector* (1962).

[79] Education Act 1870, HMSO, (1970).

[80] George Edwards, *From Crow-Scaring to Westminster* (1922).

[81] George Ewart Evans, *Ask the Fellows Who Cut the Hay* (1965 edn.).

[82] George Ewart Evans, *The Pattern under the Plough* (1966).

[83] George Ewart Evans, *The Horse in the Furrow* (1967 edn.).

[84] George Ewart Evans, *The Farm and the Village* (1969).

[85] George Ewart Evans, *Where Beards Wag All* (1970).

[86] J.H. Fearon, 'Some Notes on Bodicote', in *Cake and Cockhorse*, Vol. 3, No. 7, (1967).

[87] A. Wilson Fox, 'Agricultural Wages in England and Wales during the last Fifty Years', in *Journal of the Royal Statistical Society*, Vol. LXVI, (1903).

[88] Charles Freeman, *Luton and the Hat Industry* (1953).

[89] Charles Freeman, *Pillow Lace in the East Midlands* (1958).

[90] Sir Henry George, *Old Memories* (1923).

[91] P.H.J.H. Gosden, *The Friendly Societies in England 1815–75* (1961).

[92] P.H.J.H. Gosden, *How They Were Taught* (1969).

BIBLIOGRAPHY

[93] Brian Harrison, *Drink and the Victorians* (1971).

[94] Brian Harrison and Barrie Trinder, *Drink and Sobriety in an early Victorian Country Town, Banbury 1830–60*, Supplement 4, English Historical Review, (1969).

[95] J.F.C. Harrison, *Learning and Living, 1790–1960* (1961).

[96] W.C. Hazlitt, *Faiths and Folklore* (1905).

[97] Christina Hole, *English Custom and Usage* (1950).

[98] Pamela Horn, *Joseph Arch – The Farm Workers' Leader* (1971).

[99] Pamela Horn, 'The Country Child – 1850–70', in *Cake and Cockhorse*, Vol. 4, No. 10, (1970).

[100] Pamela Horn, 'Education in an Oxfordshire Village', in *Catholic Education Today*, September/October, (1968).

[101] Pamela Horn, 'Northamptonshire Agricultural Labourers in the 1870s', in *Northamptonshire Past and Present*, Vol. IV, No. 6, (1971/72).

[101a] D.L. Howard, *The English Prisons* (1960).

[102] L. Rider Haggard (ed.), *I Walked by Night by 'The King of the Norfolk Poachers'* (1935).

[103] Marion Johnson, *Derbyshire Village Schools in the Nineteenth Century* (1970).

[104] Barbara Kerr, *Bound to the Soil* (1968).

[105] Fred Kitchen, *Brother to the Ox* (1963 edn.).

[106] John L. Langley, 'Further Memories', in *Cake and Cockhorse*, Vol. 3, No. 3, (1966).

[107] R.J. Lambert, 'A Victorian National Health Service', in *Historical Journal*, Vol. 5, No. 1, (1962).

[108] Revd J.E. Linnell, *Old Oak – The Story of a Forest Village* (1932).

[109] Dorothy Loveday, 'Wardington Memories and Hearsay', in *Cake and Cockhorse*, Vol. 3, No. 3, (1966).

[110] P.H. Mann, 'Life in an Agricultural Village', in *Sociological Papers*, (1905).

[111] Revd J.H. Marlow, *Bozeat Village* (1936).

[112] Sybil Marshall, *Fenland Chronicle* (1967).

[113] D. McClatchey, *Oxfordshire Clergy 1777–1869* (1960).

[114] R.E. Moreau, *The Departed Village* (1968).

[115] Hesketh Pearson, *The Smith of Smiths* (1934).

[116] E. Royston Pike, *Human Documents of the Age of the Forsytes* (1969).

[117] Wm. Plomer (ed.), *Kilvert's Diary* (1971 edn.).

[118] Margaret Powell, *Below Stairs* (1970 edn.).

[119] John Purser, *Our Ilmington* (privately printed, 1966).

[120] Edward Rainsberry, *Through the Lych Gate* (1969).

[121] W.J. Reader, *Life in Victorian England* (1964).

[122] Eric E. Rich, *The Education Act of 1870* (1970).

[123] Robert Roberts, *The Classic Slum* (1971).

[124] Maud Robinson, *A South Down Farm in the Sixties* (1938).

[124a] F. Gordon Roe, *The Victorian Child* (1959).

[125] L.T.C. Rolt, *Waterloo Ironworks – A History of Taskers of Andover* (1969).

[126] Walter Rose, *The Village Carpenter* (1946 edn.).

[127] Walter Rose, *Good Neighbours* (1942).

[128] Rex C. Russell, *The 'Revolt of the Field' in Lincs.* (1956).

[129] Rex C. Russell, *A History of Schools and Education in Lindsey, Lincolnshire, 1800–1902* (in four parts, 1965–7).

277

[130] Eileen Samuels, 'Cropredy and Bourton National School in the Nineteenth Century', in *Cake and Cockhorse*, Vol. 2, No. 6, (1963).

[131] 'Lord' George Sanger, *Seventy Years a Showman* (1910).

[132] T.E. Schultz, 'The Woodstock Glove Industry', in *Oxoniensia*, Vol. III, (1938).

[133] R. Sellman, *Devon Village Schools in the Nineteenth Century* (1967).

[134] Ernest Selley, *Village Trade Unions* (1920 edn.).

[135] Brian Simon, *Education and the Labour Movement, 1870–1920* (1965).

[136] E.M. Sneyd-Kynnersley HMI, *Some Passages in the Life of One of H.M. Inspectors of Schools* (1908).

[137] L. Marion Springall, *Labouring Life in Norfolk Villages* (1936).

[138] Noel Streatfeild (ed.), *The Day Before Yesterday* (1956).

[139] George Sturt, *A Small Boy in the 'Sixties* (1927).

[140] George Sturt, *The Wheelwright's Shop* (1963 edn.).

[141] Mary Sturt, *The Education of the People* (1967).

[142] Gillian Sutherland, *Elementary Education in the Nineteenth Century* (1971).

[143] Joan Thirsk, *English Peasant Farming* (1957).

[144] Flora Thompson, *Lark Rise to Candleford* (1963 edn.).

[145] Flora Thompson, *Still Glides the Stream* (1966 edn.).

[146] J.J. Tobias, *Crime and Industrial Society in the Nineteenth Century* (1967).

[147] B.S. Trinder, 'Banbury Fair in the Nineteenth Century' in *Cake and Cockhorse*, Vol. 4, No. 2, 1968.

[148] A. Tropp, *The School Teachers* (1957).

[149] Ronald Webber, *The Village Blacksmith* (1971).

[150] Alfred Williams, *A Wiltshire Village* (1912).

[151] Alfred Williams, *Villages of the White Horse* (1913).

[152] Alfred Williams, *Round About the Upper Thames* (1922).

[153] Gordon Winter, *Country Camera* (1966).

[154] John Woodforde, *The Truth About Cottages* (1969).

[155] Miss K.S. Woods, *The Rural Industries Round Oxford* (1921).

[156] Thomas Wright, *The Romance of the Lace Pillow* (1919).

[157] 'Banbury at the Turn of the Century' – material from a 'Reminiscences' meeting held by Banbury Historical Society in November, 1970, and included in *Cake and Cockhorse*, Vol. 5, No. 2, Spring, 1972.

(E) Novels

[158] Thomas Hardy, *The Return of the Native* (1971 edn.); the book was first published in 1878.

[159] Thomas Hardy, *Tess of the D'Urbervilles* (1963 edn.); the book was first published complete in three volumes in 1891; the story relates to the late 1860s and early 1870s.

[160] Thomas Hardy, *Jude the Obscure* (1957 edn.). Hardy completed the novel, 'with the exception of a few chapters', by the end of 1894.

Index

Counties where given, are those applicable prior to 1914.

279

INDEX